GOVERNMENT BEYOND THE CENTRE

SERIES EDITORS: GERRY STOKER AND STEVE LEACH

The world of sub-central government and administration – including local authorities, quasi-governmental bodies and the agencies of public–private partnerships – has seen massive changes in recent years and is at the heart of the current restructuring of government in the United Kingdom and other Western democracies.

The intention of the *Government Beyond the Centre* series is to bring the study of this often-neglected world into the mainstream of social science research, applying the spotlight of critical analysis to what has traditionally been the preserve of institutional public administration approaches.

Its focus is on the agenda of change currently being faced by sub-central government, the economic, political and ideological forces that underlie it, and the structures of power and influence that are emerging. Its objective is to provide up-to-date and informative accounts of the new forms of government, management and administration that are emerging.

The series will be of interest to students and practitioners of politics, public and social administration, and all those interested in the reshaping of the governmental institutions which have a daily and major impact on our lives.

GOVERNMENT BEYOND THE CENTRE

SERIES EDITOR: GERRY STOKER AND STEVE LEACH

Published

Wendy Ball and John Solomos (eds)
Race and Local Politics

Richard Batley and Gerry Stoker (eds)
Local Government in Europe

Clive Gray
Government Beyond the Centre

John Gyford
Citizens, Consumers and Councils

Steve Leach, John Stewart and Kieron Walsh
The Changing Organisation and Management of Local Government

Yvonne Rydin
The British Planning System

John Stewart and Gerry Stoker (eds)
The Future of Local Government

David Wilson and Chris Game (with Steve Leach and Gerry Stoker)
Local Government in the United Kingdom

Forthcoming

Richard Kerley
Managing in Local Government

The Changing Organisation and Management of Local Government

Steve Leach

John Stewart

Kieron Walsh

MACMILLAN

© Steve Leach, John Stewart and Kieron Walsh 1994

First published 1994 by
THE MACMILLAN PRESS LTD
Houndmills, Basingstoke, Hampshire RG21 2XS
and London
Companies and representatives
throughout the world

ISBN 0–333–54927–9 hardcover
ISBN 0–333–54928–7 paperback

A catalogue record for this book is available
from the British Library.

Copy-edited and typeset by Povey–Edmondson
Okehampton and Rochdale, England

Printed in China

Contents

List of Figures

List of Tables

List of Abbreviations Used

CCT	compulsory competitive tendering
DoE	Department of Environment
DLO	direct labour organisation
GMWU	General and Municipal Workers Union
HMSO	Her Majesty's Stationary Office
LACSAB	Local Authority Conditions of Service Advisory Board
LEA	local education authority
LGMB	Local Government Management Board
LGTB	Local Government Training Board
LMS	local management of schools
NALGO	National Association of Local Government Officers
NUPE	National Union of Public Employees
PPBS	policy planning/budgetary systems
SLA	service-level agreements

Acknowledgements

The authors would like to thank their colleagues at INLOGOV for stimulating in discussion and debate many of the ideas in this book; the many officers and members in local authorities in Britain who have spared time to talk to us over the years about organisation and management issues in their authorities; and Kathy Bonehill for typing the typescript so professionally, and revising it so patiently.

S. L.
J. S.
K. W.

1 The Changing Context of Local Authority Organisation and Management

This book is about the changing approaches to and patterns of the organisation and management of local authorities in the UK at a time of rapid and destabilising change. In this introductory chapter we set out the basic assumptions which provide the starting-point for the analysis contained in the chapters which follow, and introduce the conceptual terminology which will be used throughout the book.

The starting-points for our analysis can be summarised as:

- The organisation and management of local authorities has to be grounded in an understanding of their *distinctive purposes, conditions and tasks.*
- Although there are some useful parallels between the principles and patterns of organisation and management in the *private sector* and in local government, there are *several important differences* between the two institutional worlds.
- The most fundamental of these key differences is that the local authority is not merely a *provider of goods and services*, it is also both a *governmental and a political institution*, constituted by *local election.*
- It follows that the assumption and conclusions of *organisational theory*, in so far as these are grounded in experience in the private sector, have to be modified and reinterpreted before they can be applied to the particular circumstances of local government.

- The role of local government as an institution within the governmental fabric of the country is changing fundamentally. The key element of this is the move from being the direct providers of services to acting as agencies which specify and purchase services rather than providing them directly. This direction of change is captured by the term *'enabling authority'*.

- Although the broad direction of change is clear, the term 'enabling authority' is currently open to a wide variety of interpretations. There still exists an important *area of choice* as to what *kind* of enabling authority particular local authorities wish to become.

- The past assumptions and practices of local authorities are not, however, included as appropriate choices of direction. The *'traditional bureaucratic'* authority, dominated by values of self-sufficiency, uniformity, direct provision, professionalism and departmentalism *is no longer appropriate* and is best seen as the historical starting-point from which radical change has become necessary, and with which new forms of authority can be compared.

- The appropriate structures, processes, strategies and cultures adopted by local authorities may therefore be expected to reflect the interpretation of 'enabling'. *There is no uniform set of specific ingredients for good management in the current circumstances.*

- In the present turbulent and uncertain climate it is important that local authorities appreciate the need for, and achieve, an appropriate degree of *organisational balance* in the structures, strategies, processes and systems which they adopt.

- The increased emphasis on the enabling role strengthens the relevance of the *inter-organisational dimension*, i.e. the understanding of the relationship between a local authority and the network of other private, public and voluntary organisations with which it interacts – to an understanding of the organisation and management of local government.

These ten key assumptions are reflected in the structure of the book, and in the contents of the chapters which follow. In this chapter we develop the arguments about the specific nature of local government and the implications of its particular qualities for a book about organisation and management.

Studying local government as local government – not as the private sector

The organisation and management of local authorities has to be grounded in an understanding of their distinctive purposes, conditions and tasks. It is a mistake to believe that all organisations are, or should be, structured in the same way or that there is a generic approach to management that can be applied in any situation. Organisation theory is as much about the differences between organisations as it is about the uniformities. Management studies can provide tools for analysis and concepts to guide that analysis, but the meaning given to concepts in actual management situations depend on that analysis.

In Chapter 3 we shall describe the contribution that organisation theory can make to the understanding of management and organisation in local government. That contribution can only gain meaning in application. It should certainly not be assumed automatically that local authorities should take the private sector as their model either in their organisation or in their management.

First, there is no *one* private sector model. Service industries have different requirements from manufacturing industries. Both service and manufacturing industries differ in organisation and management according to their technology.

Second, if technology and task affect organisation and management, so also must the purposes of the organisation. Responsibilities are placed in public organisations in general or in local authorities in particular to be carried out in accordance with public purpose. If instead it is decided they should be carried out as if they were in the private sector then the appropriate course is to place them in that sector.

Failure to appreciate these points can lead and has led to problems in the development of approaches to organisation and management in local government. For example, it can mean that the political process in local government is seen as a constraint, an obstacle for management in local government, because it has no ready parallel in private-sector organisations. We would argue that far from being seen as an obstacle, management in local government should support and express the legitimate political process. This requires the development of management approaches based on understanding of the political process.

If unthinking application of management approaches developed for the private sector can lead to neglect of organisational conditions inherent in local government, it can also lead to distortion if such approaches are applied without adaptation to local authorities. In local government there is an increased emphasis on the need for local authorities to be responsive to their customers. Such an emphasis has played an important part in making local authorities open to their public, but it can lead a local authority into serious difficulties if the 'customer' is seen in the same terms as in the private sector.

Whereas in the market conditions of the private sector, the customer can be identified by the sale of goods or services, the customer of local authorities services is not so clear. For many services there will be more than one customer and they will not always be the direct users of the service. Nor will the 'customer' necessarily be entitled to service. Services in local authorities may be directed at need, rather than provided on demand. Management in local government has to place an emphasis on the public for whom services are provided and to whom local authorities are accountable, but the complexities of the relationship with the public should not be confined by the word 'customer'.

Neglect of the political processes and the inadequacy of the word 'customer' are examples of the danger of applying to local government approaches to organisation and management derived from other organisations with different purposes, conditions and tasks. The starting-point for this book on the organisation and management of local authorities has to be a consideration of the local authorities' nature as organisations.

The nature of local government

Local authorities are not only providers of services: they are also political institutions for local choice and local voice. The key issue for management of local government is how one achieves an organisation that not merely carries out one role but carries out both roles, not separately but in interaction.

The phrase 'public service' reflects the interaction between the local authority as service provider and as political institution. As a service provider the organisation aims to meet the demands, needs or aspirations of those for whom the service is provided. But the service has to be provided in accordance with public policy as determined by the local authority or defined by national legislation. This may mean that some of those who want a service may be denied it, because the local authority has to ration the service according to the resources available, laying down criteria for its use (as when houses are allocated to would-be tenants according to a points system). The local authority may refuse a planning application as being contrary to its policy for an area. In public services, public purpose and responsiveness to those for whom the service is provided have to be reconciled.

The local authority is an elected political institution responsible for making choices both on the nature and level of the services provided and on the interrelationship of those choices in forming and shaping the ways of life of the communities which live and work within their area. As a political institution it can express local voice, giving expression to the aspirations and concerns of local communities. A local authority is governed by a process of debate and discussion in which different interests and values are expressed. The party political process underlies the local election, the composition of the council and the conduct of its business, but public pressure and protest are also part of the debate and discussion that inform decision-making.

There is a tension between a local authority as an organisation for effective service delivery, and the local authority as a political institution constituted for debate and challenge. Whereas service delivery, whether direct or indirect, requires shared aims and an agreed task, the governing process of the local authority involves argument and disagreement. Aims once set can be challenged, tasks when specified can be contested. The challenge for organisation and management in local government is to achieve both organisational effectiveness in service delivery and an effective political process. Those concerned with organisation and management should not resolve this dilemma by emphasising one at the expense of the other, because both should be achieved.

A special organisation

The local authority is distinguished from many organisations by a number of features that reflect its dual role. It is based on *local election*. From that basis a number of characteristics derive. The local elections are normally contested by political parties. They bring on to the governing body of the authority councillors who are not selected to meet internal organisational criteria, but are chosen by the political parties and elected by the citizenry. Their background is almost inevitably sharply different from that of the officers of the authority. They are lay men and women, while the officers are professional. Councillors can come without relevant experience and can be removed when they have gained it.

The local authority exercises substantive powers, but for those powers it is subject to *public accountability* enforced through the electoral process. Public accountability places its own requirements on the organisation and management of local authorities. It requires access to information, and an openness in decisions (if not always of decision-making) not often found in private sector organisations.

The local authority does not necessarily have to charge for its services. Indeed, it may be prohibited from doing so. It raises much of its *revenue from taxation*, either through local taxation or from grants from central government financed by national taxation. The budgetary decisions of a local authority are exercised in local choice (not business forecasts of likely sales and the costs of meeting them) both on the level of local taxation – although this choice is increasingly restricted by central government – or on the allocation of those resources to different services and the activities that sustain them. At the heart of organisational process is the management of rationing, since resources are limited in relation to demand.

The local authority is a *multipurpose organisation* providing not just one service but many. It has no single overriding objective, but differing objectives which may be in conflict with each other not merely for resources, but also in action, as when proposals for economic development raise environmental concern. The local authority cannot resolve such issues by reference to overriding objectives. It has to determine not only what to do but also what to value and to do it continuously in its working.

Yet there are choices it cannot avoid and others it cannot make. For the local authority is a creature of *statute* on which certain duties are laid. It can only act within its statutory powers. While both duties and power provide scope for choice, a local authority cannot abandon a service because of unfavourable conditions, as would a market (or even a voluntary) organisation. Indeed, it is often when the market has failed to provide services that local authorities have to act.

Local authorities gain their *identity from the area* for which they are responsible. Within that area they have to act and they will not normally act outside that area. Because of the identity with the area and the basis in election, the local authority can speak on the affairs of the area beyond the scope of its formal responsibilities. Because of the range of its powers and resources, it can shape the environment of that area.

Local authorities are *multi-contact organisations* within the area for which they are responsible. They impinge upon their publics at a myriad of points in a way unmatched by any other organisation, apart from central government itself. They construct much of the physical infrastructure of roads and services. They license, order and regulate. They remain responsible for the education of most of the children, and for social services. They own much of the property and employ many of the population. It is the cumulative impact of these interactions that constitutes a distinctive challenge for the organisation and management of local government.

It is because the local authority as an organisation:

- is based on local election;
- is subject to public accountability;
- has the right to tax;
- is a multipurpose organisation;
- is constituted by statute;
- gains its identity from its area; and
- is a multicontact organisation

that it is a special type of organisation requiring study in its own right.

The conceptual framework

In this introductory chapter, it is helpful to introduce the key concepts and framework of analysis which will be used in the book.

In texts on organisation and management most emphasis is typically placed on the formal organisational structures and management processes within the type of organisation concerned, and on the management systems utilised. In a textbook on local authorities it is in our view important to include an explicit discussion of the role and purpose and of the strategy or strategies which such organisations typically deploy, as a precursor to a discussion of structures, processes and management issues. We are also concerned to give due weight to the importance of organisational culture (or shared values). Figure 1.1, which is a modified and simplified form of the famous '7 S's' (shared values, strategy, structure, systems, style, staff and skills) figure developed by Peters and Waterman (1982, p.10), sets out the key variables which form the building blocks of this text.

'*Role and purpose*' is included as a category in the figure to emphasise the scope for interpretive choice which exists for local authorities and to highlight the argument that preferred patterns of organisation are likely to reflect this more fundamental choice of direction (typically expressed in the form of a *strategy*). *Culture* is seen here as the largely informal pattern of assumptions about ways of working which may be common or may be differentiated, for example between different departments. In relation to '*processes*

FIGURE 1.1   Key dimensions of analysis

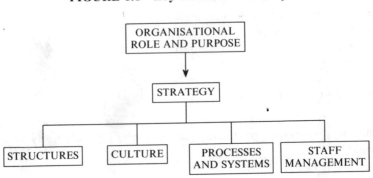

and systems' most emphasis is placed on key aspects of local authority operations such as the budgetary process and informal/ formal decision-making processes involving senior officers and members. We are less concerned here with the detailed operation of specific management systems which have been introduced in local authorities over the past five years or so (e.g. service-level agreements, staff appraisal systems, performance-related pay) except where their introduction has been central to the pursuit of some strategic objective (e.g. decentralisation, customer care). In general, the emphasis is on a *macro*-level of analysis of local authorities. *Micro*-level analysis – e.g. individual managerial behaviour and team-building – whilst not ignored, is not the main focus of the book.

Our broad approach to organisational theory (see Chapter 3) may be summarised as follows. There are a number of external factors (such as local government structure, legislation, finance) which are strongly influential in relation to organisation and management structure and processes within local authorities. One only needs to refer to the structural impact of compulsory competitive tendering (CCT) to underline this point. In exploring the way in which local authorities have adjusted their structures, processes and systems to such external and fixed factors, a number of familiar dimensions of analysis can helpfully be used, in particular organisational differentiation/integration, centralisation/decentralisation of decision-making, high formalisation/low formalisation of procedures, specialisation/ generalisation of staff and independence/interdependence of working practices. All authorities have to find some kind of balance between each of these polar opposites in their attempts to respond to external circumstances, and internal priorities.

We do not view external pressures as determinants of organisational approach. They may constrain the scope for organisational choice; they may indeed come to be interpreted as imperatives requiring a particular organisational response. But the type of response to such pressures depends upon a different set of factors which reflect the values, interests and relative power of such factors within the organisation. These factors are of particular importance in organisations whose constitutions are built upon the principle of political democracy *and* which are multifunctional in nature because value conflict and differences of interest are an inherent part of the organisation's character (see p.7 above). Both these qualities make it less likely that there will be the more direct causal relationship between external pressures and organisational choices, for example, structural form, which may be found in non-political, single-purpose, private-sector organisations. Consider, for example, the likely response of a left-wing Labour-controlled authority and a right-wing Conservative-controlled authority to the very tangible external pressure of the CCT legislation. On the one hand the former are unlikely to welcome it, and are likely to put considerable emphasis on creating the right conditions for contracts to be won 'in-house'. On the other hand, the latter are much more likely to welcome the legislation, and may not mind whether contracts are won in-house or by outsiders. In these circumstances one would anticipate very different patterns of response in terms of organisational structures and processes.

Consider also the likelihood of disagreement between a director of technical services and a chief executive over the appropriate organisational location for an engineering services direct labour organisation (DLO). The former may well argue strongly for the retention of such a unit within his department and overall span of control, reflecting his own interest position within the authority. The chief executive may see considerable advantages in an arms-length engineering services DLO, under the direct responsibility of a DLO manager (and separate DLO committee). The outcome of this difference of view will reflect the relative strength of bargaining power of the two participants which will itself be partly dependent on the views and concerns of the politicians. In one authority the outcome may go one way; in another quite the opposite way.

The reality of non-determinate relationship between contextual pressures and organisational response can be illustrated by three different types of local authority response to the pressures for change:

1. *Dynamic conservatism* In recent research (see Walsh, 1991; Leach, Walsh *et al.* 1992), it has been possible to identify authorities which have sought to 'muddle through', striving (in organisation and management terms) to retain as much of the status quo as possible in the face of formidable external changes. It can be argued that this approach represents a 'mismatch' between

external context and internal change, and cannot be regarded as an appropriately responsive adaptation.

2. *Indiscriminate 'fashion-following'* There is a commensurate danger in what might be termed as *over*-response to external pressures. There is an increasing range and variety of managerial innovations in the fields of strategies, structures, systems and staff management – which have developed and been drawn to the attention of local authorities in recent years. The danger is one of an unconsidered embracing of this whole range of current managerial fashions, without a proper appraisal of what is appropriate for the specific circumstances of the particular local authority (especially in relation to its interpretation of role and purpose) or indeed whether the fashion was appropriate for local government at all. We found examples of authorities in which at least some changes were adopted simply to be seen to be changing.

3. *Selected response* There are, however, local authorities which are *selective* about which core values they adopt, which systems they develop and which structural changes they introduce. Change in these circumstances is positive and active, rather than simply reactive, and embraces the authority's own sense of direction and unique political and organisational culture.

It is important to bear these three possible responses, or strategic directions, in mind – 1. dynamic conservatism; 2. unselective trend-following, and 3. integrated but selective response and adaptation to change – in exploring the relationship between external pressures and organisational choice.

One particularly important element in the contrast between dynamic conservatism and genuine adaptation is the attitude to *external* organisations. To caricature the issue somewhat, it can be argued that authorities in the first category continue to emphasise the notion of the self-contained, self-sufficient authority (see Chapter 2) whilst those in the latter category accept the importance of viewing themselves as a focal organisation within a network of other public, private and voluntary-sector organisations, which will inevitably play an increasingly vital role in their activities. This switch of emphasis from an inward-looking to an outward-looking perspective is one of the key themes of this book.

In Figure 1.2, an attempt is made to present in summary form the different elements of the conceptual framework which will be

**FIGURE 1.2   Framework for analysing a local authority's approach
to organisation and management**

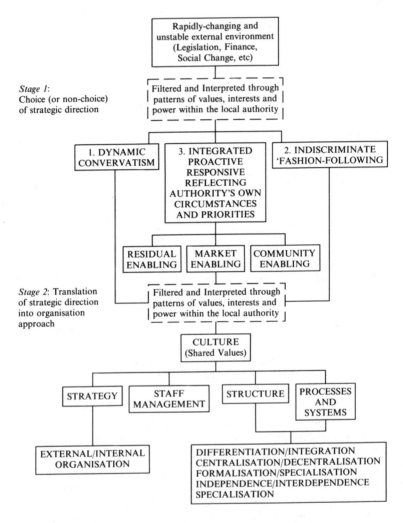

adopted in this book, and the relationships between them. Our aim
is to identify and operate in the 'middle ground' between formal
theories of high generality (but questionable relevance to practical
activities in local government) and practical generalisations drawn

from a mass of detailed management experience in local authorities. The framework set out is intended to put into operation the oft-reported maxim in local authorities that a 'top-down approach should be combined with a bottom-up approach'. It is intended to draw selectively from organisation theory, interpret it in the specific circumstances of local government and use it to give pattern and meaning to the detailed practical experience of local authority organisation and management.

The structure of the book

The remainder of the book is structured as follows. In the second chapter, we contrast the models of the 'traditional bureaucratic' authority with the different interpretations of 'enabling authority', which is proving to be the central concept around which discussion about the future role and purpose of local government is currently focused. The argument is put forward that although local authorities have necessarily to make radical *changes* in their structures, processes and systems, *continuity* is also important. In Chapter 3, the potential contribution of organisational theory to an understanding of organisation and management in local government is discussed (the key 'organising concepts' involved are identified later in this chapter). In Chapter 4 two key elements of organisation and management in local authorities – structures and processes – are singled out for particular attention. In Chapters 5 and 6 two key dimensions of organisational analysis – centralisation and decentralisation – are singled out for discussion, as much of the debate – in particular about structural change in local government – has focused especially upon the role of the centre and the scope for decentralisation of services and decision-making. In Chapter 7 the impact of the political dimension of these structures and processes – identified earlier as the major factor which distinguishes local government from other types of organisation – is highlighted. Chapter 8 analyses the changing role of staff management in local government. In Chapter 9 we explore the implications of the move towards the enabling authority for inter-agency working. Finally, in Chapter 10, we explore the implications of three different ideal types of enabling authority (residual, market-oriented and community-oriented) for organisation and management approaches in local government and reintroduce the concept of 'organisational balance' as an important component of the debate.

2 Organisational Continuity and Organisational Change

Although local authorities are, to a large extent, free to determine their own organisational structure and management procedures, there has been a remarkable degree of uniformity in the way local authorities have managed themselves. Local authorities generally have shared a set of organisational assumptions which have moulded their way of working over the years and ensured organisational continuity.

Those assumptions, we shall argue, have expressed and supported a view of local authorities as predominantly agencies for the delivery of large-scale services on a uniform and predetermined pattern, required for the maintenance and development of the welfare state. Those assumptions give expression to what in Chapter 3 we describe as organisational culture. Those assumptions have been so readily accepted as a part of local government that until recently they have rarely been challenged. They formed the concept of what local government should be. The term 'traditional bureaucratic' authority has been identified as encapsulating the qualities of this concept of local government (see Chapter 1). In this chapter we explore the nature of the challenge to past patterns of organisation and management. That challenge can be distinguished from past reviews, because it is a challenge to organisational assumptions previously accepted without question.

There were, between fifteen and twenty-five years ago, a series of major reviews of the organisation and management of local government (the Redcliffe-Maud Report, 1969; the Mallaby Report, 1967, and the Bains Report, 1972). New local authorities were created in 1974 in England and Wales and in 1975 in Scotland and while there were changes in the organisation and management of local authorities reflecting the development of corporate management, they did not involve significant challenge to many of the organisational assumptions.

Recently, however, the combination of legislative change brought about by the Conservative government elected in 1987 and the impact of societal change has begun a more fundamental process of reconsideration of the role of local authorities. As a result those organisational assumptions which had come to be accepted as part of the working of local authorities have begun to be challenged. The boundaries of organisational choice, previously constrained within those organisational assumptions have been extended.

In this chapter we shall set out those organisational assumptions, discuss the reviews of local authorities organisation and management, and past movements for change and set out the extent and nature of the current challenge to the organisational assumptions. In so doing, we shall identify issues which will be explored in later chapters as local authorities face not only the requirements of organisational change but also the continuing pressure for organisational continuity.

The role of local authorities, and their organisational assumptions

Local authorities are agencies for the delivery of services, prescribed by national legislation, but they are also political institutions constituted for local choice of both the service provided and the development of local communities and for the expression of local voice on the needs and concerns of those communities. They are concerned with both local administration and local government and as such have to have the capacity for organisational continuity implied by the provision of established services, and for organisational flexibility to meet the changing requirements of the communities they serve.

The growth of the welfare state after the Second World War gave an important role to local authorities in the provision of the services. Political parties both nationally and locally were committed to the growth of those services. Local government expenditure grew in real terms year by year and the main task of local authorities came to be seen as the provision of those services on well-established lines, often, in accordance with the dominant professional views, reflecting an acceptance of authoritative expertise. Local authorities in effect came to see their task more as local administration than local government, although of course that was never completely true. The organisation of local authorities and the assumptions on which it was based reflected the dominant task of the provision of services.

Organisational assumptions

Into any organisation are built assumptions about the way it should be organised and run. Organisations depend upon such assumptions to ensure their working, guarantee continuity and reduce the search for organisational solutions. The characteristic of such assumptions is that they are so much a part of the working of the organisation that they do not need to be stated. They reflect – and are supported by – powerful organisational interests.

When we think about local authorities and their way of working we naturally take for granted that their structure will be based upon committees and departments. As we shall see, past reviews of the structure and organisation of local authorities have also made that assumption. They have proposed modifications to the committee and departmental structures, but have taken for granted that the basic building blocks of the structure will be committees and departments in their traditional form. The organisational assumptions have, in effect, limited organisational change.

We shall highlight a set of such assumptions. The first set of assumptions relates to the basic structural elements:

- the necessity of the committee system;
- the tradition of departmentalism;
- the enforced role of the centre.

The second set of assumptions relates to the processes (or ways of working) within those basic elements:

- the assumption of self-sufficiency;
- the presumption of uniformity;
- the assumption of direct control;

- the dominance of professionalism;
- the formalities of accountability.

The basic elements

Any large organisation has to divide up its work. The local authority as a large organisation has, therefore, to find a principle of division on which to structure the work of both councillors and officers. That structure becomes a part of the experience of local authorities so that they come to be seen as necessary to the working of the authority, even when not required by statute.

(a) *The committee system*   The responsibility for all that is done by a local authority rests with the council consisting of all the elected councillors. A council will normally exercise that responsibility through committees composed of a number of councillors and in certain cases co-opted members, although since the Local Government and Housing Act 1989, those co-opted members will not normally have voting rights.

A local authority is not required to appoint committees except for certain defined purposes (education, social services and police) none of which apply to district councils. The power is permissive, but is universally exercised, although one district council (Monmouth) prior to reorganisation with only twelve councillors, and more recently Clackmannanshire district council, also with twelve councillors, decided to abolish all committees, with the council instead acting directly. That was and is so exceptional that it shows how deeply ingrained is the assumption of the necessity of the committee system.

It is not merely the necessity of the committee system that is assumed but that the main work of the council will be conducted through that system and that it will be the main setting for the work of the councillor. The council will either have delegated most of its work to committees or if decisions have to be referred upwards, will normally approve committee minutes almost automatically.

The committee system is not merely assumed to be an organisational necessity, it will normally be assumed that the committees will be structured around the main services of the local authority (e.g. education, housing, social services, etc.) along with certain central committees. The combination of service committees with central committees as the main basis for the work of the council both predated reorganisation and continued after reorganisation. In 1974 only one local authority – West Norfolk – departed significantly from that model and based its structure on area committees. The service committee was and remains the norm to which the structures of the local authority conform.

That structure had a logic which derived from the perceived role of the local authority as an agency for the administration of a series of prescribed services. The committees are the means by which the council controls the provision of those services. As such they have a regular cycle of meeting which can vary from a four-weekly cycle in some authorities to quarterly in others. The committees are likely to have subcommittees responsible for particular aspects of their work.

The committee provides the authoritative basis for decisions taken on the services for which it is responsible. Its procedures reflect that role. It has an agenda backed by reports and filled with issues for decision and information, many of them concerned with the workings of departments. It has a formality of procedure necessary for its role. Around the table will be arrayed the members of the committee and officers drawn from the departments responsible for the services and from the central departments. Conduct at the meeting will be governed by the conventions necessary to the formal conduct of business.

The committee is the formal setting for decision-making in the authority. In practice decisions may well be made elsewhere. The committee may merely ratify officers' recommendations or recommendations agreed between the chief officer and the chair. The real settings for decision-making by councillors are likely to be the political groups which are constituted by the different parties on the council and which will meet regularly to take key decisions for the council as a whole. As well as the Council party groups there may well also be committee party groups which meet before the committee.

Although the committee may be a formal rather than an actual arena for decision-making, the committee and its way of working still mould the working of the council. The committee, its cycle and its agenda set the conditions and the tempo for both officers and councillors. Group meetings will be time-tabled according to the committee cycle and their agendas will reflect the agendas of committees. Councillors define their roles largely by membership of committees. Chairs of committees hold positions of authority in the working of the council, even though their formal authority is limited to chairing the meetings. Their actual authority derives from their ability to command a majority in committees and the position of a chair in hung authorities is therefore significantly reduced.

The committee system, its service-based structure and its way of working are so much a part of the working of local authorities that thinking about organisation and management often starts from that basis. The assumption commonly made has been that the committee system is a basic element in the working of local authorities.

(b)   *The tradition of departmentalism*   In local authorities the key divisions are the departments of the authority which can vary both with the type of authority according to its functions and within types of authority according to decisions of that authority.

The departments reflect the main functions of the authority – either the services provided by the authority to the public or the services provided to, or controls exercised over service departments by, the central departments of the authority. This structure is again grounded in the role of the local authority as an agency for the delivery of a series of services and the definition of the services or functions as the main building blocks of the departmental structure reflects the key professions of local government.

The departments of local authorities have a characteristic structure. They are headed by a chief officer normally drawn from the dominant profession in that department. Below the chief officer is a multi-tiered hierarchy, which can be broadly divided into senior management (chief officer, deputy chief officer, assistant chief officers), middle management, and field workers or basic worker. The hierarchy enforces control of service provision reflecting an emphasis on the continuity of working, in accordance with established practice.

It is not the existence of departments that constitutes the tradition of departmentalism, but their dominance in the working of the authority. Departmentalism is grounded in a structure which is based on the services and in which the boundary walls of departments are buttressed by the committee system and by professionalism. Officers' loyalties are more to the department and its services and their profession than to the authority.

The departmentalism of local government is written into the structure of local authorities. The main method of working lies within departments and hence the main patterns of organisational thinking lie within the department. Departmentalism is based on the provision of services as defined professionally.

Departmentalism based on service departments is so much a part of local government that it has been almost unknown until recently for local authorities to consider alternative patterns of organisation, although again West Norfolk in 1974 developed an officer-structure based on areas. The traditional departmental structure as an assumed organisational necessity has been a basic building block for the organisation and management of local authorities.

(c)   *The enforced role of the centre*   Although the role of the local authority has been seen as the provision of a series of services, there have also been a series of central departments and central committees, whose role has been concerned to a lesser or greater degree with the overall working of the authority and with both support and control of the service departments.

To an extent, there has been change in the structure of the centre. Prior to reorganisation the structure of the centre was based upon the Clerk as the legal advisor of the council and the leading officer of the council responsible for the working of council and committees, and the Treasurer as the chief financial officer, with the possibility of other subordinate roles such as that of Establishment Officer responsible for a limited range of personnel matters. Reorganisation saw the creation of the position of Chief Executive which was often separated from the legal and administrative roles which were then carried out by the County Secretary or Director of Administration. The Treasurer's role remained unchanged, but the role of Personnel Officer replaced the Establishment Officer, reflecting an aspiration to a more developed personnel role. At the same time at Council level there emerged in most authorities a Policy and Resources Committee, with subcommittees concerned with the main resources of the authority and with performance review, replacing the more fragmented structure of central committees in previous authorities.

These changes followed the recommendations of the Bains Committee and the aspirations to corporate management discussed below. What is important, however, is that while the structure changed, there was much less change in the role of the centre. The centre's relations with service departments had been and remained based on:

- its role in servicing the committees of the authority (often successfully resisted for long periods by education committee and education department);
- its role in providing support and advice to service departments;
- its role in control over the use of resources or powers by departments.

The relations of the centre with the departments has been based on the assumed necessity of these roles. The centre had to service committees. The centre provided support and advice, irrespective of whether the department wished for it. Indeed support and advice were not distinguished from control, the nature of which was based, as we shall see, on detailed scrutiny of departmental decision.

The centre could change in form and structure, but the assumed necessity of its roles meant that its ways of working remained unchanged.

Processes
The committees, the departments and the enforced role of the centre – itself composed of committees and departments – are the basic building blocks assumed to be a necessary part of local government. The local authority also has assumptions built into its processes, or ways of working.

(a)   *The assumption of self-sufficiency*   It has been assumed almost without question that when local authorities have been given responsibility for a function they would carry out that function directly through their own organisation. If local authorities have been seen largely as agencies for the delivery of services required by the welfare state, then it has been seen as inevitable that they should provide them directly.

It has been assumed not merely that local authorities should provide services directly, but that they should themselves normally employ all the staff (and other resources) required for the delivery of the services. The identity of the authority has been seen as deriving from the services provided and the staff engaged in that provision.

The assumption of self-sufficiency can best be illustrated by the long debates that underlay the process of reorganisation. One of the most powerful factors in those debates was the argument for larger authorities to secure efficiency in the provision of services. The Royal Commission on Local Government concluded on the basis of very little evidence that for an authority responsible for education, housing and social services, 'only an authority serving a population of some 250 000 or more will have at its disposal the range and calibre of staff, and the technical and financial resources necessary for the provision of the whole group' (Redcliffe-Maud, 1969, para. 257).

As a result local authorities were created in this country which were:

> larger than anything else in the Western world. Local authorities in England and Wales have an average population of around 123 000. In Sweden, the next largest in Western Europe, the figure is around 30 000 and in most countries the average is nearer 10 000 or smaller (Goldsmith and Newton, 1986, p.140).

But the argument for an increase in size assumed that a local authority necessarily provided services directly and must itself employ all the specialists it required. Even the sharing of, for example, educational advisers between authorities was assumed to be impossible. The assumption of self-sufficiency determined the size of local authorities. What is significant was that assumptions made by the Redcliffe-Maud Commission were not challenged at the time. Rather, the issue was seen as a balance between local democracy, which perhaps equally uncertainly was seen as requiring smaller authorities and efficiency which was equated with size. The assumption of self-sufficiency set boundaries of organisational thinking.

(b) *The assumption of uniformity* It has been assumed that local authorities should provide a uniform standard of service throughout their area. Indeed it has almost been as if the identity of the authority was seen as depending on uniformity of service. One of the first actions taken by the newly created local authorities after reorganisation was to reconcile the different policies and practices of the constituent authorities, so that the new authorities should be

able to provide a common standard of services. The possibility that
the differences reflected real differences in needs and wishes was
not even considered. It was merely assumed that a local authority
had to provide a uniform standard of service.

This is not surprising. Sound public administration is normally
associated with the impartial application of rules or the effective
implementation of agreed policies. Differences have to be justified.
Uniformity justifies itself. Where local authorities were seen as, in
the main, agencies for the delivery of national services, uniformity
appeared not merely to be justified but to be inevitable.

The emphasis on uniformity of service however, can, lead to the
neglect of differences in needs and wishes. The search for equal
opportunities has exposed the reality that uniformity can lead to
neglect of real needs. Uniformity becomes discrimination when
needs differ. At its simplest, for meals-on-wheels to offer European
food to Asian old people is to deny them a service, rather than to
provide it. In the end such differences have been recognised in
authorities, but with difficulty because they require justification
when the assumption of uniformity is the norm and the structure
and procedures of local authorities reflect that assumption.

(c) *The assumption of direct control* The workings of local
authorities were based on the assumption of direct control. The
task of local authorities was the provision of established services
and the organisation was structured to ensure that happened.

In any organisation there is a potential clash between the
organisation as a collective institution and the individuals who
constitute the organisation. The problem of organisational control
is to ensure that activities are carried out in accordance with the
purposes prescribed by the organisation while recognising that
activities are carried out by individuals with their own potential. In
local authorities the established services defined the purpose.
Organisational control was therefore based on direct control. The
assumption of direct control is that control has to be exercised as it
happens. The aim of direct control, although impossible to achieve
in practice is that control will be as continuous a process as the
activities themselves.

The assumption of direct control is reflected in the working of
the committees and the departments into which local authorities
are divided. Committees meet on a regular cycle of meetings with

agendas structured to ensure control as it happens. The departments of local authorities are normally structured on the hierarchical principle with narrow spans of control resulting in multi-levelled tiers, whose justification lies in the assumption of direct control. So strong is the assumption of direct control that the workings of committee and the hierarchical structure of departments are seen as part of the normal mode of operation of local authorities.

(d) *The dominance of professionalism* In each department of the local authority there has been a dominant profession associated with what are seen as the main tasks of the department. In the social services department the main profession is that of social worker, while other departments will be structured around the work of engineers, architects or teachers as education officers. Not all professions have the same status so the degree of dominance may vary.

The dominance of the key profession in the workings of departments means that in departments the chief officer and the majority of the senior management will be drawn from the dominant profession. The boundaries of the department will reflect to a large extent the concerns of that profession. It is rare for a profession to be divided between departments.

The dominance of professionalism is reflected in the organisational culture of local authorities. Professionalism informs the values of departments, their accepted pattern of behaviour and even the way work is defined. Thus an engineer will define the work of a highways department and a social worker the work of social services in terms of their professional knowledge and skills. The professionals' basic training inculcates that knowledge and those skills and builds up professional norms. Careers reinforce professionalism and the primary loyalty of staff is to their profession and the department in which it is embedded rather than to the authorities.

Because professionalism both defines the tasks to be carried out and underlies the structure of departments it becomes difficult to envisage a local authority in which professionalism is not dominant. Professionalism ensures the continuity of local authorities as it ensures that cultures and staff attitudes reproduce themselves. It fits the model of a local authority as an agency for the delivery of services on a national basis ensuring both continuity and uniformity through professional standards.

(e)   *The formalities of accountability*   Accountability is required for the exercise of public power in our society. Those who exercise such power are accountable to those on whose behalf it is exercised. To be effective accountability has to be expressed in organisational practice.

Accountability in local authorities has been seen as being expressed through the electoral process and through the observance of 'proper procedures'. The representative system therefore has been the first condition of accountability. Accountability to the elected representatives is ensured by the observance of proper procedures reinforced by direct control. Formal accountability supports detailed control by ensuring authority for action taken.

The representative system legitimates the actions taken by the local authority. Yet the representative principle can be used to limit accountability reducing the relationship between the authority and the public to the periodic process of election. Reliance on the representative principle has served to limit the search for active processes of accountability.

Movements for organisational change

Administrative reform

While the basic elements and the working assumptions have remained unchanged, there have been movements for organisational change in local authorities. Broadly these can be divided into two periods.

The first can be described as the movement for administrative reform and in the post-war period could be dated from the Treasury 'O and M Reports on Coventry Corporation' in 1953 (although the same approach can be found earlier, as in the Hadow Report of 1934) and which influenced the Maud and Mallaby Reports.

The second can be described as the corporate movement which was highlighted in the Bains Report but which developed from the Maud Report, as the point of transition between the two movements.

It will be argued however that both movements to a large extent accepted the organisational assumptions which characterised the working of local authorities. They were concerned with moving the building blocks about in new committee and departmental structures rather than with transforming the building blocks, with one exception – a challenge to departmentalism.

The movement to administrative reform was directed to securing administrative efficiency. Thus the Treasury 'O and M Report on Coventry' recommended the addition to the position of the Town Clerk, a new role as Chief Administrative Officer. The duties of this role were clearly related to the administration of the council, rather than to advice on its policies. They included:

1. taking a continuing interest in the effectiveness and economy of all administrative arrangements throughout the council;
2. ensuring that administrative activities with which two or more departments are concerned are effectively coordinated (Treasury 'O and M Report', 1954, p.83).

In many ways the movement to administrative efficiency drew much of its ideas from advocates of classical organisation theory. Its emphasis was on administrative coordination, uniformity, hierarchy and span of control. It was expressed in the Maud Committee on Management's recommendations for streamlining committee and departmental structures and in separating off the councillors' role from the administration of services on grounds of administrative efficiency:

We recommend that the number of committees of a local authority should be drastically reduced and that similar or related services should be grouped and allocated to one committee (Maud, 1967, para. 169)

We make no recommendations on the way in which departments should be grouped, although, in our view their number should be reduced to half a dozen or so (ibid, para. 227)

While it is clear that the overall development and control of services should be the responsibility of members, in our view the day-to-day administration of services, the decisions in casework, the routine process of inspection and control should normally be the functions ~of paid officers and not of the members (ibid, para. 147).

The emphasis of the Maud Committee's recommendations for the role of the Clerk also stressed administrative efficiency. They recommended that the Clerk be recognised 'as head of the authority's paid service, and have authority over the other principal officers in so far as this is necessary for the efficient management and execution of the authority's functions' (ibid, para. 179).

These recommendations did not challenge the organisational assumptions underlying the existing structure. Nor did they challenge the concept of a local authority as an agency for the delivery of a series of services. As a result they had an impact on local authorities and led to a marked reduction in the number of committees, and, to a less extent, of departments, and to changes in the definition given to the role of the Clerk (e.g. Greenwood *et al.*, 1969a, 1969b, 1969c).

The corporate movement

Although grounded in the movement to administrative efficiency the Maud Report can also be seen as the starting-point for development of the corporate movement in local government. What distinguishes the corporate approach is its emphasis on considering the activities of the authority as a whole as a means both of ensuring the effective use of resources *and* of reviewing the activities of the local authority in relation to the needs and problems faced. The corporate approach led to both *corporate management*, which involves corporate working in relation to the continuing activities of the authority, and *corporate planning*, which required the setting of objectives for the authority and reviewing activities in relation to those objectives. The Maud Committee prefigured the corporate approach in its recommendation for a management board. That proposal was significant because it challenged existing organisational assumptions – and in particular the assumptions embedded in the traditional committee system.

The management board which would be 'part of a new organisation in which the principle that committees administer the services is replaced by the principle that day-to-day management is the responsibility of officers' (Maud, 1967, para. 161). In effect committees were to lose their executive role except 'in exceptional circumstances' (ibid, para. 167) and 'become deliberative and representative bodies' (ibid, para. 166). Authority was to be clearly given to a management board of between five and nine councillors. The Management Board was:

(a) to formulate the principal objectives of the authority and to present them together with plans to attain them to the council for consideration and decision;

(b) to review progress and assess results on behalf of the council;

(c) to maintain, on behalf of the council, an overall supervision of the organisation of the authority and its coordination and integration

(d) to take decisions on behalf of the council which exceed the authority of the principal officers, and to recommend decisions to the council where authority has not been delegated to the management board;

(e) to be responsible for the presentation of business to the council subject always to the rights of members under standing orders (Maud, 1967, para. 162).

The reception given to this proposal was very different to that given to the other proposals in the Report. It was rejected by every authority in the country (Greenwood *et al.*, 1969a, 1969b, 1969c) because it challenged the committee system and therefore the traditional role of the councillor. It lay beyond the boundaries set by the dominant organisational assumptions.

Nevertheless it had an impact. While local authorities were not ready to accept the effective disappearance of the traditional committee system, the need was widely recognised for a policy committee concerned to maintain an overview of the council's policy. To that extent the emphasis of the Maud Report on the Management Board's role in setting objectives for the authority as a whole had stimulated a response, which could be described as an early recognition of the need for a corporate approach. For the report had highlighted the dangers of departmentalism and expressed their concern at 'the lack of unity inside the authority' (Maud, 1967, para. 108). It saw the Clerk as chief administrative officer as helping to establish leadership so that 'principal officers work as a team' (ibid, para. 180).

The years succeeding the Maud Report saw a growing number of authorities developing corporate management. This was expressed in the appointment of Chief Executives rather than Clerks, the development of the role of the policy committees and an emphasis on the corporate roles of the management team of chief officers. Still lacking were adequate organisational processes to give expression to corporate planning. Some authorities introduced planning programming and budgeting (PPB) systems which sought to relate expenditure on activities to the objectives of the authority, while others introduced modifications of that system (cf. Greenwood and Stewart, 1974).

A new emphasis was given to the corporate approach by the Bains Working Group set up prior to local government reorganisation 'to produce advice for the new local authorities on management structure at both member and officer level' (Bains, 1972, p. *v*). Its starting-point challenged the assumption that a local authority was merely an agency for the delivery of a series of services:

> Local Government is not, in our view, limited to the narrow provision of a series of services to the local community, though we do not intend in any way to suggest that these services are not important. It has within its purview the overall economic, cultural and physical well-being of that community, and for this reason its decisions impinge with increasing frequency upon the individual lives of its citizens. Because of this overall responsibility and because of the interrelationship of problems in the environment within which it is set, the traditional departmental attitude within much of local government must give rise to a wider-ranging corporate approach (Bains, 1972, p.6).

The Bains Report focused on the structure required to support the corporate approach. At the heart of their recommendations were the proposal to set up:

● a Policy and Resources Committee which would 'aid the council in setting its objectives and priorities and, once the major policy decisions have been taken, will be instrumental in controlling the implementation of those decisions' (Bains, 1972, p.23). The

policy and resources committee would also have ultimate
responsibility for the major resources of the authority,
finance, manpower and land ('with which we include buildings' (Bains, 1972, p.24). It would be supported by resource
subcommittees and a Performance Review subcommittee;

- a chief executive who 'must act primarily as the leader of a team
  of chief officers and coordinator of activities. In that capacity
  he must ensure that the resources and organisation of the
  authority are utilised effectively towards the attainment of the
  authority's objectives. In addition he is the Council's principal
  adviser on matters of general policy and as first officer has a
  particular role to play as the Council's representative in
  contacts outside the authority' (Bains, 1972, p.41). The chief
  executives would be drawn from any profession or none and
  would have no department, since in effect the whole authority
  was their department. The report therefore proposed the
  creation of a separate department for the legal and administrative roles.
- the chief officers' management team was presented as the main
  instrument through which the Chief Executive would develop
  the corporate approach.

The Bains Report's emphasis on the corporate approach
challenged the departmentalism of local government. It was
however a limited challenge, first, because that was the only
organisational assumption challenged and second, because it gave
only limited consideration to the nature of departments on which
after all departmentalism is based. For the most part the report is
about rearranging the building blocks of committees and departments.

The Bains Report did however appear to challenge the service
basis of committees recommending that:

The committee structure of the authority should be linked to the
objectives of the authority and the programmes necessary to
achieve these objectives, rather than to the provision of
particular services. Each programme committee should be
serviced by the skills and experience of appropriate departments
(Bains, 1972, p.124).

By breaking the link between committee and service and between chair and chief officer, it was hoped that the new committee structure would support the corporate approach.

In practice, programme committees both as proposed in the Bains Report and as they developed in practice were not all that different from the service committees which they were supposed to replace. The organisational assumptions embedded in the existing committee systems constrained thinking. Most statements of objectives reflected the services – and the committees and departments – into which a local authority was divided.

The Bains Report also considered an alternative to traditional departments bringing together a number of previously existing departments under a directorate system. They expressed reservations about such changes where the role of the Director was merely that of coordinating what in effect remained separate departments. They saw possibilities where the departments could be integrated together, but clearly did not see that approach to be of general application.

The Bains Report had a major impact. The new local authorities had to determine their structure quickly and the Bains Report with its diagrams and its terms of references for the Policy and Resources Committee and for the Chief Executive was an immediately available guide. Broadly its recommendations were followed. Those recommendations, however, focused on structure. They gave structural support for the corporate approach. The establishment in particular of the position of Chief Executive created a counter-balancing role to that of chief officers which contained a potential for corporate working.

There was much less emphasis on processes and ways of working. Although a number of local authorities set out to develop processes of corporate planning which led to the production of corporate plans setting out details of each activity of the local authority over the period of the plan, such processes were often abandoned in authorities under the financial pressures to which local authorities became subject. The processes which had been viewed as instruments appropriate for circumstances of growth were inappropriate for the necessities of constraint. The very detail of the corporate plans gave them a rigidity unsuited to changing circumstance. The comprehensive plan did not focus attention on issues of corporate importance or even on key areas of change. It did not involve a challenge to the traditional incremental budgetary process.

Apart from the emphasis on the corporate approach which had a limited, if significant, impact on the working of local authorities, the Bains Report was constricted by existing organisational assumptions, and set the new local authorities' organisation and management within those assumptions. Changes took place within the organisational structures set up at the time of reorganisation but for a time at least they did not significantly challenge the basic elements and the dominant assumptions of local authorities.

The pressures for organisational change

The challenge of a changing society

In Chapter 3 (p.49) it is argued that organisational strategy must reflect 'the state of the world'. The 'state of the world' has changed for local authorities. Whereas in the post-war period there was an apparent certainty about the tasks to be carried out and the needs to be met as expressed in patterns of service provision, the extent of societal and economic change in recent years has meant that past patterns of service cannot merely be carried forward unchanged into the future. It is not the extent of change alone that is significant, but the number of dimensions on which change is taking place. Major economic restructuring, periods of prolonged unemployment, change in the demographic structure, new social norms, the recognition of a multi-ethnic society and growing environmental threats have combined to pose new challenges for local government and to throw doubt on established patterns of service.

Many of the policies on which that pattern was based have become subject to increasing questioning. The accepted solutions based on professional expertise have not always realised the hopes placed on them. Many town-centre developments and major housing development brought disillusion rather than acclaim. The growth in educational expenditure did not realise the hopes of those who advocated it.

Local authorities have had to recognise that the public does not necessarily accept that the way services are provided is responsive to their needs and wishes. The actual experience of services has sometimes led to frustration rather than satisfaction.

These changes were taking place at a time when central governments – both Conservative and Labour – sought constraint in local government expenditure. That meant that local authorities were unable to respond to economic and social change through growth in expenditure. Growth stabilises because it provides the opportunity for change without disturbing existing activities. Given constraint, change can only be undertaken through reconsideration of existing activities and that implies choice.

Local politics have themselves been changing as a result of these changes and the choices faced (see Chapter 7). Councillors have become more assertive and committed to policy change.

Councillors however, have, been concerned not merely with changing policies but with the working of the local authorities. In this they have responded to the changed public attitude. It is increasingly appreciated that it is not merely a question of what services are provided but how they are provided. The way of working of the local authority goes a long way to determine the nature of the service as received. Left, right and centre use the same phrase to describe the organisational issue – the problem of professional bureaucracies that determine what the public need. Many of the issues with which councillors are increasingly concerned – decentralisation, privatisation, community control, customer choice, equal opportunities – are about the way the authority is run.

All these changes are leading to a challenge to the role of local authorities in providing a series of services on a well-established pattern and implicitly (if not always explicitly) to the organisational assumptions supporting that traditional role. Local authorities have begun to give a new emphasis to their role as local government and to recognise that an emphasis on local choice and local voice requires new relations with the public and new ways of working.

Local authorities have responded as local government to the problems of their local economy by the development of a new role in economic development. The local authority's role in economic development necessarily involves working with and through other organisations and cannot be contained within the organisational boundaries set by the assumptions of self-sufficiency. Growing awareness of discrimination has led local authorities to question whether uniformity of service may mean that the needs of ethnic minorities are neglected.

Local authorities have begun to reconsider the relationship between the organisation and those for whom the services are provided in response to changing public attitudes. It has been recognised that there is a need to make the services more responsive to those for whom they are intended and this has challenged past ways of working and the assumptions on which they are based.

The challenge of government legislation

While local authorities themselves, with a new emphasis on local government, have been led to challenge many of the organisational assumption, they have also been subject to a series of legislative and policy changes imposed by central government which have themselves challenged these assumptions. These legislative and policy changes can be regarded as the government's own response to the social and economic changes described above. They combine with those changes to challenge the accepted role of local authorities in the provision of services.

The main challenge has been to the assumptions of self-sufficiency and of direct control. The Local Government Act 1988 required local authorities to submit to external competition a specified range of services which, whether awarded internally or externally, are then governed by the terms of a contract rather than by direct control. The local authority remains responsible for the service, but need not necessarily deliver the service. The government has applied these provisions for compulsory competitive tendering (CCT) mainly to manual work such as refuse collection but can extend the provisions and is doing so to include a wide range of professional services.

The introduction of CCT has implications beyond its direct effects, leading to the separation of the client and contractor roles in local authorities, with implications for the organisation of departments and for the workings of committees. The development of CCT challenges the role of the centre, since direct services organisations (DSO) that have won contracts under CCT do not readily accept the overheads charged or the services provided (see Chapter 5, pp.123–6).

The government policies for community care will also lead to similar challenges through the division between those providing care services and those assessing the need for care and making arrangements for their provision. The emphasis of government policy is on a variety of provision including direct provision by the local authority but also provision by the private and voluntary sectors, challenging assumptions about uniformity.

The Education Reform Act, by the introduction of the local management of schools giving governing bodies responsibility for the direct management of schools and for control of their budgets, challenges assumptions of direct control. It requires a fundamental reconsideration of the roles of both education departments and education committee.

The housing and education legislation which respectively permit opting-out by estates, or by schools becoming grant-maintained schools, challenges assumptions about the relationship with the public based on the formalities of accountability. It has led to an emphasis on responsiveness to the public, which will also be encouraged by the emphasis given by the government (and indeed the Labour and Liberal Democrats) in the Citizen's Charter:

> All public services are provided for individual citizens, either directly or though their taxes. They are entitled to expect high-quality services responsive to their needs, provided efficiently at reasonable costs (Citizen's Charter, 1991, p.4).

A stress is placed on customer choice which again challenges the assumption of uniformity. In different ways, all political parties are committed to a change in the way that services are provided, which must entail a challenge to many of the organisational assumptions.

These examples do not exhaust the list of changes brought about by government legislation, although they are those that most directly challenge the organisational assumptions of local authorities' traditional ways of working.

The main emphasis of government legislation has been on the control of local government – first, through penalties based on the grant system, then through selective capping limiting the right of local authorities to set their own level of taxes. The abortive introduction of the community charge was another step, followed by the general introduction of capping. The impact of financial constraint has already been discussed, but the process of change itself has been an important although often destructive influence on the working of local authorities.

There was legislation to abolish the metropolitan counties and the Greater London Council, leading to joint boards for certain services. Further reorganisation is now proposed in the remainder of the country. Functions have been removed from local authorities and given to appointed bodies such as the Training and Enterprise councils. These changes have meant that local authorities have increasingly had to see themselves as part of a network of agencies, meaning that the management of influence becomes as much a part of the working of local authorities as the direct provision of services.

Legislation and changing policy has covered the conduct of business by councils since the Widdicombe Report, the regulatory functions of local government, separating inspection from provision in the organisation of departments such as social services, and the use of competition for grants in the Government's City Challenge initiative designed to encourage local authorities to work with the private sector and voluntary bodies in urban regeneration.

From all these changes a challenge has come not merely to the organisational assumptions, but to the role of local government as an agency for the direct provision of services. The challenge is clear; what is not so clear beyond a broad statement of the enabling role, is the future role of local government.

A search for role: the enabling authority?

Whereas the dominant role of local authorities had been the direct provision of services the enabling role stresses other ways of working. Direct provision is seen as only one mode of operation. A local authority can of course provide services through a contract with a private contractor or with a voluntary organisation, but that does not exhaust the modes of operation. A local authority can, and does, act in a variety of ways. It can:

- give grants to the voluntary sector;
- form partnerships with the private sector or other organisation;
- open its resources of information, skills and knowledge to other organisations;
- use its statutory powers on behalf of other organisations;
- make land and property available;
- regulate, license or inspect;
- influence, advocate or campaign.

In the past local authorities have used many of these modes of operation, but they have not been seen as central to the role of the local authority. The local authority has been structured to support direct provision of services, rather than alternative modes of operation. The enabling role changes the emphasis to the development of those alternative modes. Because the enabling role can include many modes of operation, different emphasis and different meanings can be given to it. The development of the concept shows the effect of different influences.

One of the first references to the enabling role was in the Report of the Duke of Edinburgh's Inquiry into Housing (Duke of Edinburgh, 1985) which developed the concept of a local authority playing an enabling role in meeting housing problems, acting through other agencies rather than relying on direct provision. The 1987 White Paper on Housing echoed the phrase (HM Government, 1987).

Prominence was given to the enabling role by the publication of a pamphlet, *The Local Right*, by Nicholas Ridley, the then Secretary of State for the Environment. This pamphlet had the eye-catching subtitle of enabling not providing. While the actual text did not completely rule out any form of direct provision, the emphasis was placed on enabling as distinct from direct provision:

> The role of the local authority will no longer be that of the universal provider. But it will continue to have a key role in ensuring that there is adequate provision to meet needs, in encouraging the various providers to develop and maintain the necessary services, and where necessary, in providing grant support or other assistance to get projects started and to ensure that services are provided and affordable for the clients concerned (Ridley, 1988, p.17).

At the same time the enabling role was being emphasised in other quarters because this was a period when the role of local authorities was increasingly recognised to be changing. The Institute of Local Government Studies' project on 'The Future Role and Organisation of Local Government', sponsored by the local authority associations discussed the assumptions of self-sufficiency and suggested drawing on European experience that a local authority need not provide directly or itself employ all the staff required, but could act in a wide variety of ways in what was in effect an enabling role.

The concept of the enabling authority has been explored in a series of Local Government Training Board (LGTB) publications (Clarke and Stewart, 1988, 1989a, 1989b, 1990) and the task of managing an enabling authority has been described by Brooke in a book (Brooke, 1989) setting out the alternative modes of action to direct provision.

A widely used phrase such as 'the enabling authority' gains many meanings. What, in this case, these meanings share is a challenge to the role of local authorities as an agency for the direct provision of services. The assumptions of self-sufficiency are rejected by the enabling role, but it is easier to reach agreement on what an enabling authority is not than what it is. The LGTB publications by Clarke and Stewart have highlighted the fact that there is a spectrum of meanings given to the phrase, 'the enabling authority'.

At one end of the spectrum is a limited view. The local authority must stop doing a lot of the things it does at the present. It must put more and more of its business out to competitive tender, hand over activities voluntarily to third parties or even be required to do so. Residual responsibility will continue to lie with district, metropolitan or county council, but its important job will be to pass on the **doing**. The local authority will be about **enabling** others to act on its behalf providing local services (Clarke and Stewart, 1988, p.1).

At the other end of the spectrum is a much broader view. The local authority accepts that its direct provision of services is but one means of providing for the community among many. Its role as an 'enabling' council is to use all the means at its disposal to meet the needs of those who live within its area. It will produce some services itself. It will work with and through other organisations – in the public, private and voluntary sectors – aiding, stimulating and guiding their contributions (ibid.).

There are two important distinctions. The first is between the purposes of the enabling authority. The second is between the means that it will use to achieve those purposes. In the more limited concept of the enabling role the emphasis is still upon the services provided by the authority, which are seen as defining its role, while in the wider concept the emphasis is upon meeting community needs and problems. In the more restricted version the emphasis is upon contracting-out services, while in the wider version the emphasis is upon a plurality of modes of operation, that does not rule out direct provision. If the limited role is enabling other organisations to provide the services for which the local authority is responsible, the wider role is enabling the community to meet its needs and problems in the most effective way possible.

The narrower view could be seen as a development of the role of local authorities as an agency for the delivery of services, with the modification that instead of providing the services directly the local authorities are agencies for contracting-out services. The wider view can be seen as a rediscovery of the role of local authorities as local government, concerned with the needs of their community and ready to meet them in the most effective way, which can include external agencies but does not necessarily exclude direct provision. There is an 'intermediate' interpretation of enabling which recognises an important role for local authorities in stimulating economic development within their areas, but falls short of the more comprehensive approach to enabling based on community needs. The significance of these three concepts of enabling – residual, community-oriented and market-oriented – for future change is developed in Chapter 10.

Local authorities have always had an enabling role, but it has normally been treated as of limited importance compared with their role in direct provision. The local authority has been organised for the direct provision of service.

The enabling role is becoming important to local authorities. Ennals and O'Brien carried out a survey of local authorities in 1990 to establish 'what local authorities are doing on the ground to develop the enabling role' (Ennals and O'Brien, 1990, p.3). Their conclusion was that:

> Most local authorities see themselves as enablers, whatever their political control. They express their idea in a variety of different ways but the common thread is that under its enabling role the authority seeks to meet the needs of the community in the most effective way . . . Not only do most authorities see themselves as enablers but their definition of the role is closer to the wider version than the narrower one, even though they may not have fully developed the role themselves (Ennals and O'Brien, 1990, p.5).

Michael Heseltine as Secretary of State for the Environment emphasised the enabling role. He explicitly rejected the narrower concept:

> I reject, therefore, the caricature of the enabling authority as a passive organisation concerned only with the renewal of annual service contracts. Nothing could be further from my vision of the local authority of the twenty-first century.

Rather:

> The enabling authority will be an active authority. The enabling authority will be central to the future of our local communities from great cities to the rural villages (Heseltine, 1991).

In this speech he adopted the wider concept of the enabling authority which, as we have argued, represents the role of local authorities as local government. What is in doubt is the means to achieve that role. The enabling role needs points of leverage in powers and resources. A commitment to the enabling role in its widest sense should involve a commitment to give the local authorities the necessary powers and resources to fulfil that role.

The enabling role in all its forms challenges the organisational assumptions which supported past ways of working, because it involves a change in the role of local authorities. The narrower concept of the enabling role challenges the assumptions of self-sufficiency and direct control, transforming thereby the nature of committees and departments. The wider ·concept involves a fundamental reconsideration of the organisation and management of local authorities which cannot be confined within the boundaries set by past organisational assumptions.

The government has recognised that an emphasis on the enabling role has implications for the organisation and management of local government as it has for the structure of local authorities (Department of the Environment, 1991a). In its consultation paper on the Internal Management of Local Government (Department of the Environment, 1991b) it argues that the development of the enabling role along with other factors adds to the pressure for more responsive management structures; challenging the traditional committee system as 'time-consuming and cumbersome' (ibid, para. 23). The paper emphasises not only contracting-out but also the role of civic leadership. It proposes as models to be considered – although not necessarily to be universally applied – organisational structures based on strengthening the executive in local authorities through the creation of a cabinet, of a directly elected executive or mayor, of a council manager or through adaptation of the committee system, and suggests pilot projects to test out these approaches. The importance of the consultation paper is that it shows that changing concepts of the role of local government challenge existing ways of working and the assumptions underlying them, although the paper itself had a limited perspective focused only on the issue of the executive, perhaps because it gave a limited definition of the enabling role – more limited than Michael Heseltine's speeches had indicated:

In the Government's view local authorities' role in the provision of services should be to assess the needs of their services and ensure the delivery of those services. There are also fields in which local authorities will continue to have important regulatory functions and providing roles . . . But councils should be looking to contract-out work to whoever can deliver services most efficiently and effectively, thus enabling the authority to be more responsive to the wishes of the electorate (Department of the Environment, 1991b, p.2).

This is of course only one response to the organisational implications of the enabling role, which will inevitably vary with the meaning given to that role.

Other roles have been suggested for local authorities. The Audit Commission's management paper setting out the requirements of 'the well-managed council' is entitled *The Competitive Council*. The competitive council is one that has to compete with other organisations both 'for work' under the legislation for compulsory competitive tendering and 'for customers' (Audit Commission, 1988, pp.3–4) under the opting-out provisions for housing and education. There could be a wider sense in which the local authority is required to compete. As other public agencies such as urban development corporations and the Training and Enterprise Councils take over work that was previously the responsibility of local authorities, the local authority can again be regarded as in a competitive position, having to show that it can be effective if it is to retain its responsibilities. 'Local authorities are no longer regarded as necessarily the only, or best, providers of their traditional services' but the Audit Commission argues that:

> In any period of uncertainty and change, the well-managed organisation survives more successfully than the rest. That will be true of local authorities in the next decade (Audit Commission, 1988, p.1).

This model can, however, be seen as a variant of the narrower approach to the enabling role.

Another model is of the local authority as community government or as the community governing itself, but this again is related to the wider vision of the enabling role since:

> As community governments, local authorities' primary role is concern for the problems and issues faced by local authorities. They are the means by which communities confront and resolve those problems and issues that are beyond the scope of individuals or of other modes of social action (Stewart, 1989, p.240).

The significance of this model is that it implies 'a broad base of local accountability' if a local authority is to be the community governing itself. Both these models, whether regarded as models in their own right or as variants on the enabling local authority, imply change in the organisation, and management of local authorities.

Continuity and change

The argument of this chapter has been that the workings of local authority have been built for organisational continuity around a concept of local authorities' role as agencies for the delivery of service, and sustained by organisation assumptions built around that role. The organisation continuity is challenged by the need for organisational change, as social and economic change and legislative change challenge organisational assumptions and new concepts of the role of local authorities develop. Organisational change is taking place, as those new roles develop, but in any organisation, continuity is also required for past roles cannot be totally disregarded. That continuity in local authorities must reflect their continuing responsibilities, the stability as well as the changing nature of society and their basis in local democracy. Local government involves change but also continuity. Many of the issues before local authorities reflect that search for a balance between organisational continuity and organisational change. In later chapters organisational change will be discussed in the context of organisational continuity reflected in past and present practice.

3   The Contribution of Organisation Theory

Historical background

The central concerns of organisation theorists have changed greatly over the past twenty years, as the emphasis has shifted from a concern with structures, to strategic and cultural questions. Until the late 1960s and early 1970s the main area of study was organisational structure and process, typically involving such issues as the relationship between size and bureaucracy, or between technology and control. In the 1970s Marxist and phenomenological influences led to a concern with issues of power, interests and values. In the work of Clegg and others, organisations came to be seen as instruments of domination and control, which reflected and recreated wider aspects of the social structure. In the 1980s the concern for cultural questions in the organisation became dominant, while losing the more radical edge that similar issues had raised in the 1970s, and post-modernists and post-Fordists replaced Marxists. To culture was added questioning of the strategies that organisations were adopting, as the pace of social and economic change became ever greater.

A further concern that arose in the 1980s was the interest in institutions, which involved a recognition that organisations were not simply sites within which social forces played themselves out, but factors that shaped action. The new institutionalism has particularly considered the circumstances in which markets or organisations are likely to be more efficient arrangements for the organisation of production and exchange. The institutional perspective is valuable in focusing on the way that particular organisational settings create and reproduce rules and systems of behaviour. There is a sense in which institutions can be said to think (Douglas, 1987), or, at least, to shape the thought and action of individuals, as well as themselves being shaped by those

individuals. This perspective is particularly valuable when considering public services organisations, for there is a danger that
they are seen as no different from other types of organisation, and
their particular characteristics ignored. A key premise in our
argument is that the public sector has its own character shaped
by its own organisational dynamics, and that the institutional
structure and dynamics of local government make a difference to
patterns of organisational behaviour.

The final change in the agenda of organisation theory has been
the growing concern for the role of networks rather than, or in
addition to, independent organisations. Post-modernist and post-
Fordist theorists, as well as less portentous students of social
change, argue that the traditional large, mass-production-based
organisations of the past are no longer appropriate to modern
conditions. There is need for flexibility in order to cope with rapid
change and with the need for diversity, as opposed to the pursuit of
standardisation that characterised the mass-production era. The
development of more flexible patterns of working will depend very
much on the creation of cooperation between organisations and of
loosely coupled systems through partnership agreements, subcon-
tracting or franchising (Child, 1987). The evidence for change is
limited, but some have argued that it is rather more characteristic
of the public than the private sector (Pollert, 1988). It is not our
intention to test this comparative argument, but we will consider
the evidence that the public sector is undergoing fundamental
change in its approach to organisation and, in particular, whether
more flexible patterns are emerging. Relationships between local
authorities and other organisations, public, private and voluntary,
will form a key theme of this study.

The focus of organisation theory has mirrored the practical
concerns of those involved in deciding the form that public-sector
organisations should take. In the 1960s and early 1970s there was a
preoccupation with the structure of the National Health Service,
local government and central government, and the dominating
questions were how large health or local authorities or government
departments should be, and what should be their internal
structures, if they were to be efficient. It was assumed that each
organisation would be largely self-sufficient and that the normal
pattern or organisation was bureaucratic and hierarchical. Ideas
about appropriate systems of behaviour were adopted from the

private sector and the particular institutional character of the public service was ignored. The National Health Service and local government were both reorganised in the mid-1970s, in ways that emphasised size and structure. Questions of planning were raised but were treated in a rigid and formalistic fashion. The National Health Service, for example, adopted an ambitious and highly rationalistic planning system, that had limited success in practice, and many local authorities adopted elaborate corporate planning systems, that had little real impact on the organisation. Central government tended to pursue 'giantism' – for example, with the amalgamation of departments, as in the case of the Department of the Environment. Policy and planning systems such as Policy Analysis and Review, and Policy, Planning and Budgeting Systems were adopted, but had limited impact.

Processes of organisational management and change were given relatively little attention in the reorganisation of the public service, which tended to be discussed in terms of organisational roles and positions, and simple concepts of implementation. For example, the Bains Report, on the management systems to be adopted after the reorganisation of local government in 1974, argued the importance of management and systematic organisational planning but, in practice, considered these issues largely in terms of the appropriate structures for the new local authorities. There was an assumption that we knew what that we were doing and that the requirement was simply to create the right organisational and structural conditions in which it could be done effectively. Behind the formal changes of the 1970s little actually happened to change the nature of public-sector organisation and management. The institutional character of the public sector largely remained what it had been throughout the post-war period. The 1980s and 1990s, by contrast, have seen real change, as the public service has faced a number of challenges to the fundamental assumptions on which it had been built.

Studies of strategic management, such as Johnson's study of Foster Brothers (Johnson, 1987) and Pettigrew *et al.*'s (1992) study of the National Health Service, have shown the difficulty of change in organisations. Long-established patterns of organisation continually reassert themselves despite widespread recognition of the need for change. Quinn (1980) and others have argued that the development of strategy is a process involving many retreats and periods of stasis, as change is constrained by the pressures of the existing organisation. Hinings and Greenwood (1988) have made a similar argument in their study of strategic change in British local government. It has increasingly been recognised that it is not easy to change organisations, and that changing structures is only effective following other, more fundamental, changes.

The radical character of the change that is now being carried through in local government is bound to pose a threat to inherited structures, processes and values. It was natural for structural questions to dominate thinking in the 1960s and early 1970s, because purposes and values were little questioned. It became much more difficult to maintain that position from the second half of the 1970s, under the threat of financial constraint, criticism of the quality of the public service, and growing political differences. The debate over the nature of the organisation of the public service has become more complex as these new questions and problems have come to dominate the agenda. External pressures, both ideological and material, have provided the context for radical change, challenging the institutional character of the public service.

Schema

The purpose of this chapter is to develop, in more detail, the framework of ideas that we use to analyse the changing organisation and management of local government. It is necessary to make use of a number of concepts, and to adopt a broad approach since we are concerned to explain the overall pattern of change in the organisation of local government. *Strategy*, *structure* and *process*, on the one hand, and *cultures*, *power* and *interests*, on the other, are the key concepts that we will use in understanding the internal context of the authority, and interdependence, coupling and networking will underlie our analysis of the *inter-organisational nature* of contemporary local government. The basic argument that we are making is simple enough: local government in the 1980s and 1990s has had to make fundamental changes to the way that it works, as a result of changes in the context that it faces, and the content of those changes has been conditioned by the existing culture and structure of the organisation. The ways that local authorities have changed share many common features.

The pattern, though, is one of some organisations changing much more quickly than others, pioneering the sort of developments that are later adopted more widely. These early starters, along with outside agencies and individuals making legitimate comment on organisational matters, create both the conditions for change and the patterns which others follow (DiMaggio and Powell, 1983). Change involves processes of innovation, transfer, and the institutionalisation of new patterns of organisation. In order to develop this argument we must first consider the key concepts in our analysis.

Strategy

Organisational strategy is the approach that the organisation adopts in order to achieve its purposes, and, just as strategy precedes structure (Chandler, 1962), so purpose, or as it is often more grandly put, mission, precedes strategy. This does not mean that organisations must have strategies, or, indeed, purposes (and many do not, or have lost their original purposes) but that, if an organisation wishes to be effective, then there must be a fit between its purpose, strategy and structure. Organisations may persist while having lost purpose, or even while permanently failing, but they are not likely to be seen as effective (Meyer and Rowan, 1989). The idea of strategy has its roots in the study of war and in the theory of games, and depends upon uncertainty about the future and the existence of other players. In a certain world, in which there were no other organisations, there would be little need of strategy, because perfect foresight would allow the statement of total prescriptions of action. The future could be planned with certainty. It is only when action must be considered in the light of an uncertain future that a strategy – that is, a general plan of action that is capable of accommodating detailed changes without losing overall coherence – becomes necessary. The source of uncertainty about the future may be the lack of predictability of either the world or the actions of others.

The state of the world may be seen as encompassing either natural events, such as changes in the weather or environmental changes, or the context within which the organisation must work, such as the economic climate. In devising a strategy to deal with the uncertainty of the world the organisation is playing a game against nature, in that there is no human intentionality in the circumstances that will be faced. The organisation will rarely be able to change this material environment; only the very largest and most powerful organisations can significantly change the world within which they operate. Uncertainty may also follow from the fact that other people may act in unpredicted ways, and that they may change their actions in response to each other. The organisation will need a strategy that deals with the fact that there are other actors, whose actions will influence the outcomes that result from any given action that the organisation may take. The strategic actor cannot afford to ignore the actions of others. If I lower prices to increase my share of the market, I may simply find that everybody else does the same, and I am left with the same share of the market and less income. The fact that the result of the action of one organisation will depend upon what other organisations do, creates a number of potential dilemmas, such as the prisoner's dilemma where actors must assume that others will not act cooperatively and so themselves act uncooperatively, thereby leading to both being worse off than they would have been if they had cooperated. Increasing complexity in organisational systems, and the massive advances in the speed and sophistication of communication technology, have increased the likelihood of self-destructive cycles of behaviour, complex dilemmas, self-fulfilling prophecies, and limitations to the effectiveness or rational behaviour (Elster, 1978; Hood, 1976). Strategic management involves dealing with these problems.

There are, then, three factors which are important in the establishment of an organisational strategy – the capacity of the organisation, the capabilities and possible actions of other players, and the state of the world. Organisational capacity is important because it is foolish to adopt a strategy which the organisation is incapable of carrying out. An analysis of strategy depends upon the determination of the 'distinctive competence' of the organisation – that is, the things which it does best. As we shall argue in this book there is always a danger, at a time of change, that organisations will pursue strategies that are in conflict with their distinctive capacities. Indeed, change is often necessary because what the organisation is especially good at doing may no longer be relevant. The organisation may have a life-cycle just like the product or service that it produces – for example, the existence of the local education authority is threatened by the independence of schools and colleges. A danger faced by any organisation is that it carries on doing what it has always done because it is good at it, while demand falls rapidly away.

Strategy may change because of developments in the external context of ideas, and particularly ideas about what are proper approaches to organising and managing. The context of ideas in good currency is likely to be more significant for the public than the private sector, because there are fewer clear criteria on which to judge the effectiveness of different patterns of organisation and styles of management, and public bodies are, therefore, constrained to adopt what are seen, by externally influential people and institutions, as the correct ways of organising. As Meyer and Rowan argue, the organisation must demonstrate its legitimacy by the adoption of the latest managerial totems, whether or not they are effective, or have any real impact. This development has been apparent in the 1980s in the reaction to Peters and Waterman's book, *In Search of Excellence* (1982), which has had at least as much influence in the public as the private sector. The public services must try to give the impression of being well-managed, whatever the reality. What is seen as good management is likely to fluctuate over time, particularly as market conditions vary (Barley and Kunda, 1992).

If strategy is concerned with responding to external circumstances and the actions of others, it is also about developing organisational patterns that are appropriate to the environment – in the marketing jargon developing Strengths and reducing Weaknesses in the face of external Threats and Opportunities – the SWOT analysis. A key problem for organisations is that of responding to a complex and changing external environment, and fulfilling many potentially conflicting demands, while maintaining internal coherence. At times of external stability and certainty, when the organisation needs to give little attention to its environment, it will tend to concentrate on working out its own dynamic and creating internal coherence. As Hinings and Greenwood (1988) argue, organisations will tend to get onto 'tracks', involving movement towards a particular organisational pattern. Environmental change will challenge organisational approaches established in times of stability, and threaten patterns of influence and the structure of interests. Strategy will necessarily be linked to organisational change because it is concerned with adapting to different external circumstances, but that adaptation involves the creation of internal coherence. Our argument is that in the post-war period local authorities faced a long period in which organisational demands were relatively unchanging and certain. The result was that they adopted an approach emphasising self-sufficiency, size, and independence from other organisations. The approach was essentially non-strategic, in that the authority paid little attention to external circumstances or the actions of other organisations. The institutional character of the local authority was essentially hierarchical and bureaucratic, expressed in a strongly established culture of professional bureaucracy.

The period from 1945 to the mid-1970s can be seen as involving slow incremental development; the present changes, as we will show, are much more fundamental. Tushman and Romanelli (1985) make a distinction between two types of change – convergence and reorientation – the former involving continual small-scale change, as the organisation moves towards increasing consistency, and the second fundamental changes to the whole nature of the organisation. The changes of the 1980s and the 1990s involve reorientation rather than convergence.

Central to the development of strategy at a time of change is the role of leadership in formulating new organisational values. Processes of incremental change and development serve to embed value systems firmly in the normal rules and patterns of behaviour of the organisation. Beliefs, attitudes and values become deeply institutionalised. Leadership is necessary at times of stability but it is of a different form – transactional as opposed to transformational leadership (Bass, 1985) – from that required to manage change. The transformational leader must exhibit more than mere enthusiasm for a new set of organisational purposes, and must recognise the conflicts that are created by change, and the ethical and moral questions that will be raised by the clash of new and existing values.

Structure and process

The structure of an organisation is the pattern of rules, positions, and roles that give shape and coherence to its strategy and process, and is typically described in organisation charts, job descriptions and patterns of authority. The structure of the organisation consists of a set of patterned ways of acting. It is an expression of the organisational memory, that enables its members to behave in the same way when faced with the same or similar circumstances. Structure provides the basis of action, and reduces the need for decisions. It also creates a set of constraints on people's actions and their relationships with one another. Structure may be more or less explicit and articulated, and the actual emergent structure of the organisation may be quite different from the formal organisation, as laid out in organisation charts. It is important to distinguish between the formal and informal structure of the organisation in the public sector where, as we shall argue, the role of myth and ceremony are important, and the organisation must maintain an acceptable public face, which may well differ from the private reality.

The key elements of structure are:

- the degree of differentiation;
- integration;
- the extent of centralisation;
- the level of formalisation; and
- specialisation.

Differentiation refers to the extent to which the organisation is divided up into separate parts and units in order to get work done. Local authorities have typically been highly differentiated, with large numbers of departments and committees, despite recommendations for simplification of structures. The principle upon which differentiation has been based has been mainly that of professional function, with departments and committees being established to reflect the dominant professional groups within the organisation. More recently, the development of computers and information technology has made possible more differentiation through the fragmentation of tasks, though on a non-functional basis. It is not clear whether this has led to deskilling or the creation of more skilled work and clearly both processes are present to some degree. A further aspect of the differentiation of the organisation is the division of work based on gender, with disproportionate numbers of women filling the more junior posts in the organisation. The division of labour and the division of authority are also divisions between men and women. Technology may well have had quite different effects on the work of women compared with that of men. We will pay particular attention to the role of gender in the structuring of local authorities.

Integration refers to the extent to which there are devices intended to ensure that the various parts of the organisation are working to a common set of purposes, policies and procedures. All organisations have a central core that is intended to ensure unity of purpose and corporate control – for example, Chief Executives and personnel and finance departments. There are also various processes that are intended to have an integrating role – for example, budgetary and planning processes. Integrative devices are not necessarily synonymous with the central core of the organisation, but the role of the centre will necessarily be crucial in considering modes of integration – for example, whether it should rely on power or persuasion. Integration is not the opposite of differentiation, but a separate dimension of the structure of the organisation and it would be quite natural for there to be high levels of both integration and differentiation. The more the organisation is divided up into separate parts, the more necessary it will be to pull its activities together again.

The *extent of centralisation* will vary with the complexity and size of the organisation, the more complex and the larger the organisation, the more difficult it will be to operate through central decisions. In the case of complex problems it will be difficult for the centre to make coherent decisions, because of the loss and distortion of understanding that occurs as information is fed from the periphery to the centre. This is a particular problem for service organisations, because they cannot create their products in manufacturing units that are buffered from the world they serve. Rather they must produce their service, for example in health, social services and education, working directly with those they serve; producer and consumer cannot easily be separated from each other. Production must therefore take place on the periphery of the organisation, in the direct interaction of client and provider, and cannot be insulated in well-buffered manufacturing units. The organisation may be seen, as Daft (1974) argues, as having two cores – the operating core at the periphery and the central administrative core. The problem is one of allowing those at the periphery of the organisation, engaged in the direct delivery of service, sufficient autonomy to exercise the necessary initiative. As local authorities have attempted to decentralise in order to ensure more autonomy for those delivering services, and to become more responsive to customers, then the relationship between the two cores has become more problematic.

Size will also make it difficult to maintain central decision making simply because of the number of decisions that are likely to arise, even in a relatively simple organisation, and the problems of communication. The larger the organisation, and the more centralised its decision-making, the longer is the chain of communication through which any decision must pass from the point at which it is made to the point of implementation. Again, there is likely to be significant information and control loss as communication links become more extended. The highly centralised pattern of management that has characterised the public service has been dependent upon the development of sophisticated bureaucratic systems, characterised by hierarchy and decision making based on formal rule systems. The number of management levels in the organisation has been large, partly reflecting size, but also reflecting the division of work into relatively tightly defined specialisms. There has been a strong division of labour that has, if anything, been enhanced by the development of information technology.

The developments of the 1980s have changed the demands on the centre of the local authority. There is an increasing separation of those elements of the centre that are concerned with the provision of support services to operational units from those that are concerned with control, coordination and the strategic direction of the organisation. Support functions are either being decentralised, or provided on the basis of explicit agreements about what is to be provided and at what cost. The proper role of the centre has come to be a matter of debate and contention

Formalisation refers to the extent to which the organisation operates through stated or known rules and procedures. These may take the form of written rules or unstated but commonly known procedures – 'the way we do things here'. Rules, routines and operating procedures may lead to a degree of organisational sclerosis, but they do serve to create a certain amount of predictability which is necessary for organisational continuity.

Rules, routines and standard operating procedures, as March and Oken (1986) say, 'reduce the potential for chaos' (p.39). They are efficient in that they reduce decision-times and the amount of searching for information that has to be conducted to reach decisions. The more extensive the organisation and its activities, the more necessary is formalisation. Change involves the transition from one set of rules to another, and the process of adaptation that must be gone through, as we learn to operate in new ways. Change may also involve a move to greater or less formalisation, because of conflicting pressures, for example, increasing legislation leads to greater formalisation, but devolved control leads to pressure for less formalisation.

Specialisation refers to the degree to which the work of the organisation requires specific skills. A particular type of specialisation that is important in the public sector is that of professionalism. The departments of the local authority are typically based on particular professions, and progress up the managerial hierarchy is also professional advance. Specialisation has tended to increase as the world has grown more complex, leading to different patterns of organisation of the market for scarce skills. One result has been the growth of consultants possessing specialist skills which organisations cannot afford to employ on a full-time basis, and which they buy in as and when necessary. Again the tradition of self-sufficiency has come under pressure from the fact that the local authority can no longer afford to employ all the skills which it may occasionally need. Patterns of specialisation are changing as traditions of professional autonomy are eroded, and general management emphasised.

The concept of an organisation as having structure is an expression of its continuity – that it does not have to be created from the ground up each day – and of the fact that the actions of its members have a pattern. Structures are highly resistant to change. They are an expression of the need for both order and the maintenance of patterns of behaviour. Organisational processes, by contrast, are the various sets of activities that must be carried out in order to ensure persistence of the system. The organisation will need to plan production, and obtain and manage resources in order to produce its outputs. It will also require processes of organisational learning, in order to be able to adapt to changing needs and circumstances. In the public service, processes analogous to those that take place in the private sector have a different connotation because they happen not in response to market demands, but as an expression of political choice. The processes of public service management have their own purposes.

In contrast to structure, which points to the more static features of the organisation, 'process' refers to the notion of the organisation in action. Organisations can be seen as flows of information, resources, communication, outputs and decisions. The degree of order in these flows can vary, as the proponents of the garbage-can model (March and Olsen, 1986), emphasising the role of chance in organisational processes, have argued. We will argue that, as the rate of change in the public service accelerated in the course of the 1970s and 1980s, concern shifted from structure to process. The debate has increasingly been about processes of strategic management, budgetary control, financial management and public relations. Organisational change has made it more difficult to maintain institutionalised patterns of behaviour, embodied in organisational structures. Much of the management of the public service in the 1980s and 1990s has been an attempt to develop and institutionalise new organisational processes.

Culture

Organisations cannot only be conceptualised through analogies with machines and organisms (Morgan, 1986), using concepts such as structure and system; they may also be seen as being composed of people, seen both as individuals and as groups. A recognition of the human character of the organisation requires an acknowledgement of the role of culture and power in its working. Organisations are social and political systems, in which major life interests are pursued. Organisations are sites for people's projects. By the culture of the organisation we mean the common set of everyday understandings, beliefs and expectations with which it operates, and which allow it to persist with a degree of cohesiveness. It is the culture of the organisation which enables it to act with continuity, since it provides a set of reliable expectations about the behaviour of others.

Local authorities have been bureaucratic cultures, as, indeed, they should be, for public accountability and expectation requires that they be characterised by a degree of predictability, and that they treat similar cases in the same way. It can be assumed that rules will be followed, and that hierarchy will dominate. People can expect a degree of predictability from the bureaucracy, that they might not expect to find in a more informal organisation. There will, of course, always be subcultures within organisations, expressing the understandings, beliefs and expectations of particular groups – for example, of particular professionals or of particular departments. These subcultures will normally be developed within the limits imposed by the dominant organisational culture. Within the context of public-sector service organisations this is most importantly true of the culture of street-level bureaucrats who, as Lipsky and others have shown, will develop their own rules and patterns of discretion, in order to be able to make organisational imperatives match the world in which they must operate. The street-level subculture develops as a means of making it possible to operate from day to day in a world that will never fit perfectly with the rules and procedures established by hierarchically senior staff who lack contact with operational reality. Street-level culture only has meaning within the context of the larger organisational culture: it does not overthrow it, but adapts it to reality.

It is much easier to change structures and systems than to alter cultures, because cultures are built into our patterns of behaviour in an unconscious and, perhaps, unthought fashion. It is precisely because they have become part of everyday expectations, language and behaviour that we find it difficult to change cultures. A common culture contributes to the efficiency of the organisation through enabling communication to take place more easily than would otherwise be the case, because of common language and understanding. The pattern of organisational behaviour that has developed over long periods will be resistant to change, even if only unconsciously, because new approaches cannot easily be expressed in the old organisational language. Much of the process of change will involve the unfreezing of the existing culture so that new approaches can be considered. The purpose of organisational change is therefore likely to be one of retreat as well as advance, as dominant cultures resist replacement.

Power and interests

Organisations are arenas in which individuals and groups pursue their interests in competition with others. The concept of interest refers to the individual's or group's position in the distribution of organisational resources, such as finance, status and authority. Organisational change is likely to involve changes in the pattern of interests, as organisational advantage and disadvantage change. Alford (1975) in his study of the management of health in the USA, has distinguished between dominant, repressed and challenging interests. Dominant interests are those which are built into institutional framework of the organisation, and are expressed in the existing power structure. Repressed interests are those of the disadvantaged, who will frequently be unaware of the extent, or, perhaps, even the fact of their disadvantage. Challenging interests are those of individuals and groups who are concerned to forward change and are likely to benefit from it. We will argue that professional interests have been dominant in local government, that the interests of women and black people have typically been repressed, and that the challenging interests are those of the new managers.

A key concept in the understanding of interests in the organisation is that of career, which is the path that individuals follow in their lives within an organisation or system of organisations. Gouldner (1957) has distinguished between the cosmopolitan and local patterns of career, reflecting differences in the orientation of individuals to the organisations within which they work. Cosmopolitans are more likely to be committed to professions that have a wider reference than the individual employing organisation, and to move, in the course of their working lives, through a series of positions, and probably through a number of organisations. The individual's career expresses a process of advance, as knowledge and experience are gained. The local is likely to be limited to the individual organisation, and to experience relatively little advance up the organisational hierarchy. Patterns of organisational and personal interests come together in the concept of organisational career, with its conflicting elements of commitment to the organisation, the profession and personal advance.

Organisational personnel, then, are likely to be divided into those who are strongly tied into the individual organisation, and those who have wider patterns of commitments. Those who have wider horizons than the specific organisation are more likely to see their interests in an individualistic way. Those who are more limited, both occupationally and organisationally, are more likely to pursue their interests through common action with those in the same position and the same organisation. The nature of the attachment of these different groups to the organisation will lead to different patterns of attitude and action. The different nature of organisational interests will influence the way that staff are managed – that is, the industrial relations and human-resource-management strategies of the organisation. Changes in the nature of local labour markets have shifted power towards the cosmopolitan professional, as we shall see in considering staff management in local government.

Existing patterns of organisational culture, structure and strategy will embody particular distributions of power, and change will be seen as most threatening by those who stand to lose most, often those who are most influential in the existing system. Power may be defined as the ability to make others behave in a way that is in line with one's interests, whether or not that behaviour is in line with their interests. Power in organisations will depend upon three factors: resources, organisational processes and skill. Power depends upon resources in the sense that those who are powerful are likely to possess some or all of the bases of power, such as wealth or physical force, that give them the ability to grant rewards or impose sanctions. Hickson *et al.* (1971), Crozier (1964) and others have shown that power may also be contingent on the position of an organisational member or unit in the organisational process. The more important one's activities to the operation of the organisation and the less there are substitutes for what one does, then the more powerful one is likely to be. However well-resourced one may be and however central one's activities may be to the organisation it is still possible that one exerts relatively little power, in practice, because of lack of skill. The exercise of power is a skilled activity, and history provides many instances of those who are potentially powerful wasting either superior resources or a more advantageous position.

Power may be exercised negatively or positively – that is, to create or prevent change. In the traditional local authority power, on the bureaucratic model, depended upon position in the organisation. Power has also been built into the organisational framework, through the establishment of rules and procedures. Those with most power are typically those who can establish rule-systems that operate to their benefit, without others being conscious of the way that they are being disadvantaged. The longer the history of the organisation, the more the distribution of power becomes institutionalised. Those whose position is well established in the existing pattern or organisation are likely to resist change precisely because it will affect them detrimentally. It is for this reason, in large part, that change is so often precipitated from outside the organisation. In the case of local government since the 1970s, we will argue that change has initially resulted from changing external circumstances, which are responded to by those with the power to do so, and who have an interest in change. In well-established organisations it will be difficult to change without commitment from the organisational leadership.

Public-choice theorists have made the most explicit attempt to develop the concepts of interests and power in attempting to explain the way that bureaucracies work and the likely failings that they will exhibit. The basis of public-choice theory is that individuals are motivated by the pursuit of their own self-interest, rather than the interests of the organisation, and that this can lead to systemic inefficiencies. The problems are particularly likely to arise in the public sector, because there are only limited market mechanisms that will serve to control the freedom of the bureaucrat, compared with the private-sector company which must satisfy the Stock Exchange and the money markets, and which is vulnerable to takeover. Niskanen (1971) has argued that bureaucrats will be budget-maximisers because their own rewards will be linked directly to the size of their budgets and the number of staff that they control. Producers are more likely to be tightly concentrated and organised than are consumers or citizens, and therefore they are better placed to recognise and pursue their interests. Others, while following the general argument developed by Niskanen, have argued that there are matters other than bureau-size that will be taken into account by the self-interested bureaucrat.

The major limitation of public-choice theory is its restricted view of what it is that the bureaucrat will maximise, which may be many things other than bureau-size and budget. Dunleavy (1991) has used the concepts of public-choice theory to develop an explanation of the form that bureauxs will take and the reactions to processes of organisational change. He argues that the nature of the bureau budgets varies, creating different patterns of interest for senior bureaucrats and politicians. He distinguishes between the core budget of the organisation, compared with those parts of the total budget which are distributed to other organisations. Bureaucrats, he argues, will be motivated to maximise not only their budget or their staffing levels, but also those aspects of the organisation's spending that will enhance their own interests. For example, those – such as the Treasury – who control the budgets of others, will not derive their advantage from themselves having large budgets or staffs. Dunleavy has found some support for his arguments in studies of the organisation of British central government. These arguments will be important in examining the link between financial constraint and cutbacks, the introduction of competition, and the organisational dynamics within which these changes take place. One might expect, for example that central parts of the organisation would take an attitude to such changes, that would be quite different from that of those who were less powerful or more peripheral.

The control of the pursuit of self-interest in organisations is a crucial part of the overall steering and control process, and can take three major forms:

- punishing those who act against the organisation's interests;
- rewarding those who act in accordance with the organisation's interests;
- attempting to align the interests of the individual and the organisation.

Most organisations will use all these approaches to some degree, but they are likely to be used differently depending on the nature of the individual's attachment to the organisation. With staff whose attachment is calculative, as Etzioni (1961) puts it, there is likely to be a greater emphasis upon punishment for action that is against the organisation's interests, on the assumption that it is blameworthy. There is likely to be the development of the low-trust syndrome (Fox, 1974) and punishment-centred bureaucracy (Gouldner, 1954). This approach is not possible with staff who are more able to pursue their interests outside the organisation, and they are more likely to be dealt with by a mixture of incentives and attempts to enhance organisational commitment. In studying patterns of organisational change it will be especially important to examine the way that self-interest asserts itself, and the way that it is controlled and mobilised.

The inter-organisational context

Local authorities exist within a context of other organisations and actors, private and public, with whom they may cooperate or compete. The traditional local authority, concerned to be self-sufficient, paid little attention to the role of other organisations, but recent changes have made the inter-organisational context a factor that cannot be ignored in the internal management of the authority. It is no longer possible for the organisation to buffer itself against the influence of the environment in which it exists. The local authority has become more dependent on others for resources, and cooperative working is increasingly required in the development of functions such as social care and economic development. Legislative change, such as the introduction of competition and contracts, has often meant that authorities can only implement their policies through the use of other bodies. We will develop a number of concepts in order to understand the inter-organisational concept of the local authority, namely interdependence, coupling and networking. More generally, we will develop the concepts of hierarchies and markets, in order to understand the changing role of competitive processes in the public sector. The argument that will develop is that the authority is increasingly having to accept that it cannot effectively fulfil its responsibilities without recognising the role that other organisations play, and its dependence upon them. It must then, as part of its organisational strategy, decide how it wishes to operate, particularly in the extent to which it wishes to use markets or hierarchical processes. In effect, what is happening is that new patterns of organisation are developing that are neither independent organisations nor pure markets, but involve various types of grouping of interrelated organisations. The local authority must decide how tightly its activities are to be coupled to those of other organisations. Where hierarchy is impossible or inappropriate, then it must act to create networks, operating through contracts or other coordinating mechanisms.

Interdependence

The extent of interdependence of any organisation is the degree to which it can only operate effectively through taking account of the role of others. The large monopolistic firm will need to take relatively little account of the actions of others; small suppliers may effectively be the prisoners of larger manufacturing companies. Other organisations may be important because they possess resources or information, without which the focal organisation cannot carry out its activities effectively, or because their activities are complementary to its own. They may also be important because they may substitute for the activity of the focal organisation, which must, therefore, compete with them. The longer a particular social system has been established, the more important inter-organisational relationships are likely to be, because the various interests that exist will have had time to organise themselves. The density of the organisational context is likely to increase over time. Decision-making is likely to become more difficult as the density of the environment increases, and more interests develop explicit organisation. Pressure groups, for example, will become an increasingly important factor in organisational decision-making the longer the organisation has been established.

The more complex and dynamic the environment – the problem – the less likely it is that one organisation will be able to deal with it alone and interdependence will develop. This is particularly so in the case of the externalities that arise from failures of the market, for example, failure to deal with pollution or urban decay, which tend to arise precisely because of the failure of organisations and individuals to relate to one another, and to take each other's interests into account. The greater the pace and degree of change in the environment, the less likely it is that any given organisation will possess the skills and resources to deal with that change. Existing organisational capacities are likely to have developed in a way that will mean that they are not well-adapted to new circumstances.

Cooperation with other organisations may allow one to draw on skills and capacities that are missing from one's own resources. Local authorities increasingly face this position as they confront new and complex problems and as their environment goes through radical changes.

Dependence is the obverse of power, and to increase one's power is often to increase one's own discretion at the expense of that of others (Benson, 1975). The traditional public sector was highly dependent, having its own resources, and possessing considerable power in relation to those with whom it interacted, even central government departments. The growth of interdependence in a more complex environment is reducing the power of the local authority. The growth of policy networks, and other inter-organisational groupings, means that local authorities are becoming much less independently powerful.

Coupling

The strength of the networks within which an organisation must work can be understood in terms of the concept of inter-organisational coupling, which involves a consideration of how closely and tightly organisations relate to each other. There are three aspects of the degree of coupling between organisations that are important in organising inter-organisational networks. First, there is the tightness with which organisations are tied together. For example, an organisation that manufactures for supply to a single customer is much more tightly coupled to that customer organisation than an organisation supplying to a large number of organisations. Second, there is the extensiveness of the network – that is, the number of organisations that are coupled together to one degree or coupling is likely to be. As Granovetter (1973) has pointed out, there are considerable advantages to a loose network, which can be differentially activated in the pursuit of specific interests. Those involved in a small number of very tight relationships may well face considerable difficulty if those relationships should fail. Finally, there is the degree of formality or informality in the coupling of organisations. In some cases there may be formal contracts that are so tight that there is little difference between the organisations involved; in others, the relationships may be informal and dependent on individual relationships.

Networks

High interdependence is likely to be associated with tight coupling, in which the degree of connectedness between organisations is strong – for example, because they depend on the same sources of funds, or are concerned with similar problems. The more tightly coupled a set of organisations the more they can be seen as forming an explicit network, which involves organisations cooperating in order to build on complementary strengths. Networks will tend to be based upon concepts of reciprocity, rather than competition, and to require a degree of trust between the parties to the network. It is more difficult to operate through networks than through hierarchies, because the sanctions that are available within an organisation are not available and because knowledge and information is likely to be widely spread. The wider the remit of an organisation, whether public or private, the more it is likely to have to deal with other external organisations. Most networks, as Aldrich (1979) argues, are likely to consist of weak links that can be mobilised when they are needed for a specific purpose or activity, creating action sets. A specific requirement of legislation in the 1980s and 1990s was the requirement for the local authority to operate through cooperative networks rather than through self-sufficient bureaucracies.

Where organisational processes tend to be based on rules and routines, inter-organisational processes are based on relationships, which are often personal and therefore prone to breakdown, as individuals move or their priorities change. The importance of individuals to the management of interorganisational relationships is frequently not recognised within the organisation in terms of career advance. The more an organisation is dependent on others to achieve its objectives, the more important is boundary management. The more developed networks become the more they are likely to become based upon formal rules and procedures. For many staff the management of the organisation is increasingly likely to mean the management of linkages with others. The development of working through networks is important to the development of flexibility, and the ability to mobilise resources to meet rapidly changing circumstances. Network organisations, which play the role of creating and maintaining inter-organisational relations, are also likely to develop as networks become more complex.

Markets and organisations

Perhaps the most salient form of organisational network is that of the market, in which organisations choose, or are forced, to exchange with each other on the basis of contract. Government policy has increasingly focused upon developing the role of markets in the provision of public services, rather than providing through large and ponderous organisations. Even where it is necessary to develop large organisations, it is seen as being possible to gain the benefits of competition through the use of internal markets, as, for example, in the National Health Service. Williamson has provided the most extensive theoretical treatment of the operation of markets *versus* organisations or, as he terms it, hierarchy. He asks why it is that organisations exist. Why should we bother to create large organisations when we could purchase what we need in the market? This is a particularly pertinent question given the development of contracting-out. Why could we not get rid of the public sector altogether, purchasing what we want in the market?

Williamson's answer (Williamson, 1975, 1985) to the question of why organisations exist is that they develop because they are the most efficient means of dealing with certain transactions. A *transaction* involves an exchange of values between two parties, and, except in the very simplest cases, creates costs involving the collection of information and the establishment of the terms of the exchange. It will be difficult to conduct transactions effectively on the market the more there is bounded rationality, opportunism and asset specificity. The concept of *bounded rationality*, developed by Simon (1945), is that we are incapable of taking account of every factor that needs to be considered in making a decision because of limited cognitive capacity. *Opportunism* refers to the assumption that those with whom we must deal on the market will be pursuing their own interests as guilefully as possible. They cannot be assumed to have our interests at heart. *Asset specificity* is a measure of the extent to which the assets (both labour and capital) that are used by an organisation can be transferred to other uses.

The greater is bounded rationality, argues Williamson, the more difficult it is to be accurate about future needs, and the more difficult is the planning or the writing of comprehensive agreements. Providing services through internally employed resources is a means of dealing with bounded rationality, since it allows the redirection of resources should unforseen circumstances arise. This redirection is much easier with internally owned or employed resources because of the rights of ownership, and the open-endedness of the labour contract. Opportunism can also be dealt with more easily within the organisation because a wider range of sanctions is available should actions that are against the interests of the organisation be discovered. The organisation also has greater powers to gather information on the activities of its own employees compared with those of other – subcontracted – organisations, or individuals, for example, through supervision processes or appraisal systems. The more specific are assets, including labour assets, the better it is for the organisation to own them, because it will not then be the prisoner of potentially monopolistic sellers.

Local authorities are moving into a world in which they must increasingly relate to other organisations in the market or in other ways. They are no longer able to pursue a strategy of self-sufficiency, employing all the resources that they need. The change in the public sector is serving to blur the boundaries between the organisation and its environment, and between one organisation and another. We will use the ideas of interdependence, coupling, networks, hierarchies and markets to examine the way that inter-organisational context within local authorities' work is changing.

Conclusion

Local authorities are complex organisations, operating in diverse contexts. It is necessary to understand not only the changing character of the local authority itself, but the way that it operates in the overall context of local governance. A new institutional framework is beginning to emerge under the pressures of central government legislation, financial constraint, and the perceived need for change within local authorities themselves. Local authorities are no longer self-sufficient organisations, employing all the staff who deliver the services they provide. The traditional concept of bureaucracy is of limited value in understanding the nature of local government.

4 Internal Management: Structures and Processes

In this chapter we apply the conceptual framework set out in Chapter 1 and developed in Chapter 3 to analyse recent changes which have taken place in the management structures and processes within local authorities. Although the political dimensions of these structures and processes are briefly identified, a more detailed analysis of the role of elected members in the management of local authorities is provided in Chapter 7. This chapter commences with a brief retrospective evaluation of the changing patterns of structure and process in local authorities since the late 1960s developing some of the themes introduced in Chapter 2, and emphasising the changing relationship between structure, strategy and culture over this period. In relation to the pressures for major changes in structure and process, the sources and strength of organisational resistance to change (or 'organisational inertia') are recognised and discussed. We then identify a number of key dimensions of analysis from Chapter 3 (integration/differentiation; centralisation/decentralisation, etc.) and show how recent legislative changes have exerted pressure for a radical reassessment both of the significance of these dimensions for organisation structure and of the balance between the pairs of concepts concerned, in each case. The implications of the changes identified for some of the key structural mechanisms in local government – the Chief Executive, the management team, the service director (and his or her department) and for budgetary processes are then examined. Finally, a summary of the key changes in organisational structure and processes that have been identified is set out, and their relationship to the content of subsequent chapters is clarified.

'Structure' was defined in Chapter 2, but it is useful to reproduce the definition here. By the term 'the structure of an organisation' we mean the pattern of rules, positions and roles which give shape and coherence to its strategy and process, and which is typically given expression in organisational charts and job descriptions. The organisational structure consists of a set of patterned ways of acting that allow the organisation to act in a systematic fashion. The *formal* and *informal* elements of structure should be distinguished, although both are important topics of study. In contrast to structure, which points to the more static features of an organisation, the term 'process' refers to the notion of the organisation in action, and implies the idea of change. It is the processes of organisational operation, taking place within the structure, that constitute the organisational system.

Changing approaches to local authority structures

In Chapter 2, two (linked) movements for organisational change in local government in the 1960s and 1970s were identified and discussed; the movement for *administrative reform* and the '*corporate movement*'. Both movements addressed issues of organisational structure and process, but (as we argued in Chapter 2) were primarily concerned with 'moving the building blocks about' in new committee and departmental structures, rather than with transforming the nature of the building blocks. The one possible exception to this generality was the challenge to departmentalism inherent in the strengthened role of the Chief Executive and management team and the new emphasis on corporate planning processes. Indeed, one of the main thrusts of the Redcliffe-Maud Report was a critique of the ineffectiveness of existing approaches to policy-making. As Alexander (1982, p.67) notes:

> The Maud Committee had given official recognition to the concerns of many local government officers that the iterative incremental approach to policy-making was inefficient, wasteful and inimical to an economic and cost-effective delivery of public services.

As we shall see, it took a much more fundamental and radical challenge to the structures and processes of local authorities in the late 1980s to effect a major transformation of this traditional incremental approach.

The underlying philosophy and major recommendations of the Maud, Mallaby and Bains Reports have already been discussed (see Chapter 2, pp.26–8). The main emphasis in their recommendations can be summarised as an attempt to strengthen both corporate management and corporate planning processes in local authorities. These twin themes of corporate management and corporate planning, although they have undergone a number of transformations of nomenclature and emphasis since the early 1970s (corporate management has become 'strategic' management and corporate planning, strategic (or policy) planning) have survived as key elements in the changing patterns of local authority approaches to structure and processes since local government reorganisation in 1974.

The 1974 reorganisation in England and Wales (1975 in Scotland) provided an ideal opportunity for a break with tradition. Because a much greater emphasis was placed on *structural* change, as opposed to change in decision processes (i.e. in corporate management rather than corporate planning) and in fact much of the structural change introduced was superficial in nature, it did little in reality to change the ways in which local authorities operated. In his review of the experience of the reorganised local government system, Alan Alexander emphasised this difference between appearance and reality:

The widespread, almost uniform, introduction in the new local authorities . . . of the trappings, if not always the reality of corporate management was often the result of an uncritical acceptance of the prescriptions of the Bains Report. This acceptance, moreover, was frequently unaccompanied . . . by either a real understanding of the techniques, or an accurate perception of the political consequences implied by the new approach (Alexander, 1981, p.67).

Thus, although the Bains Report and its predecessors were clearly influential in changing the formal structures of local authorities, their impact on authorities as organisational systems was much more limited. Some of the reasons for this outcome have already been identified. The Bains Report provided an 'off-the-shelf' package of structural changes at a time when the new local authorities were desperately seeking guidance. It emphasised issues of structure to the relative neglect of issues of process; and of *formal* structure rather than more informal structural elements. It was focused much more strongly on the roles of officers than on those of members, and failed to recognise and reflect the changing nature of party politics in local government (see Chapter 7). But there is another, more fundamental reason (with the benefit of hindsight) why the Bains Report had a limited and partial impact on organisational systems. It failed to consider structure in relation to *strategy* and *culture*, and to place it in an appropriate perspective in relation to those two variables.

It was argued in Chapter 3 that there has been a marked change in emphasis amongst organisational theorists over the past twenty years, from a concern with structure to a concern with strategy and culture. That is not to say that formal and informal structures have come to be regarded as irrelevant; rather that structure has come to be viewed as a *secondary* consideration. Once an organisation is clear about its mission, its organisational strategy and its cultural values (and the nature of the changes it faces in its external environment) *then* it becomes relevant to analyse whether or not its structure is congruent with these other more fundamental organisational features, and whether changes are needed. It is the *sequence* in which organisational issues should be considered which has been reassessed and clarified.

The changing concerns and emphases of organisational theorists will not of course necessarily be reflected in the way organisations – in our case, local authorities – actually behave. As we have seen, from the mid-1960s until the mid-1980s, the main emphasis within the vast majority of local authorities when considering organisational change, was on structures, and to a lesser extent, decision processes. Strategy and culture were rarely given serious consideration. If a new problem or challenge became apparent – either externally- or internally-generated – the most appropriate response was invariably seen as changing the authority's structure. There was typically an organisational assumption that if the structure *per se* were changed, then the purpose for which the change had been introduced had been achieved. Rarely was the effectiveness of the structural changes which had been introduced subsequently evaluated.

In the early 1980s, following the publication of the influential (at a superficial level at any rate) *In Search of Excellence* (Peters and

Waterman, 1982), some of the authorities which were most concerned to respond to new management thinking (typically because of the interest in this subject on the part of their Chief Executives) began to adopt some of the Peters and Waterman terminology. Terms such as 'the entrepreneurial council', 'sticking to the knitting' and 'simultaneous loose-tight properties' began to be heard (chiefly in the Chief Executive's department) in town and county halls. With the benefit of hindsight, however, and with a few notable exceptions, the application in local government of the new management philosophy advocated by Peters and Waterman can be seen as essentially superficial (its potential relevance may anyway have been over-estimated). There was a good deal more discussion of mission, strategy and culture, but little evidence that the way in which local authorities actually operated on these dimensions had been fundamentally changed.

By the late 1980s, and in particular from 1988 onwards, these claims of superficiality of response and of over-emphasis on structure could no longer be sustained. There are, it is true, some local authorities which are still concentrating on structural responses to the new demands placed on them by legislation and other external change. Indeed, there are some authorities which have chosen to change as little as possible – in terms of structure, processes or culture – despite the strength of these external forces. But increasing numbers of local authorities are now making more fundamental changes in organisational systems. These changes, whilst they normally still include an organisational restructuring, are increasingly attempting to link structural changes to the development of mission statements and organisational strategies (see Chapter 5) as well as to the clarification and operationalisation of a set of cultural values and a new climate of operation. Such changes have often been painful, and viewed as necessary rather than desirable. But it is clear that the revolution in organisational self-image and behaviour implied by the cumulative impact of the post-1987 programme of central government legislation is now well under way. The traditional organisational assumptions of self-sufficiency, bureaucracy, professionalism and central control (see Chapter 2, pp.22–6) whilst they have by no means disappeared, are being radically reinterpreted. Structure is increasingly being seen less as a 'thing in itself' and more as a corollary of choices in respect of strategy and culture.

The dimensions of organisational change

As discussed in Chapter 3, changes in the organisation and management of local authorities (and indeed, of organisations in general) can be productively analysed on a number of different dimensions. In making sense of the organisational responses to the changes which have impacted upon British local government since the 1974 local government reorganisation, a focus on these dimensions is extremely helpful. What can be observed in relation to each of the dimensions is normally not a clear switch from one end of the spectrum to the other (e.g. from centralisation to decentralisation; from differentiation to integration), but rather a much more subtle process of internal restructuring in which (to use the two dimensions mentioned above) certain aspects of a local authority's activities have become more centralised, whilst others have become more decentralised; some more integrated and others more differentiated. It is this process of internal organisational adjustment which we explore in this section.

Before developing the argument in more detail, it is important to re-emphasise three contextual points which were first made in Chapter 1. First, local government is a large complex institution, which is currently undergoing a period of rapid and radical change. The fundamental nature of the *internal* changes, induced by the changes in the external environment of local government is quite unprecedented, as least as far as the current century is concerned. Second, however, it is important to recognise the strength of the forces of resistance to the carrying through of the internal implications of these contextual imperatives. As we briefly noted in Chapter 3, individual actors in local authorities (heads of department, chairs of committees etc.) will evaluate the implications of the external changes and the response they require, in terms of their own values and, most importantly, their own interests. All large predominantly bureaucratic organisations can be seen as constellations of established interests and career patterns, tied to the existing organisational structure (which can itself be seen as a set of 'memorials to old problems', as Donald Schon (1971, ch.2) put it). Key actors will use the power resources they possess to resist changes which they see as inimical to their own interests, in so far as the legislation leaves scope for them to do so. The extent to which those pressing for the retention (as far as possible) of the *status quo* succeed in blocking (temporarily or otherwise) the initiatives of those who recognise that the need for change depends on the relative power position of those concerned (e.g. is there a powerful 'change agent' Chief Executive with political support?) and the skill with which strategy and tactics, whether to introduce or resist change, are deployed.

This familiar situation leads to a third important contextual point. Some local authorities have changed in response to these pressures from their operating environment much more quickly than others, depending on the balances of forces for change/inertia within the authority. This has led, as we observed earlier, to a pattern whereby limited numbers of local authorities have acted as change agents, leading a pattern of innovation and change which is later adopted by others. This kind of process has been a strong feature of organisational change in local government over the past few years.

Against this backcloth, we discuss in this section recent changes in organisational structure and processes on five principal dimensions: differentiation/integration; centralisation/decentralisation; specialisation/generalisation; high formalisation/low formalisation; and independence /interdependence. Particular attention is paid to the differentiation/integration dimension as this incorporates a wide range of important changes.

Differentiation/integration

We distinguished in Chapter 3 between *differentiation* – the extent to which the organisation is divided up into separate parts and units in order to get work done – and *integration* – the extent to which there are organisational devices that are intended to ensure that the various parts of the organisation are working to a common set of purposes, policies and procedures. One of the most powerful organisational effects of the Government's post-1987 programme of legislation has been to fragment – or differentiate – the activities of a local authority into their component parts. Compulsory competitive tendering (CCT) has required separate operating and accounting units on the contracting side for the individual services to which it has been applied (although, as we discuss later, the operating unit may be reintegrated into a multipurpose Direct Services Organisation (DSO)). Recent housing legislation has 'ring-fenced' the housing revenue account and hence effectively 'sealed off' the housing function from other local authority activities. The local management of schools (LMS) provisions, and the fact that all secondary schools and increasing numbers of primary schools now have their own individual budgets to manage provides a further example of differentiation in two senses; *between* education and other services ('joint-use' of school recreation facilities has become much more of a problem under the new legislation) and *within* the education service itself.

Given the force of these legislative changes, which have been premised (to some extent) on a government view of local authorities as little more than 'residual agencies' for ensuring the provision of services which the market cannot directly provide, there has been a strong incentive in local authorities (particularly those which support this view politically) to accept the process of fragmentation involved, and to reflect it in a new organisational structure (and set of processes) which embody a much higher degree of formal differentiation than had previously been adopted. To follow this kind of logic implies the creation of a relatively large number of relatively autonomous service provision units (including but not limited to those services which have been subject to CCT) and the redefinition of the authority's integrative functions away from strategic planning (if this had ever been practised!) and detailed budgetary and manpower controls towards a weaker coordinative and contract-monitoring role.

There are indeed some authorities which have restructured in this way, emphasising in structural terms the pressure for differentiation at the expense of the (residual?) need for integration. All authorities have been obliged to treat the CCT-affected services in this way, and many others have extended the logic of the CCT process to create an authority-wide set of service-specific cost centres. However, there are two important ways in which, in many authorities, such pressures for differentiation have been countered by measures designed to strengthen integrative structures and processes, one at departmental level, and the other on an authority-wide basis.

At the departmental level, some directors have successfully argued that it is less organisationally disruptive (and more conducive to inter-service coordination and planning) to minimise the extent to which the CCT-affected contractor units are 'separated out' in organisational terms. It is quite feasible – legally and operationally – to define separate contractor units for services such as refuse collection, school catering and grounds maintenance, but to position them *within* the traditional departmental hierarchy of a department of environmental health, education or leisure and recreation respectively. In councils which adopt this approach, the head of the contractor units is likely to be located on the third (or fourth) tier of the departmental hierarchy, with an 'opposite-numbers' client-manager at the same level, both responsible to a second (or third)-tier manager in the same department (whose role has come to be known as 'two-hatted' in nature). The important point to emphasise here is that such a response has two functions. First, it retains formal responsibility for both client and contractor aspects of the affected service in the hands of a traditional service director (and is thus normally argued for by such directors because, amongst other effects, it does not erode his or her departmental establishment nor status). Second, it retains, through a traditional hierarchical mechanism a faculty for integration within the broader service area (e.g. leisure and recreation, local environmental services, etc.) which is more difficult to exercise if the CCT activities are separated-out more formally (e.g. into separate 'arms-length' DSOs, or an integrated DSO not reporting formally to the director in whose department the contractor unit concerned was previously located).

Indeed, those authorities which have responded to the introduc-tion of CCT by creating an integrated DSO covering the whole spectrum of contracted-out services within a single (arms-length) organisation have also, in a rather different way, recognised the benefits of structural integration. In this case, the argument is that a single DSO can be more competitive than a series of individual DSOs in that economies of scale can be realised (e.g. through the appointment of specialist advisers) and resources can be switched more readily from one part of the DSO to another, either to increase the competitiveness of particular contract bids, or carry them out more flexibly once they have been won. The point to emphasise here is that the variations in the form of (and balance between) structural differentiation and integration can be, and have been, adopted in response to CCT and other primarily differentia-tion-emphasising legislation.

This has been a further variant of departmental response to CCT, which is of particular interest in that it emphasises a strategic concern (see Chapter 3). If the 'differentiation into component parts' route is taken, then there is relatively little scope for a traditional head of a service department (e.g. engineering, environmental services, etc.) from a hierarchical control perspective. But if the roles of strategic management and policy planning are taken seriously in an authority at the 'programme area' level (see below for definition) as well as at the authority-wide level, then there *is* scope for a limited number of senior managers to play the role of director of a group of different but related services. This is the kind of structure which has been developed in Cheshire County Council (see Figure 4.1) and Kirklees Metropolitan District Council (see Figure 4.2). It reflects a balance between the differentiative pressures of CCT, the housing legislation, LMS, etc. and the integrative impulse in authorities which adopt a view of enabling which more akin to 'community governance' than the purchasing of a limited set of services (see Clarke and Stewart (1989) and Chapter 2 above).

The latter view of the role of a local authority has also been influential (in those authorities which espouse it) in strengthening the integrative role of the centre. In the past the centre has had a number of important roles; strategic planning; the provision of

FIGURE 4.1   Cheshire County Council: management structure

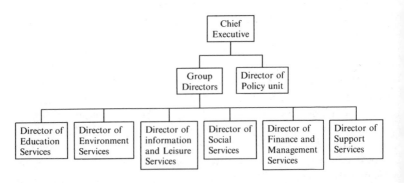

Note:
The above eight positions shown involve membership of the Management Board. There are two other Director-level posts – County Fire Officer and Chief Constable – whose incumbents are not Management Board members. Below Director level, there are 30–40 'heads of service'.

FIGURE 4.2 **Kirklees Metropolitan District Council: management structure**

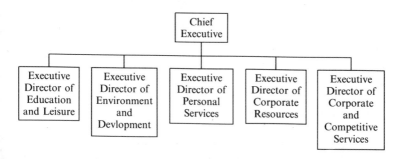

Note:
The six positions shown involve membership of the management board. Below Director level there are 30–40 chief officer posts (including Chief Education Officer, Chief Housing Officer, and Chief Officer of Social Services).

support services to service-providing departments; the control of the financial and personnel activities of service departments; and the administration of the democratic machinery of the authority. These are discussed in more detail in Chapter 5. Of these roles, the first has increased in importance in those authorities which have recognised the need for it; the second has increasingly become the subject of formalised negotiation between the central units concerned (e.g. legal services) and the service providing/purchasing units of the authority; the third has changed in nature from direct control to selective monitoring and review (and intervention at times of crisis); whilst the fourth remains (in most authorities) at the centre. The implications of these changes are that in authorities where the strategic planning role has been recognised and enhanced, the integrative role of the centre, although redefined, is still strong. In authorities where it has not been recognised (or has been rejected) the role of the centre becomes significantly reduced in scope.

The pressures for restructuring in relation to the recent legislative programme and external social and economic changes should therefore be seen as leading to a change in the basis on which differentiation and integration have been organised in local authorities, rather than a change in the balance between the two principles (except in those authorities where the strategic role has been un- or under-developed). The legislative pressures have led to the more explicit differentiation between 'client' and 'contractor' roles in an increasing number of specific services. They have led to the identification of cost centres, and unit managers with considerably enhanced devolved financial – and personnel – management responsibilities, particularly in the 'contracted' services (and other services directly impinging on the public) but increasingly within the central hierarchy of the authority also. Central support services have also been subject to the processes of differentiation and fragmentation, together with a reconsideration of the basis on which such support services are provided to service-purchasing or service-providing units, with 'service level agreements' fast replacing *ad-hoc/post-hoc* cost apportionments. These pressures have also tended to result in the break-up of the traditional bureaucratic service departments, each dominated by a particular profession or quasi-profession (e.g. planning, surveying, housing) both in terms of particular (more specific) service responsibilities and the client/contractor split. All these changes have involved a reappraisal of the basis of differentiation in the local authority.

However, the pressures for integration in the face of this process of organisational fragmentation have led to some interesting regroupings and changes in role, not just at the centre but also in the roles of service directors. The increased emphasis on strategic management and policy planning has created the scope for a new type of 'arms-length' service director, whose responsibilities are typically wider in scope than those held by their predecessors (covering what came to be known as 'programme areas'), but who do not, as their predecessors did, enjoy line management responsibility. The new role emphasis is on strategic thinking, service coordination, performance review and crisis management. In some cases the responsibility is also held for one or more particular projects, often of a specialist or entrepreneurial nature. These new integrative roles are those which are also increasingly emphasised at the organisation's centre, typically in and around the office of the Chief Executive. This similarity in role definition gives the (smaller) management team which typically results a clearer (and more specifically strategic) brief. Indeed, the new programme area directors now lean as much towards the Chief Executive at the centre, as they do towards the unit manager at the periphery. Thus a metropolitan district which dealt with the pressures for differentiation and integration in the ways outlined above would be likely to have a structure which included:

- three central directorates (Chief Executive, finance officer, central services)
- six programme area directorates (housing, environmental services, education, social services, leisure and recreation and economic development)
- an all-purpose DSO.

The management team resulting from such a structure would be ten in number, perhaps still too large to be an effective 'board of directors', but certainly smaller than many management teams of the early 1980s. In some cases fewer directoral positions are involved (see Figures 4.1 and 4.2). Clearly there are many variations around this basic pattern. However, it represents an emerging 'ideal structural type' which is being introduced in increasing numbers of local authorities. A more detailed appraisal of its implications for the roles of Chief Executive, service director and management team is undertaken later in this chapter (pp.90–7).

Centralisation/decentralisation

The centralisation/decentralisation dimension is related to the integration/differentiation dimension previously discussed but is not synonymous with it. The differentiation of an organisation into its component parts is itself a form of decentralisation of responsibility. Similarly the integration of a range of separate activities implies some degree of centralisation either at departmental or authority-wide level. But in other important respects the dimensions differ. There are important forms of decentralisation other than decentralised *managerial* responses associated with the differentiation of the organisation into its component (service-providing) parts. And centralisation can have important functions other than that of integration in the sense we have used it above. Centralisation can also involve powers of *authoritative intervention* to control the activities of particular parts of the organisation whose performance appears, in one way or another, to require such intervention.

Thus the respective pressures towards centralisation and decentralisation *per se* which have been experienced in local authorities over the past few years largely reflect external influences other than the CCT and service-related legislation which affected the integration/differentiation balance of local authorities. The 1989 Local Government and Housing Act incorporated (amongst other measures) the Government's response to the report of the Widdicombe Committee (1986) which it had set up in 1984. This response included changes which strengthened the 'control' role of the centre, particularly in its designation of the *monitoring officer* role (frequently, although by no means always appropriated by the Chief Executive). Monitoring officers are required to provide 'independent' reports to council whenever they find evidence of legal impropriety or possible maladministration. This role mirrors that of the 'financial probity' officer, which local authorities were required to designate a year earlier in 1987, following government concern about the developments in the rate-setting process in the mid-1980s. The creation of both these central supervisory positions reflects an increasing concern on the part of the government that certain aspects of the behaviour of councillors require regulation in this way – either potentially, or, in a few cases, in reality. Thus in addition to the perceived need for strategic planning which has of necessity to be carried out at the centre, the dimension of centralisation has also been strengthened by the control and supervisory consequences of the 1989 Act. Other aspects of the changing role of the centre are discussed in Chapter 5.

In addition to the decentralisation of management responsibility discussed earlier, there are two other forms of decentralisation which have made a significant impact on local authority structures over the ten years. The first – the decentralisation of points of service access and delivery – owes much to the increased consumer/customer orientation in the accessibility of services and the sensitivity of service provision, to which local authorities were becoming increasingly committed before government legislation embodied such 'customer first' principles. This type of decentralisation is becoming increasingly widespread, either on a service-specific basis (e.g. housing, local environmental services) or, less commonly on a more comprehensive basis – the 'one-stop shop' principle, which in its attempt to overcome problems of service recipients being transferred from one part of the bureaucracy to another, also reflects a form of local-level *integration*. The other major form of decentralisation – that of political power (and power to allocate resources) to neighbourhood committees – is a reflection of a political commitment to the decentralisation of power. It is discussed further in Chapter 6.

Again, it is apparent that what local authorities are experiencing (or expressing) in structural terms is a changing pattern of centralisation/decentralisation, not a move from one dimension to the other. Certain functions are becoming more centralised; others more decentralised. The fact that it is the latter that have typically received more emphasis should not be allowed to obstruct our awareness of the former.

Specialisation/generalisation

We defined specialisation in Chapter 3 as the degree to which the work of the organisation requires specific skills. What has been apparent in local authorities' structural responses to recent legislation is a switch from *professional* specialisation to *task* specialisation, with an increasing emphasis on managerial capacity as a basis for appointment at senior levels. As emphasis has become focused increasingly upon specific tasks, and the important organisational element has become the unit with the responsibility for carrying out the task (with its own budgetary allocation and devolved managerial responsibility) so the specialist skills of management *per se* become emphasised in a way that was less apparent in the professional-dominated departmental hierarchies of the 1970s and early 1980s. That is not to say that professional qualification and experience have ceased to become relevant. It is still unusual for the manager of a unit of service provision not to be qualified in the professional discipline involved. It is rather that an emphasis on managerial ability has given a much higher profile, and has increasingly operated as a criterion additional to the traditional professional basis of job appointment.

At the higher levels of management – the 'programme area' directors who, however, do not exercise direct managerial control in the way their service-department predecessors did – there has developed a similar emphasis on managerial rather than professional criteria as a basis for selection, although here a rather different set of managerial skills is involved – performance review, entrepreneurship, cultural change capacity and strategic vision are all requisite skills at this level. In some authorities, generalist managers have been appointed at this level, who have not necessarily possessed experience or qualifications in one or other of the dominant professions involved in the programme area. When Cheshire carried out a restructuring on a programme area basis in 1988, several of the appointments at director level were of managers from outside the professional purview of the programme area concerned. The fact that several were also formerly located in central departments strengthened the coherence of the management team (and reflected the fact that programme area directors belong as much in the cultural world of the centre as in that of the specific service areas).

The role of the Chief Executive, as we discuss later (see Chapter 5, pp.90–1) has in many authorities also become increasingly generalist in nature (i.e. has lost its customary legal/administration emphasis) reflecting perceived change in the nature of the Chief Executive's task, and in particular its strengthened strategic and cultural change content.

New specialisms have also developed in response to the developing *external* orientation of local authorities (Chapter 9). The skills of business entrepreneurialism, business planning and marketing have become an important part of the role of the DSO manager (and others) in the local authority. The need for a public relations specialism has been recognised in increasing numbers of authorities. Networking or reticulist specialisms in relation to Europe, the local business community and the voluntary sector have also become increasingly sought and valued.

In these various ways we can see how the changing task environment of the local authority is causing a redefinition of the specialisms required. Again a change in the nature of the tasks which are being addressed by both general manager and specialist is more apparent than any major change of emphasis between specialisation and generalisation *per se*. What is, however, becoming increasingly vulnerable is the hierarchical single-profession department which is declining fast as a basis for local authority structural organisation. However, the specific professional skills contained within it *are* still required, albeit at different locations in the organisation.

High formalisation/low formalisation

In Chapter 2 we defined formalisation as the extent to which the organisation operates through stated or known rules and procedures, which may take the form of written rules, or unstated, but widely recognised, procedures ('the way we do things here'), and distinguished between high and low levels of formalisation. In common-sense terms, one would perhaps have expected to find a retreat from formalisation in local authorities in the late 1980s, given the antipathy with which bureaucracy as a concept (and local authorities as formal manifestations of the concept) were coming to be regarded by successive Conservative governments.

In fact the changes on this dimension have been nothing like as straightforward as this. Although in certain areas of local government activity – economic development, tourism, leisure provision – local authorities are being expected to behave more entrepreneurially (and by implication, less formalistically), in other areas of activity formalisation has, if anything, been strengthened. In particular, in the field of regulatory activity, where it is essential that public bodies interpret the relevant legislation fairly (i.e. treat all cases according to the same set of principles), the extension of EEC-generated legislation, particularly in the field of the environmental health and trading standards, has led to a growth in the range of local authority activities which have to be dealt with in this highly formalised way.

Other pressures towards greater formalisation have become apparent. Many of the changes in the political management processes of local authorities, introduced by the 1989 Local Government and Housing Act required or encouraged a greater degree of formalisation. The Code of Conduct for councillors, the model standing orders, the rules governing proportional representation on committees, and the duties of the new monitoring and financial probity officers have all widened the scope of rule-based activity in local government. Partly as a reaction to these changes, and partly as a reflection of the perceived need for more informal arenas of strategic development and policy formulation, there has been an explicit and widespread search for new informal member/officer mechanisms to carry out these tasks.

At the same time, the introduction in increasing numbers of authorities of service-level agreements (SLAs), following through the logic of the likely extension of CCT, has also led to an increase in formalisation. Relationships between a service department (or unit) and a central support unit (e.g. legal services), which used to be managed informally are now regulated much more explicitly, with a consequent increase in paperwork and (in the conventional sense) 'bureaucracy'. It is ironic that a government which has been so critical of the bureaucratic nature of local authorities should have been responsible (directly or indirectly) for two measures which clearly increase the need for it!

Again we can identify a tension between, on the one hand, a number of pressures on local authorities to behave less formalistically – the exhortations towards a greater emphasis on competitiveness, entrepreneurialism, marketing, etc. – and, on the other, the pressures to increase formalisation – the provisions of the 1989 Act, service-level agreements, the spread of regulatory activity. These countervailing pressures have contributed towards the fragmentation of local authorities, with the perceived need to differentiate, in structural terms, between regulatory, promotional and service-providing units (as well as between client/contractor roles in the latter, and between service-provision/central-support roles (and units). The task for the local authority is to develop a structure which embodies an appropriate *organisational balance* between high formalisation (bureaucracy) and low formalisation, or to use the Burns and Stalker (1961) terminology, between mechanistic and organic structures. The idea of organisational balance which can be applied to the other dimensions considered, (and indeed more generally) is explored in more detail in the next section.

Independence/interdependence

The final dimension which merits exploration in structural terms is that of independence/interdependence. We showed in Chapter 2 that local authorities are increasingly having to look outwards to other organisations (public, private, voluntary) to achieve their objectives, rather than rely, as has traditionally been the case, on their own powers and resources. This change in orientation applies whether the authority adopts a limited enabling role, or a broader one, underpinned by a commitment to community governance.

This change increases the importance in local authorities of boundary personnel (Evan, 1976), that is to say officers with a specific remit to work, and negotiate, with counterparts in other organisations. Many economic development officers would see their role in this way. Senior social-services managers are increasingly being pushed in this direction (links with health authorities; the developing purchaser/provider split). Managers concerned with marketing a particular service or facility (tourism, museums and art galleries, recreational facilities) are by definition boundary personnel. 'Client managers' may be placed in this position if the contract for which they are client goes outside the authority. But just as important is the implied strengthening of the 'external relations' role of the Chief Executive. Networking skills are becoming an important part of his or her role (and are becoming increasingly recognised in Chief Executive job descriptions).

The independence/interdependence dimension is the one of the five discussed where there has been a clear shift along the spectrum – from independence (or self-sufficiency) to interdependence – over the past few years. However, the issue of organisational balance is again pertinent here. A local authority seeking to influence and negotiate with other agencies needs a strong sense of its own identity, in terms of strategic direction and organisational priorities. Otherwise, in the bargaining processes which will inevitably develop, the basis for bargaining (i.e. what the authority really wants out of the relationship) may be unclear and the consequences of the negotiation adverse. Not all 'opportunities' facing a local authority are necessarily ones which should be seized. Not all external agencies are necessarily worth cultivating. Indeed, one of the organisational skills increasingly required by local authorities is the capacity to identify important relationships in the networks in which the authority operates, and to understand the relative strengths and weaknesses both of the local authority itself, and the key organisations in its environment.

Organisational balance and organisational inertia

No organisational characteristic is absolute. Within each of the five dimensions of organisational structure discussed above, each characteristic (e.g. differentiation) has to be balanced against its opposite (e.g. integration). Thus one of the dangers faced by local authorities, particularly in circumstances where the pressures for change are considerable, is that an attempt is made to organise on the basis of one characteristic (e.g. decentralisation) as though that were an end in itself. One cannot meaningfully discuss the introduction of decentralisation in a local authority without considering the need for centralisation; nor can one sensibly organise around the need for specialisation without considering the need for generalisation. The crucial judgements faced by local authorities involve identifying the most appropriate balance between the pairs of opposites involved (e.g. between independence and interdependence) and then expressing this balance in structural terms. Indeed, the concept of organisational balance can be helpfully used to illuminate a wider set of organisational choices, and in Chapter 10 we extend our discussion of this concept to demonstrate its centrality in this process of organisational choice.

Most local authorities, of course, do not explicitly consider structural issues in these terms. They do not 'identify positions' on dimensions of centralisation/decentralisation and then express these positions in organisational terms. The reality is much more likely to involve a more specific selection and rejection process from the array of ideas which are in good currency (e.g. which other authorities have introduced and which have formed the basis of articles in the *Local Government Chronicle*). That process of selection and rejection will be heavily influenced by the values, interests and relative power positions within the local authority of those likely to be affected by the different structural innovations which are being considered. Almost any change which implies a threat to the *status quo* is likely to generate resistance somewhere in the existing structure. As we argued in a recent LGMB report (Leach, Walsh *et al.*, 1993):

> The barriers to change stem from potential resistance, at a number of organisation levels, to any kind of change which may disrupt existing status and reward systems, future career patterns or job identities/satisfactions. The very existence of 'fear of change' can itself operate as a significant barrier to change.

Thus one would not necessarily expect a District Engineer to be enthusiastic about a proposal to transfer a large section of his or her departmental establishment to an arms' length 'Direct Services Organisation' under the responsibility of the existing head of that section. Nor would one expect much support from a Director of Environmental Health for a proposal which merges his or her department with that of the Director of Housing (unless he or she expects to be appointed as the new super-director involved!). It is important to recognise that all proposals for organisational change will be viewed by those they affect in terms of the likely impact on their own values and interests and responded to accordingly (which is not to say that personal interests, such as status and position will necessarily prevail over more disinterested values such as the good of the organisation as a whole).

It is for these reasons that there is a particular need at present for *change agents* within local authorities to identify the radical nature of the changes needed (not just in structure and process, but in strategy, culture and systems also) and to develop a capacity to persuade others of the need for change and then to implement it. In particular the importance of the Chief Executive as a change agent is discussed in the next section.

Recent work on 'well-managed' local authorities (Leach, Walsh *et al.*, 1993) has shown that what differentiates well-managed authorities (i.e. those which have made effective and appropriate adjustments to the external pressures facing them, whilst retaining their own sense of identity and strategic direction) from the rest is the ability to be *selective* in deciding which new organisational initiatives to adopt and which to reject from the increasingly wide menu confronting them. There is an important difference between indiscriminate bandwaggon-jumping and careful selection (in terms of an authority's particular needs, traditions and goals) in this respect. In adopting a critical and analytical approach to the need for the introduction of particular structural changes (e.g. fewer, larger service departments) or new systems (e.g. service level agreements) an authority is in effect attempting to identify the right balance (between, for example, centralisation and decentralisation) to suit its own particular situation (although it would not necessarily perceive itself to be doing so). The fact that dogged resistance to change and a more indiscriminate and less considered introduction of new ideas are equally common responses in local authorities demonstrates the lack of a determinate relationship between external pressures and organisational change in local government. The filter of values, interests and power structures within local authorities is a crucial intervening variable.

Changes in key structural elements

In this section we look at some more specific aspects of organisational structure, and the way they have changed over the past few years. The new emphasis on strategy and culture (and the tendency to regard structure as something which 'follows from' a clarification of these two dimensions) have had a number of implications for the roles of Chief Executive, management team and service director, which have been examined in passing in the previous sections, but which are now explored in more detail. The consideration of the role of the Chief Executive is relatively brief, as this topic is considered in more detail in Chapter 5 (pp.120–3).

The changing role of the Chief Executive

Once the need for a new emphasis on strategy and culture has been accepted, the Chief Executive is typically expected to play the principal role of 'change agent' at least during the initial period of the introduction of the change. This new role emphasis has had two important implications for the Chief Executives affected.

First, the direct managerial responsibility held by many Chief Executives for some combination of committee administration, a personnel section, and/or a legal section has become harder to reconcile with the increasing demands of steering strategic development and cultural change. This has often led Chief Executives to seek ways of transferring some of these direct managerial responsibilities upon other chief officers (or of devolving them to deputies within their own departments).

Second, the task of preparing an organisational strategy, or establishing and implementing a set of cultural values is one for which the Chief Executive needs advice and help, but for which there is often no obvious existing unit within the local authority capable of providing such specialised back-up. As a result, there has been an increasing tendency for *policy units* to be set up, reporting directly to the Chief Executive, to provide the necessary developmental or progress-chasing support, not just in relation to strategic and cultural issues, but also to deal with the range of other 'new issues' which are increasingly impinging upon local authorities (e.g. economic development, equal opportunities, urban programmes and grant aid), and which transcend the responsibilities of any of the established service departments. Sometimes a number of such topic-specific units all reporting to the Chief Executive are set up, rather than one all-purpose policy unit. Planning departments are another common source of such advice and aid, either through secondment of key staff, or more directly.

The changing role of the management team

Whilst the role of Chief Executive is by definition a feature of the organisation's 'centre', the management team is the arena in which the interests of the centre and those of the service departments impinge upon one another. It is still the norm for the Chief Executive, in connection with his or her responsibility for the efficient and effective implementation of the Council's programmes and policies (Bains, 1972, p.183) to work with or through a management team. The Widdicombe questionnaire survey showed that (in 1985) 95 per cent of all authorities in Britain had a management team, and there has been no evidence of a significant change in this figure since.

The role of management teams in many local authorities has, however, has changed recently. Up to the mid-1980s the 'management team' had never really established itself firmly as the key structural element in local authority management which its title and central position would imply. Confusion over its role and reservations about its effectiveness were widely reported in the late 1970s and early 1980s (see Greenwood *et al.*, 1976, ch.3); Hinings *et al.* (1980); Alexander (1982, pp.80–7)). Stewart (1986, p.6) described the situation thus:

> The management team has survived in most local authorities, but in few does it probably retain the importance attached to it in the Bains Report. Whereas the report saw the management team as the main instrument through which the chief executive established his role, that would rarely be accepted today.

One of the reasons for the diminishing emphasis on the management team in the early 1980s was the inherent ambiguity of the management team as an expression of the corporate approach. Management teams at this time rarely operated as the main source of corporate initiative, nor as the main instrument for the achievement of corporate objectives (see Hinings *et al.*, 1980; Alexander, 1982). Given the inevitable tension between the chief officer's role as head of, and advocate for, his or her own service *and* his/her role as a member of the (supposedly) corporate team, this outcome is hardly surprising. What is surprising is the degree of suspicion with which management teams continued to be regarded by leading politicians in many local authorities. The perception of the team as a setting where officers 'stitched up deals' and decided how to sell ideas to politicians was rarely congruent with the reality of the much more mundane operations of most management teams, whose agendas were typically dominated by matters of management detail rather than major political issues!

Since 1987 the increasingly challenging and turbulent nature of the environment of the local authority (see pp.33–5 above) has strengthened the pressure for a more cohesive form of management team, as a source of mutual support in difficult circumstances. In authorities where politicisation has made member–officer relations more tense and fraught, the same argument applies. As Laffin and Young (1985, p.56) put it:

> In so far as officers have different aims and allegiances, and face different political conditions, it is difficult for them to form a united front on issues of administrative responsibility. However, chief officers are becoming more aware of this weakness, and of the potential benefits of more group solidarity. One of the main outcomes of this awareness is the greater stress that many are placing on the chief officer's management team.

The reality is that even in circumstances of external or internal (political) turbulence, individual chief officers may see their own interests (e.g. prospects for career advancement) better served by an individualistic strategy (typically linked to a powerful committee chair) than by group solidarity at the management team level. Much depends on the balance of power within and between the administrative and political hierarchies.

There is one situation where a more cohesive and generally strategic role for the management teams becomes more likely, and that is when the directors of services (or programme areas) have a relatively detached role (in hierarchical terms) from the service providing units in 'their' departments. If managerial and financial responsibility has been largely devolved, and the main role of the director defined in strategic/performance monitoring/crisis-intervention terms, then the directors are less likely to see their own careers as bound up with departmental establishments, or requiring the defence of every unit within their department. Their relatively detached role is likely to lead to stronger commitment to the objectives of the authority as a whole, and to their achievement through the efforts of the management team whatever (within reason) the implication for their particular departments.

In another way too, the effectiveness of management teams in authorities which have restructured along the lines set out above is likely to be potentially enhanced. One of the main factors militating against the effective operation of management teams has been identified as size (Greenwood *et al.*, 1976; Alexander, 1982). Large management teams, particularly those premised on a search for consensus were (and are) often little more than talking shops. Smaller management teams are potentially more effective both as coordinating instruments and as strategic management forums, but in authorities where such teams can be kept to a manageable size only by excluding a number of chief officers, feelings of status-diminishment and resentment are likely to result. By the development of a structure with a smaller number of 'strategic' directors, with a wider scope of responsibilities, such problems may be avoided.

The changing role of service director

Just as the roles of the Chief Executive and the management team have been transformed (in principle, if not always in practice) by the legislative and other external changes of the past five or six years, so too has the role of the director (or chief officer) of the service department.

We discussed earlier in this chapter the way in which the recent legislation dealing with CCT, LMS (local management of schools) and housing (increased tenant choice, the ring-fencing of the housing revenue account) had all had the effect of fragmenting the local authority and breaking down the traditional pattern of large hierarchical and relatively autonomous departments (both at the centre, and in relation to service provision). Nowhere has this fragmenting effect been felt more strongly than in the familiar role of the chief officer of a traditional service department. The large education department bureaucracies, previously seen as having a particularly high propensity to 'seek autonomy' within the local authority's structure and operations (note the very concept of the local education *authority*) have been forcibly fragmented internally by the legislation which allows schools much greater powers of self-management and resource allocation. 'Technical services' departments have been under pressure to grant independent status to the range of contracting units typically found within their ambit (e.g. highways maintenance, refuse collection, vehicle maintenance) sometimes to the extent of losing them (in departmental terms) to an autonomous DSO. The remaining activities (e.g. highways design) have typically been subject to internal pressures for devolution of managerial responsibility to cost centres managed by relatively independent cost centre managers (see pp.143–7). Where then do these changes leave the role of chief education officer and director of technical services?

It is helpful to analyse these processes of fragmentation in a rather different way. Local authorities do not merely 'provide services'; they:

- promote activities (e.g. tourism, the development of local economies);
- regulate the activities of the private sector (e.g. environmental health legislation) or the public at large (planning and building control);
- develop strategies to guide a range of public and private sector agencies (e.g. structure plans, strategic visions, etc.).

These roles can be described as the *functions* of a local authority.

We have already shown how one major impact of the CCT legislation has been to 'separate out' in organisational terms service specification (the client role) and service provision (the contractor role). That has had a fragmentary effect on most traditional service departments. But it is possible to argue that fragmentation is also implied by the developing emphasis on the promotion and advocacy, regulatory and strategic roles identified above. If service specification and provision should be separated out organisationally, so it can be argued, should these functional roles be separated out also in the interests of structural clarity. Figure 4.3 illustrates the structural implications of these principles.

Nowhere do the implications of this argument have greater impact than in a local authority's planning department. Typically planning departments have over the years accumulated an increasing range of functions. Structure planning, local planning, development control (and building control) provide their statutory *raison d'être*. But typically planning departments also deal in the promotion of economic development, the provision of a research and intelligence service (often for the authority as a whole) and the provision of a range of specialist skills (e.g. landscape design, ecology, countryside management) – again often for use throughout the authority.

In an authority reorganised on the basis of function (e.g. service provision, regulation, promotion, etc.) as opposed to professional discipline, it can be argued that the various activities of a planning department would be more appropriately located elsewhere in the organisation – strategic planning, research and intelligence at the authority's strategic centre (for should not a structure plan be an expression in spatial terms of the authority's overall strategic direction?), specialist services in a free-standing 'internal consultancy' unit, economic development in a separate promotional agency (where conflicts with environmental amenity considerations can be dealt with overtly – promotion *versus* regulation – rather than within a multi-functional department) and development control within a new department based on a more comprehensive 'environment' programme area (or as a free-standing regulatory unit).

This example clearly illustrates the potential conflict between profession-based departments and departments based on functional role (and/or programme area). The outcome of this conflict (if it develops) will depend on the relative power and bargaining skills of the key actors (in particular the chief planning officer). Thus in this respect as in many others a uniformity of outcome in structural terms would not be expected.

96

FIGURE 4.3 Organisation of a local authority based on functional roles

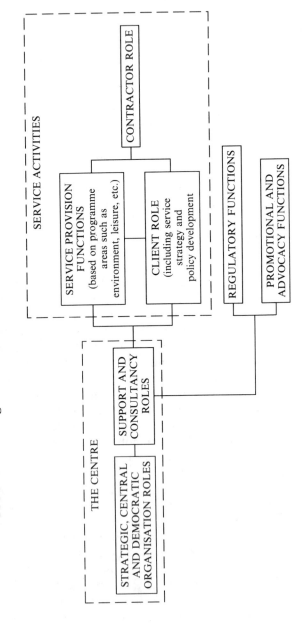

Upon whatever set of principles the departmental structure of an authority is defined, there is a clear tendency towards smaller numbers of relatively large departments, often involving combinations of activities (or functions) formerly dealt with by separate departments (there are parallels on the political side – see Chapter 7). This process leads to departments (and directors) with unfamiliar names and roles (see the Cheshire and Kirklees examples set out in Figures 4.1 and 4.2). In these circumstances the directors' role specification typically emphasises strategy and policy development, coordination, performance management and sometimes project management, rather than the formal responsibility for a large hierarchical unit. It is not surprising therefore that more emphasis is placed in selecting such directors on management experience and ability than on appropriate professional qualifications.

Budgetary processes

Traditionally the most important (and all-embracing) decision process in a local authority is the budgetary process. Greenwood (1983) has shown how during the 1900s there was a gradual change towards 'policy-led' budgeting, as opposed to the familir incremental budgetary processes (updated base with choices limited to marginal increases or decreases decided on a department-by-department – or committee-by-committee – basis).

Although there have been no comprehensive surveys of the extent to which this change has (or has not) accelerated since the mid-1980s more partial evidence from other surveys (Ennals and O'Brient, 1990; Clarke and Stewart (1990); Leach, Walsh *et al.*, (1993) suggests that this pattern of change in approach to budgeting has become more widespread. It would be surprising if this were not so. Experience elsewhere suggests that budgetary incrementalism is more difficult to sustain in times of budgetary famine or crisis (and references within local authorities to budgetary crises have become much more common over the past three of four years, and particularly in relation to 1991–2 and 1992–3). More authorities have put under scrutiny increasing proportions of their base budgets as the scope for budgetary manoeuvre has progressively reduced. From another perspective, the increased emphasis on local authority strategies (which typically identify a limited number of strategic priorities for the authority) logically implies an approach to budgeting which 'top-slices' (or at least safeguards) expenditure on such priorities. Both these influences are likely to have undermined traditional incremental budgetary processes in increasing numbers of local authorities.

Conclusion

In response to the major external changes – primarily legislative and financial in nature – which have impinged upon their operations over the past few years, local authorities have shown an increasing tendency to introduce radical changes, both to the nature of their organisational structures and processes, and to the context in which those structures and processes are seen. The most important changes can be summarised as follows:

First, there has been an increasing tendency to consider changes in organisational structures and processes *in conjunction with* (and indeed sometimes as secondary to) more fundamental questions about organisational purpose, strategy and culture. The ways in which local authorities have dealt with such issues is discussed in more detail in Chapter 5. Because of the development of a clearer sense of strategic direction and a more explicit set of cultural values, the context in which issues of structure and process have been dismissed has changed fundamentally in increasing numbers of authorities.

This change in emphasis has led to many authorities strengthening their strategic capacity structurally, through the introduction or expansion of *policy units*, attached to the Chief Executive with a remit (inter alia) to facilitate development in the fields of strategy and culture.

Second, in increasing numbers of authorities a re-examination of the role of the centre has been carried out. This re-examination has typically resulted in a strengthening of the centre's strategic and performance review capabilities, together with a devolution of the responsibility for detailed financial and personnel controls, customarily operated at the centre, to cost centres within the service departments. The new role of the centre is considered in more detail in Chapter 5.

Third, there has been some movement towards the amalgamation of specific services, previously carried out under the auspices of individual chief officers (with their own 'free-standing' departments) into larger directorates, reflecting broad programme areas (e.g. housing, leisure and recreation, technical services, etc.). Increasingly, the directors of these 'super departments' are operating in a strategic and coordinative capacity, with specific managerial responsibilities devolved to unit managers within the directorate (see pp.93–7 above) rather than in the more familiar role of direct managerial responsibility for a large hierarchical department.

Fourth, the role of local politicians in the major changes which are being made in local authority management structures and processes have been more explicitly addressed than in earlier reorganisations of internal structure.

Fifth, the changes in local authority organisation are having a marked impact on staff management. More flexibility is being required in working patterns, and increasing emphasis is being placed on relating pay to performance.

Sixth, there has developed a new emphasis on the decentralisation of decision-making and management in local authorities in three different ways:

1. the attempt to bring service-delivery outlets close to service users, and to make service provision more sensitive to social needs;
2. the development of new patterns of political decentralisation such as area and neighbourhood committees;
3. the attempt to devolve financial control and management responsibility down the organisation to 'unit managers'.

The pace of the first two of these changes of direction has slowed down significantly because of the increasing financial constraints under which local authorities have operated during the past few years. The third change is still spreading fast.

Seventh, the introduction of CCT in a range of council services has had a profound effect on local authority structures, not just in relation to the services directly affected, but also upon structures at the centre, and upon the organisation of services which it is expected may become subject to CCT in the near future.

Competition has undoubtedly been the single most important catalyst to local authority restructuring.

Eighth, as we first outlined in Chapter 1, the move towards an increased emphasis on the enabling role of local authorities, rather than, or in addition to, the direct-service-provision role is also having important repercussions on structures and processes, because of the implications for the authority's *external* relationships (i.e. its enhanced networking/facilitating role with the private sector and other public sector and voluntary organisations).

Finally, the external changes of the past few years have led in increasing numbers of authorities to a revision of the budgetary process. Increasingly larger proportions of the base budget have become subject to financial scrutiny, in an attempt to 'create space' for the funding of new strategic initiatives (see pp.97–8).

The need to consider this range of related issues of strategy, culture, structure and process has put immense pressure on the learning capacity of local authorities, and their capacity for coping with change. It is not surprising that the capacity of some local authorities has been found wanting (as in Lambeth, Brent and West Wiltshire). What is more surprising, perhaps, is that on the face of it so many local authorities have been able to respond and to incorporate the unprecedented level of organisational upheaval required over the past few years, without major breakdowns of this nature.

5 The Role of the Centre

In the previous chapter, we analysed recent changes which had taken place in the organisational structures and processes of local authorities. In this chapter we focus on one particular aspect of structure and process, which has received a good deal of attention recently – the role of the centre. In fact, the nature and role of the centre in the local authority has been the subject of debate and review since the mid-1960s. The centre typically consists of a number of services and structures that are not engaged in the management of the direct delivery of service but contribute to the overall effectiveness of the organisation, either through providing indirect services or through corporate activity. The functions that are typically organised on a generalised basis are finance, legal services, personnel management, computer services, property management and public relations. Virtually every local authority now has a Chief Executive who is the head of the organisation at the officer level. At the elected-member level there is also a central organisation, involving the policy committee, the leading elected members and leader of the council. The central organisation of the local authority tends to be large, often contributing 10 per cent or more of total costs and employment.

The centre of the authority can be conceived in terms either of structure or processes, that is, in terms of the units of which it is made up, or of the activities which it carries out, and the debate over the nature of the centre can be understood in these terms. Until the late 1970s the debate largely took place in structural terms, revolving round issues such as whether or not there should be a policy committee, Chief Executive or a management team. In the 1980s and 1990s the debate shifted to issues of what the centre should do, and how it should do it, which reflects a change in the context facing local authorities from relative stability, certainty and growth, to change, uncertainty and resource constraint. It is probably fair to argue that, in the past, structure took precedence over strategy, but that now the need for strategic management is dominant, and there is a consequent shift from a concern for what the centre *is* to a concern for what it *does*. There are also signs of change in the way that managerial leadership operates in local government, with a move away from the almost total dominance of professionalism, to an emergence of leadership that is more managerially based and which is focused on the culture of the organisation as a whole. These changes are most obviously embodied in the changing role of the Chief Executive and the Leader of the authority, and in the development of changed processes of budgeting, policy-making and performance management.

The centre in the private sector

Comparative perspectives

Surprisingly little attention has been paid to the role of the centre in organisation theory and analysis. What discussion there has been has been implicit in considerations and studies of the role of the executive, leadership in organisations and the nature of strategy. Chester Barnard (1938) presented an early analysis of the role of the executive as being at the centre of a communication network, acting to facilitate the work and decisions of others, and clarifying choices and priorities. More recent studies have focused less on the role of the individuals at the peak of the organisation, and more on questions of the changing nature of the centre in the process of organisational evolution. The main arguments are essentially that the appropriate form of organisation of the centre largely derives from the problems that are created by increasing size or product diversification.

There is some analogy, though it is limited, between the multi-divisional company and the multidepartmental local authority. Chandler argues that the role of the centre in a functionally organised company involves coordination between functions, setting direction, allocating resources, controlling performance and providing central functions, such as marketing and financial management. As companies produce a greater diversity of products the centre tends to become overloaded and there is a need to reduce involvement in day-to-day issues. The result, Chandler argued, was a shift to the decentralised divisional form as companies' range of products grew. Divisions were responsible for the running of specific businesses on a quasi-autonomous basis and were normally organised on a geographical, brand or product basis. The centre could then focus more clearly on strategy, control, and planning issues for the organisation as a whole.

Williamson argues that, as the size of the firm increases, there are problems of coordination and communication, and a consequent need to operate on a decentralised divisional basis. He states that the centre must maintain an appropriate distance from operational management, and that it should monitor the efficiency of performance, create incentives, allocate resources and conduct strategic planning. Divisionalisation alone is not enough, and Williamson argues for the importance of the general management of the organisation:

> It is also necessary that a separation of operating from strategic responsibilities be provided. The former are assigned to the operating divisions while the latter are made the focus of general management. Moreover, such a partitioning does not, by itself, assure strategic effectiveness; for this to obtain requires that the general management develop an internal control apparatus, to assess the performance of the operating divisions, and an internal resource allocation capability, which favours the assignment of resources to high-yield uses (Williamson, 1970).

The analysis of the role of the centre has most recently been taken up by Goold and Campbell (1987), who focus on the way that the centre relates to operating units and the way that it affects decision-making, distinguishing two dimensions of influence – planning influence and control influence. They found that there were three basic approaches adopted by the corporate centre – strategic planning, strategic control, and financial control. Strategic planning involved the centre working with the operational business units to develop strategy, with relatively little attention devoted to control. Performance targets were very broad, and annual financial targets subordinate to long-term strategy. The strategic-control approach involved the centre setting substantive objectives and targets, and reviewing plans that were developed by the operational units. Financial control involved the centre exercising influence through setting financial targets and budgets and monitoring financial performance closely.

The centre has a number of means which it can use to influence the activity of individual businesses:

- organisation structures;
- review of plans;
- setting strategic themes;
- specific suggestions;
- management of overlaps;
- allocation of resources.

Different blends of the means available to the centre will be adopted depending on the strategic style which is operated. Goold and Campbell (1987) find that four characteristics determine the success of the strategic style adopted. First, style needs to be matched to circumstances, as contingency theorists have long argued. Second, central managers need to have a thorough understanding of the various businesses of the organisation if they are to be able to add value. There needs to be openness and communication between the centre and the managers of units. Finally there needs to be 'a shared energy for action' and a sense of common purpose. Essentially the explanations of the appropriateness of the style adopted by the centre are a mixture of contingency and cultural explanations, with greater emphasis on the latter. There is a considerable degree of freedom open to the centre in the style that it adopts.

Hill (1988) develops a slightly different, though comparable, categorisation of the role of the centre in the industrial sphere. He argues that there are three basic types of central control. The first is strategic control, which involves the centre establishing broad strategic parameters that must be followed by business units. Second, there is market-financial control, with the centre laying down detailed financial targets, which are linked to rewards and punishments. Finally, there is operating control, in which the centre maintains direct control of key functions such as marketing, purchasing or production, acting both to support and influence individual business units. The key to determining which of these organisational control types is most appropriate is the degree of diversity of the organisation's products rather than its size. Hill concludes that the disadvantages of centralisation may have been overstated by the literature, particularly in the case of operating control – an interesting conclusion in the light of the general search for decentralised approaches to management in the public service.

The discussion of the role of the centre in the private sector has mainly focused on the development of large-scale, multidivisional manufacturing companies. The pattern in other types of organisation is likely to be different. Greenwood *et al.* (1990) studied the role of the centre in large accountancy partnerships. They found that the centre played a relatively limited role, largely concentrating on issues of quality and professional ethics. In a highly professional organisation they argued that it is much less acceptable to operate the sort of centralised control that was possible in the manufacturing sector. The findings of Greenwood *et al.* are interesting in examining the case of local government, because local authorities are highly professionalised organisations, while at the same time being large bureaucracies that produce a wide range of services. The conclusion that the role and functioning of the centre will be different depending on the nature of the organisation is also significant, and the nature of the centre in the public sector follows from the particular demands and purposes of the public service, and particularly the need for political management.

Work on other sectors provides valuable analogies in analysing the position of the centre in the public service in general, and local government in particular. The local authority is typically both large and diverse, and there are clear analogies with the multidivisional form of the private sector company. The local authority, though, is different in having a dual core, with separate central organisations for the elected members and the officers. There is at the most, only a somewhat strained analogy between the local authority and the private company with its board of directors. The fact of being public is important, as Hickson and his colleagues found in their study of decision-making:

> Public interest and public scrutiny bring government departments and agencies into the process of decision-making more often, complicating it with external interests in addition to numbers of internal interests . . . In sum, the complexity of public sector decision-making is clear (Hickson *et al.*, 1986).

The need to be publicly and visibly – accountable makes the nature of the work of the centre significantly different in the public sector. Much of the role of the centre is concerned with the organisation's need to attain legitimacy. We will also argue that the increasing complexity of the local environment and the need to work with other organisations to attain purposes play a large part in determining the changing role of the centre. The relatively recent development of the strong centre in local government is reflected in the arguments over whether certain positions, such as that of the Chief Executive should exist, as well as what they should do. The debate over the role of the centre is a debate over the nature of local government, as was apparent in the Widdicombe Report (1986a) and the debate over the internal management of the authority in the Heseltine review (Department of Environment, 1991b).

The changing role of the centre: the historical perspective

The dominant principle in the organisation of the local authority has traditionally been professional function. Officers heading departments have had great autonomy, often acting as independent barons, jealously guarding their independence, and treating the rest of the authority as of little relevance to them. This highly independent approach was, most commonly, adopted by larger departments such as education and engineering, but the culture that dominated local government as a whole has been one of professional separatism. The result was an organisation that was divided into hierarchically organised units, which were separated by fairly rigid boundaries. These baronies were supported by the chairs of the committees to which they reported, who were equally concerned to retain their autonomy. Perhaps the clearest expression of this tradition was in education departments, which saw their links if anything as being more clearly with the Department of Education and Science than with other departments of the authority. But other departments took much the same view, with professional and service links acting to create a national community of interest that was seen as being of greater significance than

links within the locality, as Laffin's history of the interaction
between professionalism and central government departments
shows. The role of the centre within this system was limited to
the ceremonial, and to those functions necessary for organisational
maintenance. The clerk, who was usually the authority's legal
officer, was largely involved in servicing committees and had little
to do with other officers. The treasurer played a predominantly
bookkeeping and money-management role.

In the 1950s and early 1960s some authorities, normally in
urban areas, though not in London, made changes that reflected
the felt need for more effective central management in local
government. Authorities such as Coventry and Liverpool introduced changes through the use of management services and
computers. In the 1960s Newcastle upon Tyne had introduced a
General Manager for the authority, Frank Harris, who came from
the Ford Motor Company, though this was more to provide
coordination of the extensive redevelopment of the city, than
integrated management of the services of the authority. Though
few authorities had made significant organisational changes by the
1960s, there was a realisation that the traditional patterns of
management would need change to accommodate the increased
scale and complexity of local authority operations. The key
organisational problem was seen as one of integration. The
structure of authorities had developed in such a way that they
were highly differentiated, but faced problems, such as urban
redevelopment and social deprivation that required an increasingly
integrated approach to service. The issue was not so much the
integrated management of the organisation as a whole, as the need
to manage problems that did not fall neatly within the responsibilities of one department. There was no explicit attempt to break
down the individual autonomy of departments. The high level of
differentiation in local authorities was to continue but there was to
be increased integration through the use of central mechanisms.
The role of the centre was to ensure coordination rather than to
exercise control.

As we have seen the perceived need for greater integration was
expressed in the findings of the Maud Committee, appointed in
1964 to investigate the management of local authorities and
reporting in 1967. Maud recommended that the management of

the authority should be more clearly integrated both at the officer and at the member level. The recommendation was for the integration of policy and not simply for greater administrative coordination. In addition to the arguments for greater coordination and policy integration, Maud argued for increased central control.

Although the recommendations of the Maud commission were largely ignored in practice, it contributed to the development of a set of ideas that were to become the orthodoxy of the 1970s and 1980s. Maud contributed to a climate of ideas in good currency concerned with how management structures and processes could be changed in order to ensure a more integrated and effective pattern of government.

The factor that precipitated major changes was the reorganisation of local government in 1974, which made it possible to reconsider management approaches without so obviously attacking established interests. Reorganisation served to unfreeze the institutional framework of organisation that had become established in the post-war years. The Bains Report (1972) recommended that there should be a policy committee, a Chief Executive without departmental responsibility, and a management team of chief officers supported by corporate groups. The centre was to become more important, but predominantly in a coordinating rather than a controlling role. The Paterson Advisory Group, which considered the management system that should operate in Scotland, took a slightly more centralised view, favouring an executive office which would assist the Chief Executive:

> in his tasks of coordinating policy planning, monitoring the effectiveness of the authority's programmes and managing the central services, by two or three officials of chief officer status. These would be a director of finance, a director of administration and, in the largest authorities of all, a director of policy planning. These officers could be designated as deputy Chief Executives (Paterson Advisory Group, 1973).

In practice the large majority of local authorities established in 1974 did establish a post of Chief Executive, though only in a few authorities in Scotland, notably Strathclyde Region, was anything approaching an executive office established. Most authorities also created a management team of officers. The degree of real change was limited in the short term, reflecting the difference between the relative ease of changing the structure of the organisation and the much greater difficulty of changing the culture. The new positions and approaches were added to the traditional system, rather than that system being transformed.

There were attempts to change process as well as structure. Before the reorganisation of 1974, there had been little in the way of integrated planning of the various services of the local authority. Following reorganisation many authorities attempted to develop a system of corporate planning, which involved the investigation of the needs of the local area and the development of an integrated plan, detailing how all the services of the authority could be integrated to meet those needs. In practice corporate plans had relatively little effect in the long term, largely because the assumption on which they were based did not hold in the rapidly changing circumstances of the late 1970s and the 1980s. Many of the corporate plans that were developed were large and unwieldy documents, that were frequently out of date before they were completed. But, despite its limited practical impact, corporate planning was important, again, in contributing to the emerging climate of ideas about how the management of local government needed to change.

A further stimulus to change was the end of the assumption of growth in local government expenditure. Until the mid-1970s there had been significant levels of growth, particularly in the latter half of the 1960s and the early 1970s. The relatively easy financial situation was reflected in the processes of the authority, and in particular the way that budgets were prepared, with each department bidding for growth in its allocation of resources, and the treasurer engaging in some marginal trimming to make the figures add up. The nature of the local government grant system was such that central government met a high proportion of the costs of services. The questions were how much growth there was to be and how additional finance was to be distributed, not how limited resources were to be allocated. The role of the centre was largely one of putting together the total budget from the individual departmental bids and, to a much lesser extent, massaging the bids to fit within an acceptable total.

In 1975 the financial situation changed, when Mr Crosland, then Secretary of State for the Environment, declared that the party was over. It was difficult for local authorities to cope with this change, more for cultural reasons than because of structure or process. So difficult was it to conceive of problems of financial constraint that many officers came to talk of any cuts in spending as 'negative growth'. The belief was that the change in financial circumstances was temporary and that growth in local authority expenditure would resume once the economy recovered. The major charge was that authorities began to develop explicit processes for budgeting, which involved the development of targets to which departments had to work in setting their bids for expenditure. The centre became more powerful because it was able to influence other departments through spending guidelines, and the adjustments made to bids before the final budgets and the rate were set. The budget process became less incremental, with less assumption that spending would be continued from one year to another, and with only the changes at the margin being subject to scrutiny. The result was the introduction of a greater degree of formal rationality into the process of resource planning, with the centre established as the embodiment of the search for rationality.

By the end of the 1970s, the importance of the centre in the local authority had grown, partly because of the institutional change of reorganisation, and partly because of changes in the financial context, but overall the level of change had been limited. There had been some limited increase in the role of the centre in the exercise of financial control. Only in a very small number of cases had there been an increase in the strategic control or influence exercised by the centre. Reorganisation had served to establish central structures, but it had done relatively little, in itself, to make them effective or influential. It was the changes of the 1980s that have had a real impact on the role of the centre. The 1970s, at the time, appeared to be a period of major change in the management of local government, and particularly in the role of the centre. In retrospect, it is clear that the level of change was small. What was more important was that assumptions that had informed the organisation of local government in the immediate post-war period were now challenged. Reorganisation had given rise to central institutions that were to take on an increasingly important role in managing the much more fundamental changes that are now affecting local government.

The development of the centre

Processes of mimesis and institutional conformity may explain why the 1970s was a period more of formal than substantive change. Changes in ideas were great but the operating environment of the local authority was not subject to radical change. Financial constraint, though it seemed great, was actually limited, mainly involving reductions in the rate of growth of expenditure. The present situation is different, with changes both in ideas about what constitutes good management in the public service, and in external constraint. The changes in the nature and role of the centre in the 1980s continued trends that were established in the 1970s, but also saw the development of new and potentially much more radical changes. The structures that had been established in the 1970s came to be effective in the 1980s. Continuity involved the increasing institutionalisation of the basic structural features that had been proposed by Maud, Bains and others. The Widdicombe studies of the mid-1980s found that almost every authority had a Chief Executive, management team and policy committee. Even those who had argued against some of these developments in the 1970s tended to return to the mainstream in the 1980s. For example, Birmingham, which had dismissed its Chief Executive, reestablished the position in the 1980s. Recent developments have been more concerned with changes in the way that the centre works, and in what it is trying to do, than in the structure.

The developing role of the centre can be seen as falling under seven headings:

- coordination;
- control;
- external relations;
- strategic planning and development;
- political management;
- new initiatives;
- support.

Coordination involves attempting to ensure consistency across the authority, for example in the treatment of staff or of the public. Many of the key developments have involved attempts to develop more integrated approaches to services that cross departmental boundaries – for example, through decentralisation of the delivery of services or the establishment of 'one-stop' shops. Central *control* is normally operated over such matters as the total revenue and capital budget of the authority. *External relations* have become important as local government has had to work more with other agencies in order to pursue its purposes. *Strategic management* on a centralised basis is at an early stage of development, but is of increasing significance, as local authorities have to interact more with other organisations in order to achieve their purposes, and because the environment in which they operate is becoming more uncertain. *Political management* is necessary in local authorities, and typically falls to the centre, and particularly the Chief Executive. It has become both more necessary and more difficult as levels of political organisation have increased, polarisation has grown, and more authorities are 'hung', operating with no overall control. *New initiatives* involve the development of organisational changes that are seen as beneficial, but unlikely to happen if left to the departments alone. Finally, the centre provides services to the rest of the authority – for example, legal services, computing, finance, management services, personnel and property management. We will examine each of the seven aspects of the management of the centre of the authority in turn.

Coordination

Two basic forms of coordination are necessary in the local authority.

First, there is the need to co-ordinate policy between the various divisions and boundaries within the organisation, notably between different services. Any set of boundaries will create problems of classification in determining what falls under the aegis of a particular department. The increasing complexity of the environment means that problems are less likely to be amenable to straightforward classification. This is particularly so as organisational categories become older since they are less likely to be appropriate to new problems. Issues that do not fall neatly into the

ambit of any particular department include coping with environmental problems, developing initiatives on crime prevention, and
encouraging economic development.

Second, there are issues that cross all intra-organisational
boundaries, and cannot sensibly be classed as the province of any
particular department. The most important source of such issues is
the development of a client or interest group orientation, for
example considering the needs of women, children, old people, or
minority ethnic groups. It is often felt to be necessary for the centre
to take a leading role in developing an organisational response to
such problems of coordination, either through establishing specific
units, such as women's or equal opportunities units, or through the
use of central, generalist staff.

Coordination is made particularly difficult in the local authority
because of the duplication of differentiation at the officer and the
member level. Studies of coordination in social policy (Challis *et
at.*, 1985) have found that it is often more difficult to establish
coordination between different departments inside the local
authority, than with external agencies. Coordination partly
involves the centre acting autonomously to forward issues, and
partly the development of approaches such as management teams
and corporate groups, that cross departmental and professional
boundaries.

Control

Central controls are normally exercised through formalisation and
standardisation of procedures rather than through command.
Although, as we shall see later, the formal power of the Chief
Executive has increased somewhat, the power of individual
departments is still considerable. Nor is there an overwhelming
centralised control at the elected-member level, for although the
influence of the leader has increased, power is normally distributed
within the party group. Control is expressed in the formal
procedures of standing orders, schemes of delegation and financial
regulations. Matters over which there are likely to be relatively
strong controls are revenue and capital spending, aspects of
personnel management and procedures for reporting to committee.

The development of devolved systems of management has led to
the relaxing of controls to some degree, but, generally, local

authority departments are subject to more detailed control than would be the case for a division within a multidivisional company. These requirements are heightened by the fact that, as public organisations, local authorities are expected to behave differently from the private sector, and to be able to show that they can account fully for the way that they use public law. The degree of control has tended to increase as the law has become tighter, and has been interpreted more strictly over the past few years. There is now far more likelihood than was the case in the 1960s and 1970s of the action of the local authority being the subject of litigation. There is a consequent tendency to operate strong central control in order to ensure the legality of action. Central control of finance has also increased as financial constraint has tightened, a tendency that has been exacerbated by the increasing complexity of the finance system. Greater control has also followed the increase in political organisation, and the desire of politicians to ensure that their ideological commitments are implemented. Central government has also legislated for stronger central control in the local authority, through requiring local authorities to designate specific officers at the centre responsible for legal and financial probity, and commenting upon management arrangements.

External relations

The external relations role of the centre involves much more than representation and public relations. As the world of the local authority has become more inter-organisationally complex, and as local government has become more dependent on other organisations, so the importance of building links has grown. Local authorities must work, for example, with urban development corporations, city action teams and a host of other bodies in the development and implementation of policies on economic regeneration and revival of the inner cities. Social services departments must work effectively with the police service, the National Health Service and voluntary agencies. Numerous reports, particularly those on specific instances of failure, such as the Butler-Schloss Report (1988) have emphasised the importance of the integrated working of public agencies. Government policy has increasingly required local authorities to cooperate with external agencies in the delivery of service. The 'new right' has argued that the local authority should operate predominantly through contracts with external agencies. As Mather (1989) puts it:

> The future of local government should be seen in this sense of a series of contracts: with central government for the 'purchase' of particular grant-supported services; with contractors for the operational execution of functions and services; with residents through more closely defined charging mechanisms, including the community charge; and with partners, including the voluntary sector and the business community (Mather, 1989).

The local authority is increasingly defined as a network agency, within a tightly coupled inter-agency framework.

Much of the responsibility for maintaining the inter-organisational network of local government falls on the centre of the authority for three reasons:

1. The problems that need to be dealt with on an interorganisational basis tend not to fall within the responsibilities of any single department.
2. There is a tendency to centralisation in organisations relating to one another, because the responsibilities of subordinate staff are normally defined within the organisation, and it is difficult for them to be clear on their power and responsibilities in relation to external bodies. It is simpler to pass problems up the line and let those at the top deal directly with one another.
3. Local authorities have become more conscious of the need for, and the possible uses of, public relations. Particular policy areas such as economic development and tourism are highly dependent on the authority being able to market the local area effectively. Local authorities have been developing marketing normally as a central function of the authority.

The role of the local authority as a focal point within the network is explored in more detail in Chapter 9.

Strategy planning and development

We have argued that the need for strategy has grown because of the changed demands that face local authorities, increasing uncertainty, and the fact that the effectiveness of their actions depends in part upon the actions of others. Strategy involves an attempt to think and plan in broad terms and for the medium- and long-term future. It also involves considering the development of the organisation as a whole rather than the needs of individual departments. There will be strategies for individual areas of the authority's functions, but these are increasingly likely to be seen as part of the overall strategy of the authority, developed on a centralised basis.

The strategic planning approach that is beginning to emerge in local government can be compared with the corporate planning movement of the 1980s. The latter grew out of policy planning/budgeting systems (PPBS) and other highly rationalistic techniques that had been developed, primarily in the United States of America, in the 1950s and 1960s. Corporate planning was based upon the premise that total planning was both sensible and possible, and depended on a world of relative certainty, which allowed the present to be projected into the future, and on slack resources, so that unexpected events could be coped with without diverting resources from the plan. It is clear that this sort of highly rationalistic planning is inappropriate to the less certain and more constrained 1990s. Planning cannot be based upon the assumption that the future will be like the past.

Strategic planning and development is based upon flexibility. Caulfield and Schultz quote one authority, which describes what it is doing as follows:

> It is proposed that an emphasis be placed on . . . a strategic process rather than . . . a corporate planning document. The output of the process would be a bundle of consistent, comprehensive and well-targeted 'policy vehicles' . . . e.g. the annual budget, the Transport Policy and Programme, the unitary Development Plan, the Housing Investment Programme, the Council's economic strategy, etc . . . These would be prepared so that each is consciously oriented to the achievement of the Council's strategic objectives (Caulfield and Schultz, 1989).

This form of strategic planning tends to overlap with control because of the need to be able to respond quickly to changing circumstances. The production and management of strategy is not therefore divorced form the process of organisational management, but needs to be integrated with it. Local authorities are increasingly adopting what Goold and Campbell (1987) describe as the strategic control approach.

Political management

The local authority is an organisation with a dual core, the managerial core and the political core, and a key role of the centre of the organisation is to weld together the two cores so that an effective system of political management is created. This role of the centre has become both more difficult and more significant as the saliency of political organisation has grown. The political-management role of the centre at the officer level involves two main activities. The first is the political maintenance of the authority – that is, ensuring that the formal political system of elections, committee administration and decision-making is effective. The second is ensuring that there are adequate and acceptable links between the political and the managerial levels of the authority. In carrying out the activity of political management the centre plays a linking-pin role.

The political-management role of the centre is different from any comparable role carried out in commercial organisations. The politicians are not in the same position as members of the board in a private company. Nor is the link between politicians and officers analogous to that between the company and its share-holders The elected members have become more involved in the management of the authority over the period since reorganisation, and the need for more effective means of enabling members to carry out their role has grown. Local authorities have increasingly established specific support services for elected members, and the role of senior officers, and particularly that of the Chief Executive has become more explicitly one of political management. Strategic and political management are linked through the role of the centre. As a Local Government Management Board (LGMB) document on strategic management says:

> Strategic management sits between the day-to-day activity of the local authority and the political aims and values of its members. The key benefit is to enable members to accomplish whatever

they see as their central aims and purposes despite all the other pressures on them (LGMB, 1991).

The strategic management process is also an expression of the process of political control in the authority. These issues are explored in more detail in Chapter 7.

New initiatives

The centre may play the role of starting initiatives that may be take up by other parts of the organisation. There are developments that are seen as desirable but which are unlikely to develop without the specific impetus that the centre can provide. Examples include the development of customer-oriented approaches to service, or the development of equal-opportunities policies across the range of the authorities services. There is also a need to coordinate major change that does not fall within the introduction of competitive tendering. The centre can act to mobilise the resources of the organisation in a way that individual departments cannot. The ability to develop initiatives depends upon the availability of slack resources, or, at least the ability to reallocate resources, which is more feasible with generalist policy staff at the centre, than those involved in the operational management of services. The role of the centre is particularly likely to be important in the initial development of initiatives, which are subsequently taken up by service departments.

Support

Local authorities are large and complex organisations, which means that they create considerable need for support services – for example, in financial management or computer services. Support services are provided on a centralised basis to benefit from economies of scale. It would be difficult for every department to have its own lawyer or accountant, and, certainly, it would be impossible for each department to have within each profession the range of skills and knowledge that it is possible for a centralised organisation to provide. The very largest departments may have their own capacity, but are still likely to rely on the centre for particular skills and specialisms. The advantages of economies of scale may change as technologies change – for example, with the development of information technology that allows decentralisation, but there are always likely to be advantages to the centralisation of some support services.

The provision of support services through centrally organised departments not only results from technical imperatives, but also reflects the career interests of central professionals. The existence of a central department offers opportunities for careers and independence that would not be possible in a more decentralised structure. The decentralisation of support services is frequently resisted by central professionals because they see their power as being reduced and because their individual career paths may be disrupted. Even where support staff are decentralised they frequently remain on the establishment of the central department. The delivery of central support services is increasingly being established on an internal trading and quasi-contract basis, and subjected to competitive tendering.

Conflicting pressures

The traditional role of the centre, the management of the committee system and the exercise of ceremonial functions, has continued. But it is increasingly overshadowed in importance by the new and developing roles of the centre. Both the external and internal context within which the centre must work has changed. The centre faces conflicting demands and pressures both in the roles that it fulfils and the way that it carries them out. There is strong pressure for decentralisation, but, paradoxically, this is frequently centrally driven, often against opposition from departments and committees, which see it as against their interests. Decentralisation threatens the traditional hierarchy of departments more than the centre of the authority. The role of the centre has become more prominent because of the need to manage change, which leads to the need for a more articulate organisational strategy. Even if, in the longer term, the role of the centre were to decrease, its short term influence is increasing. The dominant role of the centre is the management of change – that is, the creation of new structures, process and culture within the organisation. The centre itself is changing in order to be able to carry out the role of change management. There is an emerging concept of and demand for organisational leadership, as local authorities experience the difficulties and tensions of organisational transformation. These developments are most clearly expressed in the role of the Chief Executive.

The Chief Executive

The local authority did not traditionally have a Chief Executive at its head, but, after the Bains Report, the majority of authorities did formally establish the position. By the early 1980s the position of the Chief Executive was more or less universally accepted; there was less common agreement on the role that she or he should play. The Bains Report had recommended that the Chief Executive should not have a department, but should have authority over all other officers. Neither of these arguments was accepted in practice. The majority of Chief Executives were either established with departments or gradually took on specific responsibilities. In some cases they were given or took on responsibility for the secretary's department and committee administration, thus continuing in the tradition of the Clerk. In other cases they took responsibility for functions that were relatively new and did not fit easily into other departments, for example economic development. The debate continues. One Chief Executive recently argued:

I have consistently argued against the model of the Chief Executive without the department believing that certain key strategic functions should be directly accessible and the Chief Executive should not become isolated from the day-to-day business of the council. However I recognise the council's concern that I should avoid becoming preoccupied with departmental management. I believe that a balance can be struck by ensuring that the functions within my department operate relatively autonomously for day-to-day purposes with their most senior officers being responsible for the management of staff and budgets and reporting to committee in their own name on non-strategic matters. The benefit of the proposed department lies in the opportunity it provides to draw key functions together with a single direction and to ensure very close working with short lines of communication and decision-making. (Private communication)

As time has gone on the majority of Chief Executives have acquired some departmental responsibility, notably for central policy staff, for staff engaged in relatively new developments such as economic development, or for some of the central services such as personnel. The role of the Chief Executive is developing as the strategic management of the authority and the management of relations with the politicians.

Traditionally, the Chief Executive had relatively limited authority over other chief officers. This too has changed, and the authority of the Chief Executive has increased as the role of the centre has become more important. Though authority over other chief officers is nebulous, and to a degree can exist only as long as it is rarely exercised and then only in relatively extreme cases, it is clear that authority exists. As one Chief Executive put it:

Chief officers are expected to have a good deal of autonomy in managing their departments and have therefore only a limited day-to-day responsibility to the Chief Executive for corporate matters. The responsibility is in my experience very poorly defined, although most Chief Executives probably have some authority to instruct chief officers in the final analysis. Whilst I can only recall using the power to instruct on two occasions in more than ten years the fact that it exists is a significant influence on the relationship between the Chief Executive and the chief officers. (Private communication)

Since the Widdicombe report the position of the Chief Executive has become slightly clearer, as defined in the Local Government and Housing Act 1989. But it is still the case that the position and authority derives not from formal rules or statute but from accepted understandings within the authority. The position is nebulous, at least in terms of authority, because it is not yet fully developed, and because the Chief Executive is typically involved in the management of change, conflict and politics. The position of the Chief Executive is one of emergent rather than of defined leadership.

The role of the Chief Executive has been expressed by one officer holding the position as:

- head of the paid service, responsible for overseeing the performance of the organisation as a whole;
- management of the interface of the political process and the management process;
- responsible for maintaining and enhancing the authority's position in regard to the wider impact on the community within which it operates;
- giving the organisation leadership, vision, purpose and direction;
- troubleshooter and arbiter.

The political role is the one that is most characteristic of the management of local government. The position of the Chief Executive in industry involves no such role, and the nature of management in the Civil Service, with its ministerial system, is quite different. The Chief Executive must interpret the needs of management to politicians and the needs of politicians to officers. The role is particularly difficult in highly politicised authorities.

Chief Executives in urban authorities, in particular, spend a great deal of their time with the leadership of the political group in control. The development of a large number of hung authorities in the 1980s has meant that the political-management role of the Chief Executive has become both more difficult and more salient. It has been necessary to manage the complex relationship between the officers and the elected members. The political role may involve attendance at political group meetings, but, as the Widdicombe research showed, this only take place in a minority of cases. There are regular contacts between the political executive and the political leader; in 88 per cent of cases they will meet weekly or more often. For the officer structure the link to the policy committee is typically through the Chief Executive.

The leadership role of the Chief Executive is particularly significant at a time of change. As the Audit Commission argues:

He or she must be both the authority's centre of continuity and its agent of change. This means managing the interface between politics and management, converting policy and strategy into action, developing processes, people and management skills to ensure that the authority is capable of delivering its strategy, reviewing its performance against stated objectives and thinking and planning for the future (Audit Commission, 1989).

The Chief Executive has a crucial role to play in the process of transformational leadership that is necessary to the reorientation of local government.

Central costs: from command to trading

The tensions and conflicts that characterise the debate over the role of the centre are apparent in the debate over central costs and the way that they are controlled. The development of devolved management and internal trading accounts has led to questioning of the costs of central services. Traditionally the costs of the centre have been distributed to departmental budgets by means of a variety of more or less sophisticated mechanisms, such as use of floor-space or the size of the budget. The distribution of central costs have been seen as necessary to ensure both that the full costs of services are known, and that accurate comparison of costs between authorities can be made. In practice the distribution of central costs was largely a paper exercise, because they were treated as 'below the line' and not properly part of the budget of the service department. The process was not seen as having any influence on the managerial process, but was a purely accounting exercise which impinged relatively little on service managers. Departmental managers had little knowledge of and were little concerned with the costs of the centre. The accuracy of the allocation and apportionment of costs in relation to use was little questioned, because they did not affect the interests of service departments.

The development of devolved management, and the introduction of trading accounts for services that are subject to competition, has made the cost of central services a matter of interest to service managers because it has moved these costs above the line. They now fall directly on the budgets of the managers of direct service organisations or of devolved management units. The former are concerned that central costs will be so high as to make it difficult for them to compete against the private sector. The latter are concerned that money spent on central services is not available for the provision of services. The result is that there is pressure to reduce central costs and to give devolved units more control of the central costs that they incur. Central services have to account more clearly for the costs that they recover from other services, and have moved towards more detailed methods of determining those costs. The relationship between the centre and direct service providers has moved from one of distribution on the basis of command, towards allocation on the basis of exchange, that is, from hierarchy towards market processes. More radically, the local authority has been led to re-examine what the centre is for, because service departments question their lack of control over the nature of the services that they receive. The change is not simply one of management accounting methods, but a response to much more fundamental changes. As Ahmed and Scapens (1991) find in a study of the development of the allocation of common costs in the private sector, it is 'shaped by a diverse set of institutional, economic and social factors', rather than being a purely technical matter.

Managers given responsibility for their own budgets resent their residual dependence on the centre, especially where, as has traditionally been the case, central costs are added to accounts at the end of the year. The question that arises is of the relative power and organisational significance of the centre. An extreme approach, adopted in only a few authorities is to make the centre totally dependent on service managers. This is done by allocating to service managers an element of their budget that would pay for services such as finance and the personnel, and allowing them autonomy to decide whether they actually spent their money in that way, and if they did whether they bought services within or outside the authority. This approach shifts power within the organisation to the periphery, with the size of the centre depending upon the extent to which the periphery is willing to contribute.

While there has been little movement towards the extreme of 'contribution' costing for central services, they are generally being required to monitor costs more closely. The most common development has been time-charging systems involving detailed monitoring of the way that central service officers spend their time, often involving time-recording. The costs of central services are then allocated on the basis of the standard unit cost or the service. It is argued that this approach focuses attention on the efficiency of central services through highlighting the relationship between the number of hours that a service is able to charge out and the unit cost. The centre is put onto a trading basis with the service department, and it is easier to operate where the service provided can be broken down into units, whether of time or service – for example, the hours that the legal officer might spend working for a particular department. In other cases block prices are agreed.

Many authorities have developed 'service-level agreements', which involve the centre making an explicit agreement with each service department at the beginning of the year. These agreements can take two forms:

• One possibility is an agreement based on stated units of service and the cost per unit. The service department will then agree to pay a certain price for a certain amount of service. For example the treasurer's department might charge service departments for the costs of making up wages on the basis of the cost per week per employee.

• The alternative form of agreement is more common where it is difficult to specify the nature of the units of service and to predict in detail what the need for the service will be. It may be difficult, for example, to know how much legal work or personnel work will be needed in any given year. In these cases, a service-level agreement that consists of a block payment, a retainer, for a certain maximum level of service, with specific charging above that rate, is common. The service manager is effectively buying insurance up to a certain level and the central department gains a minimum degree of certainty of the resources that it needs to have. The sort of agreement that emerges depends upon the interests and power of the respective parties.

If the first method is adopted then the risk will tend to be left with the centre, through a process of unit-pricing with the option to purchase being left with the service manager. Few have taken this route. More common is the second, risk-sharing approach of block booking.

The move to trading for central services forces the authority to consider which services are there because they are needed to support direct-service provision, and are most efficiently and effectively provided on a central basis, and which are there because of the corporate needs of the organisation. It is impossible for the latter costs to be put onto an effective market basis, because they are effectively public goods within the organisation, which all share, and over which there is no choice of usage. It makes no logical sense to put such services onto a trading basis. In some cases authorities have been led to separate central support services from those services that form the corporate centre. In Northamptonshire those services that exist at the centre because of the corporate nature of the authority as an organisation are part of a central executive office, with all support services being organised in a single 'professional services' department. This approach is unusual, but distinctions are increasingly being made in the various roles that the centre plays in order to develop appropriate processes of charging and cost-recovery.

The development of trading and the devolution of managerial control and budgets are forcing authorities to think more clearly about the nature of the organisation as a whole. Those services that exist because of the corporate nature of the authority continue to be organised on the basis of command and bureaucratic control. Those services that exist to support the departments engaged in direct service delivery are, by contrast, organised on the basis of contract and market-based exchange. These tendencies may be enhanced by the development of competition for services such as law and computing, with the private sector being allowed to tender against internal providers.

Conclusion

The changing context of, and pressures on, the local authority have changed the role of the centre significantly. It is no longer there in a primarily legal and administrative role to service the committee system and to play a largely ceremonial role. Rather it has become necessary for the centre to play a strong role in transforming the organisation. This has involved the reconciliation of conflicting pressures. On the one hand there is the strong argument for devolved management and greater autonomy, and on the other the need for organisational cohesion. This dual pressure is reflected in the apparent paradox that centralisation tends to go along with attempted decentralisation – a tension that is apparent in other public service organisations. The role and position of the centre is much more diffuse than in the private sector as portrayed by Chandler (1962) or by Goold and Campbell (1987). The centre in the local authority is developing an increasingly clear executive role, and the executive office is developing. The conflicting pressures and contingencies which impinge upon the local authority are felt particularly at the centre of the organisation.

6 Decentralised Organisation and Management in Local Government

In Chapter 5 we analysed the changing role of the centre in local authorities in the new legislative and financial circumstances of the late 1980s and early 1990s. Changes in the role of the centre imply changes in the role of the organisation's periphery. A balance has to be achieved between the forces of centralisation and those of decentralisation. In this chapter we look at the different ways in which decentralisation has taken place in local authorities since the 1974 reorganisation.

Decentralised organisation and management developed in the 1980s as a response to changes in society, to government legislation and to changing concepts of management. Distinctions can be drawn between:

- geographical decentralisation for better access and more responsive services;
- political decentralisation for community involvement and strengthened representative democracy;
- management decentralisation for greater organisational effectiveness;

even though in practice they may be linked in authorities. Each organisational change challenges the continuities built into the workings of local authorities.

The tradition of centralisation

The traditional local authority had a centralised structure symbolised in our large urban authorities by the town halls dominating the city centres in their pride and grandeur. In and around those town halls were offices in which many of the routines of the authority were carried out and to which many of those who required services had to travel. The degree of geographical centralisation was less in the counties, where the distances involved created their own organisational necessities. Indeed, in many counties, education divisional executives had a degree of independence until they were abolished by the 1974 reorganisation. Some, but not all, counties introduced a new area organisation for education. In general, however, the emphasis, remained upon the central council offices as the seat of local power – it was after all, in some counties, the former centre of justice. Indeed in some counties those offices were built on the site of the old medieval castle which represented the centre of power.

It is not, however, merely a question of geographical centralisation. Geographical centralisation was matched by organisational centralisation. The basic elements of the organisation both supported and expressed centralisation. Because the committee, on behalf of the council, was the source of authority for all that happened in the services for which it was responsible, decisions tended to be drawn up the hierarchy to the committee.

The committee system had its impact on the working of departments. Subtly the effect was to undermine management responsibility. 'The committee has decided' avoids management responsibility, even when the committee merely accepted the recommendation of a particular officer. The (often long) hierarchies of the departments were built for detailed and direct control centred on the formal position of the committee, and, with limited spans of control could result in seven or eight tiers between fieldworker and chief officer.

'Organisational centralisation' can also refer to the central control exercised by the central departments of the authority over the working of service departments and discussed in Chapter 5. The Treasurer's Department and the finance subcommittee have often exercised detailed budgetary control, restricting departments' freedom to vire between budget heads. The personnel officer and the personnel committee exercised detailed control over grading, the establishment of posts and even the filling of vacant posts.

Organisational centralisation in all its forms both supports and expresses the organisational assumptions set out in Chapter 3. The assumption of direct control is centralising in effect, since it presumes that a committee or a chief officer has to be directly involved in decisions in order to exercise control. The rationale for detailed control lies in the assumption of uniformity. Without such control, there could be growing and undesirable variation in the services provided. Detailed control is reinforced by procedural accountability. Financial control in detail is exercised to ensure that the budgets are spent as planned and 'proper authority' is required therefore to move items from one budget head to another.

The reorganisation of 1974 confirmed the centralised local authority. Attention was concentrated by the Bains Report on the corporate management of the authority, which was seen as involving the Chief Executive and the management team of chief officers. The diagrams in that report focused attention on the structure of committees and upon chief officers. There was little recognition in the report of the potential of decentralisation.

The creation of larger authorities meant that both geographical and organisational distance grew between the centre of the authority, the fieldworkers and the public. While a natural response might have been thought to be to emphasise decentralisation (which happened in a few authorities such as Stockport, Devon and especially West Norfolk) most authorities adopted a centralised structure.

In many authorities the dominant consideration was the perceived need to establish the identity of the new authority and that was seen as requiring the establishment of authority-wide policies so that services could be applied on a uniform basis throughout the area. That need justified centralisation. In most authorities there was a reluctance to decentralise the running of services to areas which resembled those of the predecessor authorities, since their traditions were often seen as a threat to the new authority.

Moves towards decentralisation

While the dominant pattern of organisation in the new local authorities, as in the previous authorities, was based on a centralised structure of committees and departments, there were some counter-influences.

A number of local authorities saw decentralisation as a natural response to a reorganisation which created larger authorities bringing together what had previously been separate communities. West Norfolk went so far as to run certain services through area committees with an officer organisation responsible to them (Bolton, 1974).

The main influence, that led to a consideration of the need for area decentralisation came, however, from a concern for urban deprivation with its concentration in parts of the inner city. The community development projects, launched by the Labour Government of 1964–70, had focused attention on particular areas, even though the analysis carried out by those projects was later to suggest that their problems reflected wider structural problems (Community Development Project, 1977).

The Conservative Government of 1970–74 initiated urban guideline studies and inner area studies. These studies contained suggestions for area organisation. Thus the Sunderland study argued that dealing with problems on an area basis would enable the local authority 'to identify problems that might be overlooked by using only a functional division' (Department of the Environment, 1973). The Government was to encourage a series of experiments in area management 'as a means of adapting local government organisation so that it can respond more sensitively and effectively to the particular needs of areas' (Department of the Environment, 1974). This led to a series of pilot projects either in response to this initiative or, as in Stockport, building on projects already undertaken. These and a limited number of other initiatives constitute the area management movement of the latter half of the 1970s.

Different approaches were adopted by different authorities. Stockport had created area committees playing an advisory role throughout the authority composed of local councillors, supported by area organisation. Newcastle set up priority area teams in the deprived areas of the city to allocate special finance for new projects and local priorities. Other projects as in Liverpool and Haringey focused on a single area.

On the whole the projects had a limited impact because their powers were limited. To give them more powers or more resources would have challenged the dominant pattern of organisation:

Given the extent of these challenges which area management, by its very nature, represents to the existing organisation and ongoing decision-making processes, it was perhaps predictable that its powers would be limited (Webster, 1982, pp.194–5).

The area management projects did not therefore lead to any major development of decentralisation in local authorities. While inner-city policy continued to focus attention on particular areas, the interest in decentralisation that was to develop in the 1980s had other sources.

New developments in decentralisation

An interest in decentralisation developed as one response of local authorities to the changes discussed in Chapter 2. Local authorities have recognised the need to develop more responsive services in the face of changing public attitudes. There has been a recognition of the need to create a more flexible organisation, and the centralised procedures of the local authority have been seen as a source of rigidity. At a time of financial constraint centralised controls, far from ensuring the efficient use of resources, have restricted the capacity of managers to deploy them effectively in relation to the problems faced. There has been a wide-ranging concern in political parties at what are seen as the rigidities of bureaucratic working in local authorities.

The legislative changes imposed by the government are also challenging centralisation in local authorities as they are challenging the organisational assumptions on which it is based. Compulsory competitive tendering (CCT) means that control is not exercised directly but only through the terms of the contract. We have already noted in Chapter 2 the impact of CCT on the role of the centre, a subject explored further in Chapter 5. Contracting-out necessarily removes direct financial and personnel controls and the same degree of freedom is required by internal contractors if they are to compete effectively.

The legislation providing for local management of schools means that Boards of Governors of schools will have direct management responsibility over their budget, being free to determine its allocation and to exercise control over its use, within the resources allocated to them. They take over direct management responsibility for running the school. This legislative change clearly decentralises within the education service as well as changing fundamentally the role of the centre, creating an awareness in local authorities of the possibilities of decentralisation in other services.

Organisational *and* geographical centralisation are also challenged by the approach of the Citizen's Charter and by the approaches initiated by local authorities themselves that have led to a new emphasis on closeness to the public as customer and as citizen.

In Chapter 3 we have suggested that in organisations there 'are conflicting pressures for centralisation and for decentralisation, which reflect conflicting managerial imperatives, but also the interests of different groups and units'. The changing framework of ideas brought about gave support to the pressure for decentralisation. The dangers of centralisation are being given greater emphasis in thinking about organisations as is shown in Chapter 5 on the role of the centre. Handy (1985) has even suggested that decentralisation may not be enough and that the organisation of the future may have a federal structure:

> Federal organisations . . . will rely on a small nerve centre coordinating a range of small, nearly autonomous operations which can be widely dispersed geographically. The concept of a holding company which has been a financial and legal reality will begin to mean more in strict organisational terms and will be as common in the integrated manufacturing company as it is in the financial world (Handy, 1985, p.407).

All these different factors have contributed to the interest in decentralisation that has developed in local government. Decentralisation in authorities takes many different forms reflecting in part the different problems in the centralised structures at which they are directed:

- concern about the lack of accessibility caused by geographical centralisation and about the style of working encouraged by centralised offices is leading to the development of local offices both on a service basis or on an authority-wide basis, normally called neighbourhood offices.

- concern about the lack of control by people over the services provided is leading to proposals for extending community control, or for developing the role of the councillor as representative of an area;
- concern about the constraints upon effective management resulting from organisation centralisation is leading to schemes for devolved management which may stress either the need for greater management effectiveness in deploying resources or greater responsiveness to the public.

Decentralisation for accessibility

Local authorities have normally centralised control over their services in offices in the town hall or in offices close to the town hall. The position has, of course, varied from service to service. Some services are necessarily provided locally because they are delivered by field-workers, such as environmental health officers, housing maintenance staff, home-helps, social workers, or refuse collectors. But the fact that a service is delivered locally does not necessarily mean that access to the service can be achieved locally, or business about the service be conducted locally. Thus, although council housing is necessarily a local service, until recently access to the service in many authorities could only be secured through the central offices. Indeed under the impact of the dominant organisational assumptions, the trend was to reduce direct contact with the tenants on estates.

> Meanwhile other pressures were at work within the arena of public housing management, mainly the desire to minimise the cost and staff commitment of an exploding service. The influential Metropolitan Boroughs' Committee produced in 1963 a series of recommendations on how to cut the costs of management in line with local authorities' general feeling that housing management could work perfectly well for the majority of 'normal tenants' remote from tenants themselves and with a minimum of contact. Each of these recommendations represented a retrograde step into the centre and a withdrawal where it hurt most (Power, 1987, p.82).

Other services such as education, libraries and leisure and recreation services are necessarily provided in local premises to which access is normally possible – at least for those who have found their way in the local authority system.

Social services had recognised the need for area organisation at the time of the formation of the new departments, based on the Seebohm Report (1968) which placed an emphasis on community work and proposed the creation of area teams of social workers, a proposal which was generally adopted by the new departments. Highways departments, particularly in counties, had an area organisation as had many education departments. Area organisation was, however, generally seen as a technical requirement of the service, rather than as a means of improving accessibility. A well-publicised study by Liverpool Shelter Neighbourhood Action Project published in 1972 highlighted 'the lack of coterminous boundaries which made it quite impossible for district officers to attempt a coordinated service' (Shelter, 1972, p.139). Area organisational structures reflected the requirements of each separate service organisation and not the needs of the people served.

In the 1980s, however, a new approach was adopted to area organisation which focused on the people served through the development of neighbourhood offices. The issue of access was seen as important, but more was involved than access. The intention was to create 'a new style of working' focusing on the needs of the public. It was often associated in rhetoric, if not always in reality, with an emphasis on community control. The change to local offices was likely to lead to management decentralisation, but the emphasis was on 'going local' to ensure greater access by, greater responsiveness to, and even greater control by, local people, and in some instances the management implications were not fully worked out.

The introduction of neighbourhood offices by the Housing Department in Walsall received considerable national attention. First proposed in 1981, the neighbourhood offices served an average population of 8000. Environmental health and social services also had a presence in the offices. The intention was to extend the coverage of neighbourhood offices more widely and in particular to social services generally, but this was stopped when Labour lost control of the authority in 1983. The use of decentralised offices for particular services is fairly widespread. What distinguished Walsall was the attempt to create new styles of working, based on offices to which the public had easy access.

Islington created twenty-four local offices each serving an average population of 7000. These offices deal not merely with housing but also with social services, environmental health, planning and welfare benefits:

> The aim of the reorganisation of the Council's work in Islington is to make the service more accessible and to increase the speed of service delivery once need has been identified. To achieve this the Council is advocating, in the first instance, a partial reversal of the bureaucratic tendency towards centralised decision-making. Obviously major policy initiatives will continue to be the prerogative of councillors. An element of neighbourhood control, however, will supplement the established system of representation and, it is intended, will permit local needs and wishes to influence the nature of council services. In addition, the decentralisation proposals advocate an increase in the autonomy and decision-making capacity of those staff dealing directly with the public. Most of these staff will be housed in neighbourhood offices, the independence of which is to be ensured by the staff's capacity to manage an element of their own budgets (Henry, 1984, p.47).

There were organisational changes through the creation of the position of the neighbourhood officer who was responsible for the overall management of the office. The intention was to create a style of working in the neighbourhood offices that challenged traditional departmental working.

Lucy Gaster has described the developments of pilot neighbourhood offices in Harlow as a result of an Organisation Review Working Party which confirmed decentralisation and democratisation as major objectives of the council and argued that neighbourhoods should be the council's basic unit of organisation backed by corporate support services. The pilot projects were established in three areas with the opening of neighbourhood offices and the appointment of neighbourhood services managers and neighbourhood support managers. Chief officers began to act as twin-tracking neighbourhood managers to whom the neighbourhood offices were responsible. Area committees were later established.

Harlow has extended the neighbourhood approach, but the research study covered the pilot phase. It showed that 'considerable success has been achieved in creating a welcoming – and untraditionally non-bureaucratic – atmosphere in the neighbourhood offices' (Gaster, 1993, p.47). It also showed the difficulty of carrying out organisational change – when policy has not been fully worked out beyond a general aspiration to neighbourhood working and when the remainder of the organisation is structured on traditional lines.

Neighbourhood offices on a cross-service basis which have also developed in other authorities such as Birmingham have been effective in improving access and in encouraging a style of working that is responsive to the public within the limits of the discretion available to staff. Whether the creation of neighbourhood offices involves more fundamental change is less certain. There was an aspiration amongst the advocates of decentralisation that challenged traditional departmentalism. In practice, neighbourhood offices have often been added on to structures that remain based on departments.

Even in Islington professional staff remained for a time responsible to their departments – rather than to the neighbourhood officer – and those departments remained responsible to committees. Political and professional power remained departmental. The staff from housing and social services in Islington, however, have now been made responsible for a Department of Neighbourhood Services, although there has recently been criticism of the consequences for social services.

Neighbourhood offices in the widest sense of the term have not developed to anything like the extent to which its advocates hoped. A number of local authorities which attempted to develop neighbourhood offices had to abandon the attempt (e.g. Hackney, cf. Puddephatt, 1987). In 1987 the Decentralisation and Research Centre in listing the major developments of the last decade recorded only three authorities which had actually introduced neighbourhood offices catering for more than one service and the number has not greatly increased since. The reasons why local authorities have not pursued their aim varies. Cost is clearly a factor. In some authorities trade-union attitudes were seen as creating problems.

It may well be that there is a more fundamental reason. Where the wider local authority organisational and political structures remain departmental, neighbourhood offices that aspire to a new style of working are in effect operating against the basic assumptions of the structure.

In practice it has been much easier to create local offices on a departmental basis. There have always been such offices but recent years have seen a marked extension in housing, where it has also been associated with the growth of the generalist housing officer. Under the stimulus of the Priority Estate Project, estate-based management and the use of estates offices has developed, but to be successful estate management has to challenge traditional ways of working:

> It is relatively easy to diagnose the problems of estate management under historic local authority regimes. The tenants are a loosely knit group of disparate households required to liaise from time to time with a housing district or housing department, usually both. There is no focal point. A local management office replicates all the central confusion if it is simply a referral point for tenants. Everything hinges on the local manager having delegated authority and being clearly in charge of the total housing service to the estate (Power, 1987, p.245).

Similar issues are raised by the development of patch working in social services (Hadley and McGrath, 1984).

Although movement to geographical decentralisation has proceeded furthest in particular departments, to an extent the point remains the same as for wider decentralisation. By itself it has limited value. Access is improved, but geographical decentralisation changes little else, unless the department or the authority is prepared to change its way of working at the centre of the authority – and that must involve political change as well as change in officer structures.

Political decentralisation

The changes discussed so far have been concerned with geographical decentralisation of the officer structure. They have been mainly concerned to improve access for the public as customer, although they have also been concerned to alter the style of working. Those approaches can be regarded as largely representing what Hoggett and Hambleton (1987) have described as consumerist approaches. One theme that runs through such approaches is 'the desire to focus more attention on the quality as distinct from the quantity of service' (Hoggett and Hambleton, 1987, p.20).

There have also been (sometimes associated with these changes) movements towards political decentralisation or devolution. These belong to what Hoggett and Hambleton describe as collectivist solutions, which embrace wider objectives 'relating to strengthening local democracy (as a contribution to sustaining democracy as a whole) and diffusing power and responsibility within society' (Hoggett and Hambleton, 1987, p.24).

A broad distinction can be drawn between decentralisation based on the representative structure of the council and decentralisation directly involving the public although in practice development of the former approach can lead on to the latter.

In the traditional local authority, the role of the councillor in the working of the authority is focused on the service or central committees of the authority and no recognition is given in the committee structure or in any other part of the organisation to the role of the councillor as representative for an area. Of course, the councillor raises issues on behalf of his or her constituents and they are dealt with in the officer structure. Councillors hold advice bureaux in their wards or electoral districts and are generally concerned with their areas. However such activities and concerns lie outside the working of the council, as represented by its formal structure and processes. Concern for the area runs counter to the traditional ways of working. A councillor who is elected to represent an area is turned by the working of the authority towards a concern for the running of services – from being a representative of the public into an advocate for the service. Councillors whose main concern is for their area are often spoken of as 'parochial' or as mere 'political welfare workers'.

Strengthening the accountability of the authority to the public and the responsiveness of the organisation to the political process can build on the role of the councillor as an elected representative through the development of new settings within the working of the authority. There is a distinction between local authorities which have created settings to give expression to the representative role of the councillor within a structure still organised on traditional lines and the exceptional authority that has changed that structure.

Birmingham's area committees are an example of the first approach. In 1984, the newly elected Labour Council created twelve area committees, corresponding to the twelve parliamentary constituencies. They were composed of the nine or twelve councillors for the three or four wards and the MP (originally before abolition of the metropolitan council they included county representatives). They met in the area and the public were encouraged to bring issues to the meeting. They considered such issues and issues affecting their area, referred to them by service committees. They had very limited powers mainly in relation to grants to community groups. They may be regarded as of limited importance but their significance lay in the legitimacy and support they gave to the councillors' representative role, providing a setting in which it could be developed and ensuring that the organisation had to consider and respond to an area perspective. It provided the means to put issues on the agenda within the normal working of the authority. Recent changes have reconstituted the area committees on a ward basis, although with the possibility of also meeting on a constituency basis. South Somerset has set up four area committees which, while playing a similar role, are also being given greater budgetary responsibility.

Tower Hamlets is an example of the second approach involving fundamental change in the councillor and the officer structure. The Liberal administration elected in 1986 created seven neighbourhood committees composed of the councillors elected in those areas. These committees took over the main responsibilities of the council. As a result all central committees were abolished except the policy and resources committee and, because of statutory requirements, the social services committee. The centre of the authority is concerned with resource allocation and a limited range of issues requiring borough-wide action. (Thus a housing sub-committee of the policy and resources committee was created to deal with borough-wide transfers and homeless families).

Because the membership of neighbourhood committees consisted of the elected councillors for the area, three of the committees (and after a by-election, four) were controlled by the Labour Party – the opposition on the council – although this was reduced to two after the 1990 elections. The committees represented a commitment to decentralised working, and seven neighbourhood Chief Executives were appointed with their own officer structure. In effect area-based working has replaced service-based working. The changes in Tower Hamlets had a number of aims. There was a desire to improve service delivery but there was also a commitment 'to remake local democracy, to create a new relationship between councillors and their public' (Stoker and Lowndes, 1991, p.32). The decentralisation co-ordinator for the Liberal Group described the developments in these terms:

> Decentralisation in Tower Hamlets is a means to an end, not an end in itself. It is a means to a local government system which is responsive and does serve the needs of local people (Hughes, 1987, p.36).

Stoker and Lowndes analysed the experience of Globetown neighbourhood. As they point out, it was a part of the change that each neighbourhood could develop in its own way:

> Each neighbourhood has developed a particular character and way of working, a reflection of the political priorities of its councillors and the managerial quality of the senior staff that were appointed to operate in each neighbourhood (Stoker and Lowndes, 1991, p.5).

Their conclusion about Globetown was that it was successful as a platform for its customer orientated policies. It ensured that officers serving the public were accessible, knowledgeable and keen to provide services (ibid p.29). They identified problems, however, in handling strategic issues and in providing specialist cover. Decentralisation does not necessarily remove a role for the centre.

The research did not find that the relationship with the public was significantly different from other authorities who have used other means of community involvement and they highlight the importance of other community concerns:

> This is not an argument against opening up a neighbourhood channel of communication but it does suggest that there should

be an awareness of the need to provide other routes for those interests not readily organised and expressed through the neighbourhood (ibid, p.33).

While decentralisation brought advances, the need for a centre remained.

Some of the local authorities that have adopted the first or more limited approach have created new institutions for community involvement. The area committees of Birmingham are in part a means to public involvement with the public invited to contribute, and the council intended to complement their decentralisation policies with parish councils. Authorities which have introduced neighbourhood offices have also developed new forms of community involvement as have other authorities. Islington introduced neighbourhood forums representing local residents and community groups which it 'is envisaged will exercise a full range of decision-making powers with the exception of letting and staffing' (Hoggett and Hambleton, 1987, p.249). In Tower Hamlets different approaches have been adopted by different Area Committees. Thus in the Globetown area an open advisory committee was established (Stoker and Lowndes, 1991).

Middlesbrough has introduced community councils. They originally established eleven councils for part of their area:

It was realised that there was a learning experience to go through, but the intention is that every area will have a Community Council.

The prime objective of a Community Council is to extend the influence of the local community over the decisions made by the Middlesbrough Council and other agencies, which affect the lives of people living within the area. The Community Council has a right to be consulted and any views will be considered by Middlesbrough Council, prior to reaching a decision (Shepherd, 1987, p.45).

The community council meets every four or six weeks and is open to any residents or representatives of voluntary organisations. Officers attend, report on services and listen to views:

In the longer term (and subject to the availability of resources), it is hoped to identify discretion in the provision of council services. Where there is discretion then the Community Council will be given the freedom to make choices on whether, say, the grass is cut more frequently or more pot holes are filled (Shepherd, 1987, p.46).

Such developments are more about opening the local authority to greater public influence rather than the transfer of substantive powers to direct public control. They, therefore, only go a limited way in achieving the aims set out by Hoggett and Hambleton. They can strengthen local democracy but do not go far in diffusing powers. Where a transfer of power has developed it has normally been in the control of specific facilities on estates as in user control of leisure centres or tenant control of estate management, usually within policies and procedures laid down by the authority.

Nevertheless all these developments challenge traditional ways of working and the organisation assumptions on which they depend.

Management decentralisation

The traditional working of local authorities has been organisationally centralised as a result of detailed control by service committees and departmental hierarchies as well as central committees and departments. Detailed control is not necessarily effective control. Because the focus is on direct control as it happens, the emphasis is upon particular decisions. There is no need to specify what is required in advance because decisions are taken as they arise but that can mean a failure to specify requirements to be met by management. Detailed control and centralisation, whether exercised over departments by central departments or exercised within departments can weaken management effectiveness. A manager who has to seek approval for detailed decisions, on staffing changes or virement between budget heads, becomes a resource bidder rather than a resource manager, deploying resources in the most effective way to meet the authorities requirements. It weakens management responsibility and limits management initiative. Detailed control reduces the capacity of the authority to respond to the public in ways that better meet their requirements within the purposes of the authority.

Detailed control is challenged by the development of CCT and of contract management, where what is required is specified in advance. It is also challenged by the legislation on local management in schools which reflects in theory if not always in practice a concept of control described by Cooper Lybrand in their report for the Department of Education and Science on the implementation of the proposals:

> The underlying philosophy of financial delegation to schools stems from the application of the principles of good management. Good management requires the identification of management units for which objectives can be set and resources allocated; the unit is then required to manage itself within those resources in a way which seeks to achieve the objectives; the performance of the unit is monitored and the unit is held to account for its performance and the use of funds (Coopers and Lybrand, 1981, p.7).

But it was not merely government legislation that challenged the assumption of direct control. The education legislation was itself based on developments in Cambridgeshire, Solihull and other local authorities. The interest in a new rhythm of control based on specifying requirements, giving management responsibility and enforcing accountability derived from a wider search for both effective and responsive management.

The Audit Commission has argued strongly for decentralised financial management:

> If councils are to make the maximum use of their management potential and financial resources, it is essential to involve line managers more closely in the financial control process. This requires a number of developments:
>
> • every part of a department's budget should be assigned to a designated 'budget-holder' – typically a front-line manager such as a head teacher or the manager of a recreation centre who should take the lead in preparing his or her own budget;

- each budget-holder needs to receive clear and prompt reports showing what they have spent to date, and compare this with the budget. Financial systems should be aligned with management responsibilities;
- managers should then accept a greater degree of responsibility for their own financial control (Audit Commission, 1988, p.11).

and argued not merely for decentralised financial management, but generally:

The only way properly to harness politics and management is for members to assign very clear responsibilities to officers, to set a framework of accountability and then let them get on with it.

Decentralised management (the staff implications of which are discussed in Chapter 8) is not easily introduced. It requires the identification of cost centres to which both management and financial responsibilities have to be related. Financial data and accounting procedures have to be related to the cost centres, which is likely to require new financial information systems. But it is not sufficient to allocate budgets to cost centres and hold managers to account for those budgets. The management targets have to be specified for performance as well as the policy constraints within which the managers have to operate. Procedures have to be introduced both for setting targets, assessing performance and holding managers to account.

These obstacles can all be overcome. The financial information can be produced and procedures introduced, although they will need time and care. It has to be realised, however, that introducing decentralised resource management involves more than technical and procedural change. Changes in attitude are required because of the change in ways of working.

Without such changes in attitude, managers used to seeking permission for virement may be reluctant to take responsibility for their own decisions. They may not be ready to think positively and innovatively about the redeployment of resources having been trained by experience to regard such redeployment as the exception requiring special permission, rather than as a normal part of the management task. In particular they may feel ill-equipped for financial management, and may thus be reluctant to exercise their new responsibilities.

It is not merely the heads of the cost centres who have to change, the role of the central departments also have to change – as have the senior management of the service departments. Their role does not disappear – far from it. The cost centres have to operate within a policy and financial framework with which both central departments and the senior management in departments must be involved. As with other aspects of decentralisation, it does not involve the *abolition* of the role of the centre but its *redefinition*. Redefining the role of the centre and the development of decentralised resource management have to be considered together.

The centre – whether those in the central departments or in the departments themselves have to learn to stand further back, but not to stand back completely. It has to make its expertise available and yet not impose it – for it has to learn to help when it knows it would come more easily to act directly.

As Michael Frater writing about Kent has said:

Devolution In other words, getting the right balance between corporate responsibilities and service freedoms. Kent County Council, like most if not all local authorities and most large organisations, traditionally vested power and control in its central departments. They had become 'millstones round the necks' of the service delivery departments in Kent. The role of the central departments has been redefined as providing strategic direction, initiation of corporate change, monitoring and review. This requires substantially smaller central departments than hitherto. Many of the professional staff, accounts, personnel officers, information systems people and the like, are moving out to be line-managed in the service-delivery departments. Where it is, on balance, better to keep staff grouped together at 'the centre' they no longer provide their service as of right. They negotiate a service-level agreement with the service delivery department, who will have the right to buy the service elsewhere if they can't get the service they want at the price they want within the county council. All this is leading to smaller, fully accountable, 'leaner and fitter' central departments (Frater, 1991).

Has the decentralisation movement succeeded?

The different forms of decentralisation vary in the extent to which they have been adopted:

- management decentralisation within departments has been more readily achieved than management decentralisation across departments;
- decentralisation of access has been more readily achieved than decentralisation of decision-making;
- decentralisation of decision-making within the officer structure is more widespread than devolution of power to area committees or to local communities.

These conclusions are not surprising. The greater the challenge to existing ways of working, the more difficult they are to achieve.

The working of local authorities has been based on a professional tradition. That is challenged by neighbourhood organisation on a cross-departmental basis. It is even more deeply challenged by the devolution of power to the community or even to area committees.

The organisational assumptions on which the traditional workings of local authorities has been based are directly challenged by aspects of decentralisation. Decentralisation of decision-making permits a diversity of response rather than uniformity of practice. Hierarchical control is lessened, while organisation by area challenges functional organisation. The political structure of local authorities is based on representative democracy, which can be seen as limiting the devolution of power to communities. Even the devolution of power to area committees may be seen as undermining majority control if it means (as it will in most authorities) giving power to at least some area committees controlled by the opposition.

It is not surprising that, given these considerations, the devolution of management responsibility is the most widely accepted aspect of decentralisation, since this can maintain departmental control, does not necessarily challenge professionalism, and ensures the required degree of uniformity through the targets set and policy constraints on managers. Equally it is not surprising that the devolution of substantial political power to communities or even to area committees is the least accepted aspect of decentralisation because of the extent of the challenge to existing practice.

Many would see this conclusion as meaning that the movement to decentralisation had failed in its political if not its management dimensions. Certainly decentralisation has probably generally only led to modification of, rather than fundamental change in, existing ways of working. Where successful management decentralisation has released management initiative, decentralisation to local offices has led to improved access for the public, some improvement in working between neighbourhood staff drawn from different departments, and examples of more responsive service. None of these are unimportant gains, but they have not led to the fundamental alterations of political and management power that some advocates of radical decentralisation sought. Professional power remains; the local authority is still a bureaucratic organisation; political power remains with the council leadership.

The reason for the failure may well be that the advocates of radical decentralisation failed to recognise that there are strengths as well as weaknesses in those principles they wished to challenge.

Professionalism brings real knowledge, real skills and real commitment, even though it can also bring rigidity, narrowness and an over-dependence on political authority. Bureaucratic organisation ensures the large-scale delivery of service on a fair and impartial basis, even though it may unduly limit responsiveness; representative democracy can provide political leadership giving purposive direction in a changing society, even though it can limit individual participation too greatly.

Put in the context of decentralisation to areas:

- not all problems and issues are limited to a specific locality;
- major redistribution of power and resources cannot take place in a single locality;
- the organisation that has no element of bureaucracy has yet to be invented;
- the specialisms represented by professionalism are necessary for an informed society.

If the movement to radical decentralisation has failed it is because these issues have not been faced up to. The strengths as well as the weaknesses of past ways of working have not been appreciated.

The issue is then not how to overcome professionalism, but how to use professionalism to provide responsive service; not how to eliminate bureaucracy but how to modify it and not how to replace representative democracy, but how to allow space for community involvement within it. The issue for devolution of power is how to allow scope for diversity within policies and principles laid down. Often this is recognised in such areas of political priorities as equal opportunities. An authority which has a policy of equal opportunities would not be prepared to see it modified from area to area.

The issue is much wider. Would an authority be prepared to see its policies for aids for the disabled, road maintenance, expenditure on libraries, monitoring children at risk or even careers advice, modified from area to area? The issue then becomes not whether decentralisation can replace present organisational structures and practice, but how far. If decentralisation can modify that structure and practice rather than replace it, it may overcome its weaknesses and maintain its strengths.

The impact of reorganisation

These issues have become real and present issues for many authorities because of local government reorganisation and the possibility that it will lead to larger authorities based on the unitary principle. While the need for authority-wide policies is recognised, so is the need for decentralisation. This has led the Local Government Commission to argue:

> New authorities of whatever size will need to adopt devolved management arrangements, making them as local as possible and to be close to their consumers so that they respond to what local people really want (Local Government Commission, 1993, p.31).

This proposal covers management decentralisation only. However, a number of local authorities, in preparing proposals for the Commission, have seen the need to go much further – particularly some of the counties who in arguing for unitary status see the need to devolve power within a policy framework to the areas of communities within the county, which they identify as generally lying below the district level.

One of the authorities that has gone furthest in developing these ideas is Surrey County Council, which has identified twenty-five local communities each of which it proposes should be served by a Community Board with its own Community Board Business Manager. The Community Board will consist of not only the elected Surrey councillors for the area, but also twice their number of separately elected community board members. The community boards will provide 'a visible, accessible and responsive local government presence when members of the public can engage the democratic process at community level. But they will also have wide delegated decision-making powers. They will 'determine whether particular local government services in the community should be provided at or above the minimum prescribed standard, in response to locally identified needs and wishes'. They will also have 'discretion to generate additional local income or curtail expenditure within overall guidance established by the Surrey Council' (Surrey, 1992, paras 6:10).

This proposal seeks to combine the strength of the authority-wide approach with devolved power to local councillors and community representatives, facing the issues raised in the previous section of this chapter. Of course the real issues which have to be faced are what is determined at county level and what is determined at community level. The issue is complicated by the proposal that many services will be delivered through internal or external contractors. This will in any event be increasingly required by legislation, raising therefore the issue of the extent of possible variation in contracts to meet the requirements of community boards.

The minimum standards suggested can be used to highlight the dilemma. If the minimum standards are set by the county at a low level, then they will have little meaning since each community board will wish to set higher standards. If the minimum standards are set at too high a level, then they will allow the community board little discretion. The problem will be to keep the balance right. In facing that issue the authority will be adopting an approach to decentralisation which realises the strength of the local authority and of the community boards. The solution will be decentralisation within a policy framework.

This proposal is one example of the renewed interest in decentralisation as a result of the debate and discussion generated by reorganisation. It is likely that whatever the outcome of reorganisation that interest will continue and will lead to more widespread developments in political decentralisation precisely because it is realised that a balance has to be struck and that political decentralisation can be combined with political direction at the authority level.

7   The Political Dimension

The literature on organisation theory discussed at length in Chapter 3 and mentioned at regular intervals throughout the book, is a necessary but by no means sufficient basis for understanding recent changes in the organisation and management of local authorities in Britain. This is because local government has a crucial 'extra dimension' which private-sector and indeed the majority of public-sector organisations lack – the *political* dimension (see Chapter 1). That is not to say that organisations outside local (or national) government cannot be profitably studed from a perspective which focuses on their internal politics – i.e. the basis on which different actors in the organisation gain, use and lose power to influence outcomes.

A 'political' perspective of this kind, as we saw in Chapter 3 (pp.59–63), is an essential element in the understanding of intra-organisational dynamics in all types of organisation (including local authorities). But where local government, as an institution, differs is in its specifically *governmental* nature. Decisions in local authorities are the responsibility (unless they are delegated) not of managing directors or boards of directors but of *elected representatives* – the councillors who are elected to serve on each local authority. In the early 1990s councillors are elected predominantly on a party political basis, and the majority of councils are controlled by a political party holding a majority of the seats on the council. But the uniqueness (in the political sense) of local authorities is not compromised if councillors with no formal party affiliation (e.g. independents) predominate, or if, in a party-politicised council, no one party has overall control. The difference lies in the governmental nature of local councils, and the fact that council members are elected (usually on the basis of some kind of manifesto, or statement of intentions) by people living in the area to represent them. That puts councillors in a different position from managing directors (although the roles can be merged, as in the case of the *Bürgeromeister* in West Germany

152

and the city mayor in the USA) and from boards of directors (although an influential strand of thought within the Conservative Party favours the redefinition of councillor roles and responsibilities in a way which would make local councils much more similar to boards of directors of private companies).

Thus the political dimension of local government organisation and management extends beyond the system whereby power is distributed and utilised within local authorities (although that is an important element in understanding the role of councillors) and beyond the dominance of party politics in local government (although that too is a crucial analytical dimension). The political dimension incorporates two important elements: the legitimacy which elected members can claim as a result of their election, and the formal responsibility which they collectively hold to make decisions.

The political dimension (in this sense) both affects and is affected by the pressures for organisational change outlined in Chapter 3 (and discussed throughout the book). The externally-generated legislative changes and the pressures resulting from socio-economic change impinge on local authorities as organisations *per se* and require a response from elected members as much as they do from leading officials. The special position of the elected members, however, means that it is *their* response to these externally-generated pressures which will ultimately form the basis of the organisational response (although, of course, elected members will be subject to a stream of advice from leading officials about what is best for the organisation). But, *in extremis*, if there is a pressure for organisational change which officers interpret as pointing in a particular direction (e.g. the formal separation of client/contractor roles following CCT), but that direction is one to which elected members are resistant, then unless there is a legal requirement to change, the change will not take place. This situation can be interpreted in another way. To the officer part of the organisation (represented by the chief officers and the departmental structure) the political dimension is often itself interpreted as an 'external pressure', on a par with legislative change, socio-economic change etc. In non-governmental organisations it would be much more unusual for the 'political' level (e.g. board of directors, board of trustees) to operate the kind of proactive role which is played by councillors in local authorities. Elsewhere, the 'organisation' is typically allowed to make a much wider range of decisions (within a set of broadly identified organisational goals) than in a local authority, with 'political' intervention taking place only in crises or in other special circumstances (e.g. a company takeover). Because in local authorities intervention from the political level takes place much more regularly and over a much wider range of decisions, it not only appears as an 'external factor' to officers but also merits a much more central position in the analysis of organisation and management issues. Elected representatives frequently have their own views about such issues in a way which is much less common in non-governmental organisations. Thus an analysis of the changing context of local government organisation and management must necessarily incorporate an awareness of the unique qualities of its political dimension as set out above.

In this chapter, we look first at the way in which party politicisation has intensified as a force within local government since the Second World War, and highlight some of the key changes which this intensification has brought about in organisation and management in local authorities. We then re-examine from a specifically political viewpoint the five major dimensions of organisation change first identified in Chapter 3 (and applied systematically in Chapter 4), namely integration/differentiation, centralisation/decentralisation, high formalisation/low formalisation, specialisation/generalisation and independence/interdependence. The major changes in political management structures which have resulted are identified.

We go on to examine the values and interests which underpin the behaviour of elected members. An analysis of political roles is then developed in which it is argued that the changing legislative environment within which local authorities operate has generated a good deal of role confusion amongst politicians, in relation to their involvement in organisation and management issues. Currently, there is a lot of frustration apparent amongst councillors, as the traditional roles of local authorities (and of members and officers within them) are quickly becoming superseded by different roles (and implied relationships). The alternative ways in which such roles (both for politicians in particular and local authorities in general) may develop in the future are explored at more length in Chapter 10.

Party politicisation and its impact on local authority organisation and management

The Widdicombe Committee on the Conduct of Local Authority Business in its influential report published in 1986, referred to party politicisation as a 'tidal force' in its impact on local government. The extensive domination of most councils by party politics (and party politicians) which had by then resulted should not, however, be seen as the outcome of a sudden metamorphosis. It is more realistically seen as the product of a cumulative, though by no means uniform, development which Young (1986, p.1) has described in the following terms: 'a steady long-term trend, beginning in the nineteenth century, first through the major cities and then, if less evenly, to the shires'. Even in the mid-nineteenth century:

> it was not uncommon for an active politician to be appointed to the post of Town Clerk (an early example of 'political appointments') and then to be replaced, if political control changed, by a politician of the victorious party (Gyford *et al.*, 1989, p.8).

However, the most pertinent historical contrast to be drawn is that between the role of local politics in the periods of 'nationalisation' (1935–77) and 'reappraisal' (1974 to present date) (Gyford, 1985, p.84). Gyford sees the 'nationalisation' period as one in which there was a 'coming together' of local and national politics which owed less to the considerable efforts made by the two major parties to secure better coordination of the local and national efforts than to the general measure of bipartisan agreement which developed during the period of both levels, on the desirability of the welfare state and the mixed economy. Local politics in this period displayed an air of considerable stability; party politicisation increased, but it did so slowly. Even in nominally partisan councils, administrators rather than politicians normally dominated the decision-making process.

During the period of reappraisal, however, the domination of 'administrative politics' came to be challenged and eroded in increasing numbers of authorities. Local government reorganisation proved a catalyst in this process, as it did in relation to a range of internal structural issues (see Chapter 4, pp.70–4). However, a more significant influence upon the increasingly high-profile involvement of members in organisation and management issues which became apparent during this period was the emergence of a more ideological party politics which sat increasingly uneasily with the dominant assumptions of 'administrative politics'. Local parties (particularly Labour) began to produce more and more substantial, programmatic party manifestos which were taken much more seriously by councillors than had been previous examples of the genre. Officers were expected to familiarise themselves with manifesto contents and to implement them, in the event of a successful election outcome. The tendency to challenge professional advice grew, and the traditional claim of officers that they had the capacity to serve the interests of whichever party was in power came to be regarded in some authorities with increasing suspicion.

During the 1970s and 1980s the political dimension in local authorities became more *formalised* (a more explicit recognition of the reality of party politics in organisational structures and process); more *polarised* (increasing ideological differences both within and between political parties); more *intensified* (in relation to political involvement in issues of organisation and management) and *wider in scope* (with local councils increasingly moving beyond the traditional service- and finance-based agenda of local authorities into a range of issues – e.g. nuclear disarmament – with which they did not necessarily possess direct powers to deal). These changes were not uniform and were manifested in different ways depending on the point of development from which the authority started. But they affected almost all authorities in one way or another.

All these aspects of the increasing role of politics in local government had important repercussions for organisation and management. One-party committees (or subcommittees) grew steadily during the 'reappraisal' period until they were made illegal by the Local Government and Housing Act 1989. This legislative change, however, only had the effect of accelerating the trend towards more informal one-party policy-formulation arenas (leadership groups, strategic working parties and the like). Informal meetings between majority party leaders and Chief Executives increased in frequency, with special arrangements involving all party leaders (separately and/or together) becoming necessary in the increasing numbers of hung authorities which emerged from 1985 onwards. A wider range of committees and subcommittees were set up to deal with the expanding scope of local council agendas, particularly in Labour controlled authorities (equal opportunities; economic development; nuclear-free zones; police monitoring and community development provide a range of typical examples). Working parties of varying degrees of inform-ality and political balance involving members and officers were established in increasing numbers of local authorities to deal in depth with topics which would previously have been dealt with by the traditional process of an officer report to committee (an example of the 'intensification' dimension). Members became increasingly involved in the appointment of officers demonstrating concern in some authorities to take into account political commitment (interpreted in a variety of ways) as well as professional and managerial competence. The traditional policy/ implementation division of labour between members and officers was increasingly the subject of challenge, with members (again predominantly, though not exclusively, in Labour authorities) arguing that, as politicians, they had a legitimate interest in the delivery and the impact of their manifesto policies (e.g. equal opportunities), and that officers could not necessarily be simply 'left to get on with implementation'. The interpretation of what 'an interest in policy implementation' involved varied considerably, but in some cases put a considerable strain on divisions of responsi-bility and relationships between members and officers. Finally, there was an increasing tendency to seek external advice from consultants regarding changes in organisational structure, rather than rely on internal advice (typically from the Chief Executive).

Thus politicisation *per se* can be seen as a major force during the period 1975–91. Irrespective of legislative change, it had a number of significant effects on local authority organisation and management.

The political aspects of organisational change

In Chapter 3 we analysed recent changes in the organisation and management of local government on the basis of five dimensions (or spectra). It was argued, in each case, that recent legislative and socio-economic pressures had resulted not in a clear change of direction from one end of the spectrum to another (e.g. from a centralised to a decentralised authority or from a highly formalised to a relatively informal type of organisation) but rather to a more subtle change of balance within each spectrum with a reappraisal (for example) of which organisational elements should be centralised and which decentralised. In fact, in the areas of choice available to individual local authorities (on each dimension) political values and interests have often had a major effect on the organisational choices made. In this section the influence of the political nature of local authorities on each of the dimensions identified is discussed.

Differentiation/integration

It was argued in Chapter 4 that the logic of the introduction of CCT (and the anticipation of its future application to a further range of services, including several central support services) had been the major external factor changing the nature of (and balance between) the forces of integration and differentiation in local authorities. The main new areas of differentiation have been between client and contractor units, between specific service providing units within a broad programme area, and between different types of central support service (e.g. legal, computer, design), which were increasingly separated in organisational terms to operate in effect as 'internal consultancies' (in anticipation of enforced competition with the private sector within the next few years). The main new areas of integration have been authority-wide strategic planning, policy planning (on a programme-area basis) and authority-wide systems of performance-review/quality-control (including contract monitoring).

It is fair to say that, in general, officers have adapted more easily to these changing structural patterns than have members. The split between client and contractor roles has proved frustrating for many members, particularly experienced committee chairs who have been accustomed to overseeing the planning and delivery of a particular service (or group of services) in a way which paid little attention to the conceptual distinction between client and contractor roles. The conventional wisdom (from the Audit Commission as well as the DoE) is that councillors playing a leading role on a client-side committee or subcommittee should not do so on the equivalent contractor-side committee (or subcommittee). Indeed, in authorities where there is a separate DSO committee (or increasingly, management board) to oversee the work of an integrated DSO, the officers' recommendation is typically that members serving on the DSO board or committee should not be members of any of the major client committees which commission work from the DSO.

For the experienced committee chair (say of housing) this pressure has typically meant that he (or she) has had to opt for the chair of a (client) housing committee *or* a role on the management board of a housing maintenance DLO (or a more integrated DLO/DSO). Councillors have often resented having to make this kind of choice (just as housing directors and chief engineers have resented the break-up of their departmental empires). Thus in some authorities, the approach adopted has been to settle for the 'least disruptive' organisational solution – typically a series of DSOs/DLOs embedded organisationally within the client departments, working in conjunction with a contractor subcommittee of the relevant (client) service committee. Although it is now rare to find a situation where the same councillor chairs both service committee and its related contractor subcommittee, the principle of overlapping membership (which is not illegal) has been accepted in many authorities in response to councillors' (understandable) wish to retain an involvement in both client and contractor aspects of a familiar service area.

At the same time, the role of chair of the committee (or management board) of an integrated DSO is an extremely powerful organisational position, which has proved attractive to councillors with experience in issues such as industrial relations, and service delivery. Indeed, in a shire district, this position is possibly the most powerful political role (in terms of budget, manpower and impact on the population) outside that of the leadership role itself. Although formally most DLO committees (and in particular management boards) have terms of reference which exclude the involvement of the chair (or any other committee/board member) in the detailed operation of the DSO, in practice the chair will find that he or she is regularly 'consulted' by the DSO manager on detailed matters (indeed they would normally be in a position to insist on this). So although the formal power of control has decreased, the informal power of influence may well have increased.

In a similar way, the increased differentiation between service-providing units within a broad programme area (whether or not they are formally subject to CCT) with much greater management and budgetary responsibility devolved to 'unit managers' operating on a 'cost centre' basis, has inevitably had major repercussions for the committee(s) overseeing such activities. If management/personnel/budgetary allocation responsibilities have been devolved to officers, then by definition they cannot be exercised by service (or central resource) committees. The same point is of course true of central support service units. Again, this outcome has not proved a welcome one for many councillors, particularly those who have found the detail of budgetary or personnel control or management more comfortable than esoteric-sounding activities such as strategy formulation, policy planning or performance review. In general the powerful externally generated logic behind these internal changes has had a force which councils (appropriately advised by chief officers) have found it hard to resist. That is not to say that many a battle has not been fought between a chair of finance or personnel (sub) committee (typically supported and briefed by the director of finance/personnel) and their colleagues (suitably briefed by the Chief Executive and heads of service departments). In Labour authorities in particular the argument 'let's do the least possible we have to do to comply with this unwelcome legislation' is likely to have many supporters. The outcome then depends on the distribution of power amongst and between leading members and officers, and their relative skill in the deployment of strategies and tactics.

The development of the (relatively) new integrative processes of strategy formulation, policy planning and performance review has also caused problems for elected members. Although in principle there are clear links between the articulation of political goals and priorities (e.g. as set out in a party manifesto) and a strategy document, such links are not always emphasised by the officers who typically initiate the strategy-formulation process, and in some authorities leading members have come to regard the process as a 'technical' officer-dominated initiative, thereby almost certainly relegating any document produced to, at best, a limited influence, and, at worst, irrelevance. Similarly, performance review (a function increasingly emphasised by the Audit Commission for exercise by the centre and/or client service departments) invariably fails to capture the imagination of local councillors, unless it can be interpreted in a way which draws upon their local knowledge and their role as a vehicle for transmitting complaints. The 'softer' language of performance review is more appropriate in this sense than the more quantitative language of performance measurement. In a small but growing number of authorities distinctions have been made at service committee level to reflect these differences. Each service committee in Avon County Council (e.g. education, social services) has a main committee dealing with the strategic/planning/ policy aspects of the service, a 'service administration' subcommittee dealing with such operational matters which remain within the purview of elected members, and a performance review subcommittee. In many other authorities the agendas of service committees are changing to reflect a greater concern with strategy/planning/ policy/review and a corresponding movement away from operational detail. From what has already been written, councillors normally have to be persuaded of the need for such a change (although in 'new-right'-dominated authorities there is more positive enthusiasm for it). It is not normally in line with their own predispositions.

Centralisation/decentralisation

In relation to the centralisation/decentralisation dimension, the relevant legislative changes have focused more on the roles of officers rather than members (e.g. the designation of the monitoring officer and the financial probity officer). In some authorities some members have shown resentment at this change, and in particular at the explicit legitimacy which such officers now have to write publicly available reports warning the council of the dangers of legal or financial malpractice (or maladministration) involved in a course of action the council is contemplating (or has carried out). Such advice has always been provided by officers on an informal basis. However, formal advice in the form of a report to council, is more difficult to ignore and a source of considerable potential embarrassment to the majority party involved.

In July 1991, the government published a consultation paper on the internal management structures of local authorities (Department of the Environment, 1991b) setting out a number of possible changes in forms of political management structure which might be adopted in local authorities, which were more radical than anything that appeared in the recommendations of the Widdicombe Committee. It is not yet apparent that the government is committed to introducing radical change of this nature. But the consultation paper will require local authorities to develop a response to a set of alternatives all of which imply a significant *centralisation* of the political structure.

Most of the options being canvassed involve some kind of separation of powers between a small political executive and a larger legislative/consultative body of councillors – i.e. a move towards 'cabinet government' at the local level. The executive could be directly elected or elected from within the local authority; it could be one person (the 'elected mayor' concept), or a small group of councillors. Any political executive model would inevitably concentrate power within a smaller number of hands (i.e. centralise the political decision-making structure), create a much sharper role distinction between the members of the executive (or 'cabinet') and the other 'backbench' council members, and would also markedly affect the respective roles of executive members and chief officers. For example if the executive chose to allocate responsibilities amongst its members on a service-specific basis, a chief education officer (for example) would be faced with a full-time elected executive director of education – the equivalent of the former chair of education, but with power in his or her own right, and no committee to have to deal with!

This proposed change is also relevant to the high formalisation/ low formalisation dimension. In most politicised, majority-controlled authorities an *informal* cabinet system has already existed for a long time, although its modes of operation have been seriously constrained by the Local Government and Housing Act 1989 (e.g. one-party committees or subcommittees are no longer possible). Leadership groups of various forms and titles are widely seen as an essential part of the decision-making machinery. However, the switch from an informal to an explicit formalised status for such groups would raise major issues for the internal values and typical modes of operation of majority party groups. In the case of the Labour and Liberal Democrat parties it is likely that such concerns will lead to a predisposition to reject the move towards cabinet government, because of its centralising, anti-democratic tendencies.

Within the Labour Party, a great deal of emphasis is now placed on the internal democracy of the party group, and the policy-making role of the local party. It is difficult to see how a 'political executive' in a Labour-controlled authority could co-exist with a continuing emphasis on local group and party democracy, *unless* the executive regularly consulted with group (and party) over the issues with which they were technically empowered to deal. The main problem here would be that Labour groups (under the party's current constitution) have the ultimate power to decide on a course of action (whether it be a choice of policy direction, or a more specific decision with political implications). Labour leaders (and group executives) currently have to persuade their party group to support a particular line of action, and if they fail, would feel obliged to express in council the view which a majority of the group supported. Thus for a separate 'political executive' to operate effectively in a Labour-controlled authority, it is likely that there would have to be major changes in the party's existing rules governing leadership/group/local-party relationships. Certainly the concentration of executive power in a single figure (the elected mayor) would cut right across the traditions and practice of Labour group behaviour (which is not to say that local Labour politicians have not, in certain circumstances, been able to operate as powerful 'city bosses' in the recent past).

The same reservations as to the feasibility of the introduction of an executive/legislative split apply to the Liberal Democrats (indeed, probably more so!). The vast majority of Liberal Democrat groups operate in an open, democratic way (typically with no formal whipping system within the group). Any attempt to invest power formally in a limited number of Liberal Democrat councillors (or worse still, a single leader) would be quite alien to party philosophy.

In hung authorities, too, there would be a problem. The effective operation of a 'separate executive' could only work in such authorities in two circumstances. First, it could work if the largest (or indeed only) minority party were allowed to form an exclusive one-party 'executive'. This is a most unlikely outcome in a hung situation. Conceding a minority party the chairs (whose role is anyway inevitably weakened in a hung authority) is one thing; allowing them exclusive access to a political executive is another! The second situation which might be compatible with the operation of a separate executive is the formation of formal coalition between two (or more) parties. However, as the work of Leach and Stewart (1992, p.113) shows, this is an extremely úncommon political response within hung authorities.

It is only in relation to majority Conservative groups in local authorities that the idea of an executive seems compatible with party traditions and practice. There is a much greater predisposition within Conservative groups to accept, and indeed to expect the exercise of authority by the leader (although there is nothing in the way of party guidance that requires or encourages such a predisposition). A system which effectively concentrated power in one pair (or a limited number of pairs) of hands would be much less difficult for Conservative groups to take on board. But as we have seen in the other parties, the current models being canvassed by the government (or indeed any measure which formally concentrated power within a small subgroup of councillors) would be likely to be resisted.

Party attitudes to decentralisation of political power to neighbourhood committees (or to some equivalent sub-area of the authority) are a mirror-image of their attitudes to the centralisation of power discussed above. Conservative groups are least likely to introduce proposals of this nature (although they are likely to support the devolution of *management* responsibility within the organisation). Liberal Democrat groups and 'soft-left' Labour groups are much more likely to favour such measures (see Chapter 6).

Specialisation/generalisation

The process of fragmentation implicit both in the move towards CCT, and in recent housing, education and social services legislation has not only increased task-specialisation at the expense of professional specialisation on the officer side (see Chapter 4, pp.83–4); it has also changed the nature of specialisation at the political level. Councillors have traditionally specialised in a small number of specific service areas (for example, a councillor might devote his or her energies to the social services and planning committees in a metropolitan district) and as a corollary have little or no involvement in the service areas represented by committees of which he or she is not a member. The other major choice of specialisation is between an emphasis on constituency matters *vis-à-vis* an emphasis on authority-wide matters (although all councillors clearly have to maintain some degree of commitment to a constituency-level role, if only to maximise the probability of re-election).

The separation of client/contractor roles, not just in the CCT-affected services but in the three major service areas indicated (and indeed the general emphasis on the 'enabling' role) has meant that it is now much more difficult for a councillor to specialise in a service area *per se*. The real choice is increasingly moving towards a specialisation in *either* the client role *or* the contractor role in one or more service areas (although there is no reason why a particular councillor should not be an active member of a 'client' committee for one service, and a 'contractor' committee for another). As we indicated earlier, this choice is not a palatable one for many councillors, and has been evaded in significant numbers of authorities, although how long such authorities can maintain this stance is questionable.

In addition the removal of much responsibility for service delivery out of the hands of traditional departments (and committees) and into those of arms-length DSOs, or private contractors, has made it much more difficult for councillors whose preferred specialism is the constituency role to operate in the way to which they are accustomed. It is now much more difficult for a councillor to affect directly the detailed operation of many services, either through committee decision or direct contact with the officer responsible. In principle at least, complaints about the malfunctioning of a service from a councillor, or anyone else, now have to go through the client officer (or unit). Thus, although councillors still can, and do, emphasise a constituency role in their council activities, it is often perceived to be a less-satisfying role than it used to be, because of decreased possibility of directly affecting outcomes.

The new generalist roles which have become available – strategic direction and policy planning for a broad programme area – have yet to capture the imagination of councillors in the way that the committee/service-role emphasis did. There are authorities in which a small number of leading councillors have been able to relate the strategic role to their political priorities. But more typically perhaps this area of activity is little understood and perceived as an officer-dominated activity. We draw together the implications of the changes discussed in this section and other changes which have affected councillor role opportunities in recent years later, under the heading 'Changes in political management structures' (pp.168–74).

High formalisation/low formalisation

The formalisation of local authority decision processes which followed from the Widdicombe-based provisions of the Act 1989 have been widely seen as inimical to effective government in majority-controlled authorities. Quite apart from the complexity of the application of proportional representation principles, the main concern has been the lack of acknowledgement (in the new legislation) of the need for one-party forums for private member–officer discussion about key issues facing the authority or for policy formulation. The requirement that the composition of all council committees and working parties should be on the basis of proportional representation has lessened the scope for choice in relation to use of structural devices for this purpose. The party group (which it is now accepted that officers can legitimately attend) is not seen as an appropriate arena for such discussions, with the result that somewhat opaque informal arrangements have to be made.

The government's response to the Widdicombe Committee's range of proposals to 'strengthen local democracy' was to take up those proposals which strengthened the rights of opposition parties and to exclude those proposals which facilitated the ability of majority groups to govern effectively (Leach, 1989, p.191). In other ways too there has been an externally-imposed increase in formalisation as a result of the 1989 Act, through the increase in rule-bound behaviour which it introduced. The specification of the roles of monitoring officer and financial probity officer, the new constraints governing councillors' involvement in officer appointment, the new 'model standing orders' and 'code of conduct' are all manifestations of this trend. As noted earlier, it is hardly surprising that these changes have inspired the search for compensatory *informal* mechanisms to enable majority party groups to develop policies in private, with officer help (or for all party groups to have this facility in hung authorities).

Independence/interdependence

In relation to the final dimension, independence/interdependence, there has also been a time-lag between the logic of the changed context within which local authorities operate and the response of elected members. There is a strong and persistent attachment amongst most council leadership groups to the concept of *self-sufficiency*. If a local authority has the formal responsibility for a service, then the traditional expectation is that it should directly provide that service. The concept of working with or through other agencies to provide a service has not easily penetrated the assumptive world of councillors, although the increasing range of circumstances in which councils are obliged to operate in this way is now beginning to generate changes in attitude. The new emphasis on interdependence, with its implication for the development of negotiation and bargaining skills, requires that councillors use their positions on other bodies to achieve council objectives. When such outside bodies were less central to the achievement of council objectives, it was usual for nominated councillors to behave on them in a relatively detached way – i.e. certainly not as delegates from the council, but more as individuals for whom the position on the outside body represented some kind of *reward*.

This situation is well-illustrated by the behaviour of district councillors on the three joint boards (police, fire, passenger transport) established in the six metropolitan county areas in the wake of the abolition of the county councils (see Leach *et al.* (1992). Mechanisms for informing joint board members about agenda items, briefing (or mandating) them, and requiring them to report back (e.g. to justify their actions in terms of council priorities) were extremely uncommon. Once appointed to joint boards, district councillors have been able to behave very much as 'free agents' (although most of the Labour members choose to accept the discipline of the 'Labour group' associated with the joint board). The opportunity for the nominating authority to use its membership of 'networks of interdependence' relating to service areas which have clear potential positive and negative implications for the authority's welfare in a more proactive way has not been realised in the metropolitan areas since abolition.

There are other ways, of course, in which councillors do use external channels deliberately as a means of attempting to persuade other organisations (or individuals) to take actions which are perceived to benefit the local authority. The delegation to the government department (or minister) is a well-established example, which has probably increased in significance (though not necessarily success rate) since 1979. Similarly, relationships with local economic and commercial interests have been taken a good deal more seriously (and positively fostered) at councillor level, in recent years. But in most authorities the basic change in councillor-orientation implied by the switch in emphasis from the 'self-sufficient' to the 'enabling authority' has not yet taken place, and the opportunities of realising council objectives through networks of interdependence neither systematically addressed nor widely exploited.

The final point to emphasise in this consideration of the changing balance of emphasis within the five organisational dimensions is the sheer scale of the turbulence in the legislative and socio-economic environment in which local authorities have had to operate over the past three or four years and the impact this has had on councillors' roles and expectations. So many of the organisational structures and processes with which councillors have long been familiar have experienced radical change (or if not actually experienced it, have certainly been threatened by it). Similarly, many of the familiar roles of councillors have been changed out of all recognition. The pressures on their learning and adjustment capacity (and their motivation) have been correspondingly great.

Changes in political management structures

The changing structural configurations of local authorities, brought about by the fundamental changes in their operating environment (see Chapter 4, p.73) have had major repercussions not just for member roles but also for the familiar pieces of organisational machinery in which those roles are expressed. Just as on the officer side the role of management teams has been modified to cope with these new pressures, so too has the role of the policy and resources committee been subjected in many authorities to a critical reassessment.

In 1974, following the advice of the Bains Committee, almost all British local authorities had established a policy, or policy and resources committee (see Hinings *et al.*, 1975, p.17) and by 1985 the number of authorities without one was even fewer (Widdicombe, 1986b). However, as Alexander (1982, pp.95 ff) demonstrates, in many authorities, particularly the less-politicised shire districts, there existed major reservations about the role of a policy and resources committee (typically on the grounds that policy matters ought to be the responsibility of the full council) and such committees were often ineffective, in that *either* they did not enjoy delegated powers, *or* the matters which they considered were relatively minor issues which did not happen to fall within the remit of any other committee. Thus the observation that policy and resources committees operated largely as 'rag-bag' committees, with agendas composed of miscellaneous items not dealt with elsewhere, was by no means uncommon in the Widdicombe 'political organisation' interviews. Particularly in situations in which there was a separate finance and/or personnel committee (or where finance and personnel subcommittees of policy and resources operated with considerable devolved powers), the policy committee rarely played the high-profile central role its title implied.

Even in the more politicised authorities in which in principle at least the crucial central role of a policy and resources committee was accepted, its role was often less powerful than might have been expected. If the authority was one in which there was a strong sense of autonomy on the part of the service departments (and their respective committees) and in which the budget process was customarily incremental, and organised round a bargaining process involving chief officers and the director of finance (mirrored on the political side by a process involving service committee chairs and the chair of policy and resources – typically the leader) then the scope for a proactive role for the policy and resources committee was correspondingly limited. This committee would still be the first formal arena in which major authority-wide issues were discussed (e.g. new legislation, the Rate Support Grant Settlement, internal reorganisation). But typically the authority's stance on issues of this nature would not be resolved until a full debate in council had taken place. Thus policy and resources committees, in many authorities, typically operated in something of a vacuum between full council (where the public debates on major issues took place) and the service committees (where policy relating to the major service areas was made and reviewed).

The changes of the past few years have increased the potential impact of the policy and resources committee in a number of ways. First, the savings which authorities have been required to make to avoid rate-capping (or charge-capping) have increasingly been beyond the scope of the traditional process of budgetary incrementalism (whether applied to increasing or decreasing resources). The sheer scale of the cuts has increased pressure both for much more searching reviews of the base budget, and for the development of guidelines to provide a basis to show where the cuts should fall. Both these tasks can only really be carried out by a central committee such as policy and resources.

One of the ways in which a set of principles (or at least, some coherence) can be applied to the budgetary process, in these circumstances, is through the development of a strategic direction, which highlights the authority's priorities (and, by implication, relegates everything else to 'non-priority'). The process of strategy formulation, which has been introduced in increasing numbers of authorities in recent years (in the Public Finance Foundation survey, 80 per cent of the authorities responding claimed to have formulated a strategy for meeting the needs of their areas (Ennals and O'Brien, 1990) has provided a much more focused *raison d'être* for the policy and resources committee, as it has for Chief Executive and management team.

The other change which has strengthened the role of this committee is the increased emphasis placed in many authorities on the development of a corporate culture, involving such initiatives as the specification of core values, authority-wide approaches to customer care, and a more explicit emphasis on corporate identity (particularly in relation to marketing). All these approaches fall logically within the ambit of a policy and resources committee. In addition the seemingly almost-continuous series of crises in which local authorities feel they have been plunged in recent years (mainly through actions taken, or not taken, by central government) emphasises the need for a piece of organisational machinery on the political side to play its part in crisis management. In all these ways, the role of the policy and resources committee has been strengthened. It has to be said, however, that the majority of shire districts have not, until 1990–91, felt the kind of financial pressures experienced by other authorities (they were previously exempt from rate- or charge-capping if their revenue budget was less then £15 million); and that in those authorities which have adopted a minimalist interpretation of enabling (filling the service gaps which the external market cannot deal with directly) the strategic imperative is much less strong (and the new opportunities for the policy and resources committee correspondingly more limited).

The main alternative to a policy and resources committee – separate policy, finance and personnel committees – tended to become less prevalent in the 1980s decade, as those authorities which adopted this model came under increasing pressure to integrate policy planning with resource considerations (on both the finance and personnel side). The policy and resources committee with resource subcommittees (finance, personnel and sometimes land and property) because an ever more-dominant model in the late 1980s.

In a handful of authorities, the role of the policy and resources committee has been supplemented by the establishment of a policy board, consisting of leading (majority party) members and officers. Such boards do not have formal decision-making status, otherwise their exclusively one-party composition would breach the provisions of the 1989 Local Government and Housing Act. However, on the decisions subsequently made by the policy and resources committee is usually considerable. Kirklees has developed a Policy Board of this nature. It consists of fourteen leading Labour councillors plus the Chief Executive and the five executive directors (see Figure 4.2) and appears to operate as an extremely effective policy deliberation and formulation arena but with a more explicit formal status than in most authorities.

Similarly the role of the performance review committee (or more commonly, subcommittee of policy and resources) has also increased in significance since the mid-1980s, together with the introduction of many new examples. The performance review committee/subcommittee was one of the few Bainsian recommendations which was not widely adopted in 1974, and as Alexander (1982, p.89) shows even in those authorities where it was introduced, it was rarely a high priority for councillors, nor was its role taken particularly seriously in the rest of the organisation.

(It not infrequently became the stronghold of discontented back-benchers and/or ex-influentials). There are three principal reasons for its renaissance in recent years; first, its use as a device for identifying potential savings in expenditure on existing services (including central support services); second the need for contract-monitoring in the wake of the introduction of CCT; and third, the high profile accorded to it by the Audit Commission to this activity (particularly in its paper on the role of members – 'We Can't Go On Meeting Like This' (1990b)). However, it is clear that the role is still not one which generates much enthusiasm amongst the majority of councillors. There is also a difference of view as to whether the performance review role should be carried out at the centre, or by each client service committee (e.g. housing, education, social services) in relation to its own service. There is a case for it to be carried out at both levels – in relation to strategic objectives (and strategic savings targets) at the centre, and on a more systematic and comprehensive basis within each service area.

The changing pattern of service departments was discussed earlier in Chapter 4 (pp.93–7). Usually, though not always, committee structures have been changed to reflect changes in departmental structure. There is of course no necessary conjunction between departmental and committee structure (not to match committees with departments limits the likelihood of strong chief-officer/chair axes of power developing). Figures 7.1 and 7.2 set out two examples of committee structure which may be seen as representative of the 'vanguard' of structural change at the political level.

Figure 7.1 should be compared with Figure 4.2 which sets out the county's organisational structure at *officer* level. In this case there is a reasonably close correspondence between departmental structure and committee structure. Figure 7.2 is particularly interesting in its use of the term 'board' rather than the more traditional committee. Relatively streamlined political decision-making structures (with a gradual increase in use of the 'boards' nomenclature) are now spreading faster amongst local authorities, for three reasons:

1. the spread of 'good practice' inspired by (*inter alia*) the Audit Commission's paper 'We Can't Go on Meeting Like This';

FIGURE 7.1   Cheshire County Council committee structure

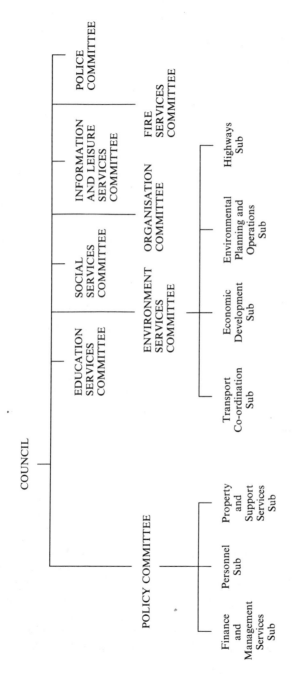

Notes:
All committees, apart from fire and police, have a policy panel attached to them. Other miscellaneous subcommittees have been omitted from the diagram (e.g. education committee has operations, professional services and resources planning subcommittees).

FIGURE 7.2   Windsor and Maidenhead District Council: committee structure

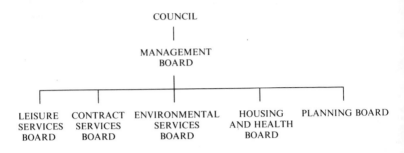

Notes:
There are no subcommittees (or 'sub-boards') – but each of the boards has a range of between two and six panels attached to it.

2. the reduction in level (and in some authorities elimination) of attendance allowances, reducing the financial incentive for large numbers of meetings (and hence committees and subcommittees);
3. outside the metropolitan areas and Greater London, the eagerness of counties and districts to demonstrate to the Local Government Commission that they have the capacity to operate an effective political mangement system, with reduced 'costs of democracy'.

There remains, however, a powerful 'countervailing' force in many authorities.

Political values, interests and roles

We argued in Chapter 3 (pp.59–63) that organisations can be seen as arenas in which individuals pursue their own interests, in competition with others. The term *interests* refers to the distribution of resources within the organisation, and the motivation of individuals and groups to maintain or enhance their own resources. Resources may take the form of income (or material benefits) status and authority (or power). It was argued in Chapter 4 in relation to the behaviour of officers that the response of key individuals to proposals for organisational change could be interpreted realistically only in relation to their respective interests. The same argument holds when considering the political dimension of the response to organisational change. It was also emphasised in Chapter 4 that an emphasis on interests in explaining responses to change should not be at the expense of an awareness of the importance of *values* – i.e. beliefs, assumptions and attitudes about good practice or appropriate organisational responses which are not tied to outcomes that would be of direct benefit to the individuals concerned in terms of material rewards, status, or power. That argument is also true of local politicians; indeed membership of a political party and commitment to its manifesto will in itself involve the commitment to a range of (party political) values which do not directly benefit the individuals concerned (cf. the professional values held by officers). Many people become councillors primarily because they wish to promote social and economic change, of various kinds. The clarification of the interest/ value basis of political orientation will help us to interpret the different roles played by politicians in local government.

It is helpful analytically to develop a broad categorisation of the typical interests and values which motivate politicians in local authorities (and elsewhere). Three interest categories can be identified: material interests, status interests and power; and three 'value' categories: political, territorial and personal.

It is rare for a councillor's job as councillor to provide his or her main source of *income*. Few councillors rely on such benefits as their main income source. The total amount of resources available for councillor allowances was only marginally increased by the provisions of the Act 1989.

However, there are ways in which material rewards (in cash or in kind) may act as a motivational force. Under a system of payment (or compensation) which includes attendance allowances, there is a built-in incentive for councillors to attend meetings. This is true even in the (typical) situation where the income gained from local council activities is of some (albeit marginal) significance in the councillors' overall sources of income (there are also significant 'fringe benefits' which result from certain types of council activity).

The second category of interest which is of relevance to an understanding of members' attitudes to organisational change is that of *status*, a term which refers to the public recognition, particularly through the local media, which comes from being a public figure. The more prominent a part a local councillor plays within the overall span of council activities, the greater the potential status rewards. The archetypical 'status position' within a local council is that of mayor (or chairperson of the council). Status rewards, such as chairmanships, are an important resource for those political leaders who can allocate them (most common in Conservative groups) or influence them (more common in Labour groups).

Power (or authority) involves a different form of personal interest. It reflects a motivation to gain (or retain) influence on the decisions and outcomes of a local authority irrespective of considerations of status, income or the achievement of political goals. Thus, for a councillor for whom power is a key interest, the achievement of a formal position of power is not in itself essential; the key requisite is a position within the organisation (which may be informal rather than informal) which enables influence to be exerted.

It would be rare to find a councillor whose behaviour was totally unaffected by each of the three interests mentioned (material benefits, status, authority) although there are still significant numbers of councillors who make a point of not claiming attendance allowance (who would hence presumably argue that the 'material benefit' interest was absent). The interesting analytical issue in any given authority is the balance of emphasis given to the three interests, particularly amongst the leading politicians.

In relation to values, a distinction can be drawn between (party) political, territorial and personal values. *Political* values will be of considerable influence in all authorities except those where the political culture is still dominated by 'low partisanship'. Although the obvious differences (with major implications for the organisation and management of the authority) are those *between* parties, differences of political value within party groups are often also important.

A second important value category for councillors is that of *territoriality*. It is rare to find a councillor who does not have a strong commitment to the area covered by his or her own authority. But just as important are the value commitments apparent in the assumptive worlds of councillors to a particular area *within* the local authority; either the ward which the councillor represents, or a particular town or sub-area (particularly if defined as a separate authority prior to 1974) within the authority (personal values are less relevant to the issues considered in this chapter and are not considered here).

How have these interests and values affected changes in the organisation and management since 1974? The spectacular increase in unemployment during particular periods since 1974 (notably 1978–85, 1988 to present date) increased the numbers of councillors who were unemployed, for whom attendance allowances (and SRAs) provided a not insignificant source of income. In the worst-hit areas – Merseyside, the North-east and parts of the North-west – the Widdicombe 'political organisation' research (Widdicombe, 1986a, p.72) uncovered several authorities in which Chief Executives and (more rarely) leaders argued that they were under considerable pressure to extend the number of committees and subcommittees to provide a greater number of committee places, which in turn generated an increased number of potential attendance-allowance claims. This influence on committee structure would be expected to diminish after the 1989 Act, in the large majority of authorities which have reduced (or in some cases eliminated) attendance allowances in favour of the flat-rate payment. This certainly was one of the reasons why the government was attracted to the introduction of the 'flat-rate' allowance (Department of the Environment, 1988). The 1989 Act has had another more insidious influence. The types of meeting for which attendance allowance can now be claimed have been redefined to cover mainly those *formal* meetings at which all parties on the council are represented (plus formal representation of the council on outside bodies, plus a limited number of other types of occasion). Informal briefing or discussion meetings for majority party members only to help them (in the company of officers) to *develop* policy rather than make formal decisions do not now qualify for attendance allowance. There is a strong fear in several authorities that this may seriously affect the motivation of at least some councillors, to attend such meetings, which are widely regarded as of increasing importance in terms of providing a political steer on authority's strategic direction and policy planning.

Status considerations, too, may have a direct effect on a local authority's organisational structure. A leader may often rely for support on a group of experienced local politicians who are accustomed to the status of a chairmanship. If, through a recent election, or because a group of less long-serving councillors are deemed to have reached a stage of development which merits a chair, then the only realistic possibility of accommodating the newcomers may well be to create additional committees (and/or subcommittees) to provide such opportunities, both directly for the up-and-coming councillors or to provide a 'sideways move'.

Similarly, restructurings involving reductions in the number of committees, or the redistribution of committee responsibilities, in response to external pressures for change, may be successfully blocked by councillors who feel that their power or status interests are threatened by such changes. The ability of a councillor in this position successfully to resist change depends (like that of a chief officer faced with a departmental restructuring) on his or her influence within the party group (is he or she one of the leader's key allies?) and the skill with which proposals for change are resisted. Certainly any proposal for changes in a political management structure have to be evaluated in terms of whose interests are threatened, whose interests are furthered, and whether it is likely that a sufficiently powerful 'constituency of support' can be built up to ensure that the change is implemented. One of the reasons why local authorities are making increasing use of outside consultants to produce proposals for structural change is that it is more difficult (although by no means impossible) to argue against proposals from such a source. Certainly accusations of self-interest cannot be levelled against consultants' proposals in the same way that proposals emerging from within the local authority (e.g. a Chief Executive or a political leadership group) are vulnerable to such changes.

In relation to values, the different political parties may have different priorities which affect the acceptability of proposals for structural change. In Labour-controlled authorities, for example, any structure which maximises the chances of internal direct labour units winning CCT contracts will tend to be favoured. In Liberal-Democrat-controlled authorities performance-review mechanisms and processes are typically advocated, whereas in Conservative-controlled authorities, structures which emphasis parallel with the private sector (management boards, devolved management responsibility) may be favoured.

The general point to emphasise is that pressures and proposals for change can rarely be considered (internally or analytically) 'on their merits'. They have been understood in the context of the complex constellation of political and organisational interests and values into which they intrude. Typically, political interests operate in favour of the *status quo* and in opposition to pressures and arguments for radical structural change. This can result in a problem of 'mismatch' between organisational tasks and roles and organisational structure, which at a time of rapid external change (particularly in legislation) can seriously impede a local authority's capacity to operate effectively. In this situation the importance of change agents on both the officer and member side becomes crucial. Local authorities faced with imperatives for change need change agents in key positions in the officer structure (typically at chief executive level) *and* enough political awareness/ support to drive the changes through.

The changing role pattern of councillors

There is a tension between the pressures for change in the role pattern of councillors (and the way this pattern is articulated in the political management structure) and the established role patterns, which have crystallised over a long period of time. The radical nature of the recent legislative changes imply, as we have already argued, changes of equivalent magnitude in the role pattern of councillors and the political management structures of local authorities. But because they threaten the familiar established role expectations of councillors they will often be resisted, with concessions to the pressures for change going no further than what is deemed the *minimum* change in roles and structure necessary to respond to the *legal* requirements of the new legislative programme. Thus there has been in most local authorities a structural tension between the *status quo* (typically defended by the majority of councillors) and what is necessary or desirable in terms of the logic of the external changes (typically emphasised by at least some of the chief officers). In the short term, the direction in which the tension has been resolved has varied, ranging from radical reorganisation to minor changes to the *status quo*. In the longer term a higher level of congruity between the external pressures for change, and the internal organisational structures adopted would be expected.

It is thus helpful to explore the kind of fundamental changes in members' roles which are implied. Clarke and Stewart (1989, p.1) make a useful distinction between councillors' *representative* and *organisational* roles. The councillor's *representative* role embodies his or her responsibilities as an elected representative both in relation to the local area for which the councillor is elected (for the interests of the area, and those who live in it) and in relation to the authority as a whole, and the community it represents. The councillor's *organisational* role embodies his or her responsibility as a member of the council, both for the policies of the authority, and for the effective working of the organisation. Although both roles (and their associated responsibilities) have long been recognised in the structures and processes of local authorities, it can be argued that the relative emphasis placed on the roles has developed, in many authorities, in a way which is hard to reconcile with the concept of the enabling authority. As Clarke and Stewart (1989b, p.2) put it:

> In practice, councils have given little support to the representative role, but have only given support to the organisational roles. Perhaps because of the neglect of the representative role, the organisational roles have been given expression in settings, and supported by processes that have given a narrow definition to the councillor's responsibilities. In effect, they have been given expression in the committee system.

The move towards the enabling authority clearly potentially strengthens some aspects of these roles and weakens others. The councillors' representative responsibilities for the authority as a whole are emphasised (at least in the Clarke/Stewart interpretation of enabling) by the enhanced importance of the development of strategic direction and a coherent, authority-wide culture and the strengthened *external* emphasis of the local authority's role. Conversely, the organisational responsibilities of councillors for the effective working of the authority are potentially greatly reduced by the separation of the council's client- and contractor-roles (not just in relation to CCT, but also through the recent legislation concerning major services such as education, social services and housing). It can be argued that the second major organisational responsibility – the policies of the authority – offers little scope for development (except in those authorities where members have previously allowed officers to play a lead role in policy-formulation, and whose role has been largely reactive) given that the policy space (or scope for policy choice) is widely perceived to have lessened in the majority of the major categories of service-provision. Thus in overall terms, the potential scope for the councillors' organisational role has been markedly reduced. As we have seen, the authority-wide aspect of the representative role has been potentially strengthened. The implications for the 'local representative' role are much less clear-cut, with the interpretation of the role arguably offering a good deal of scope.

The Audit Commission's recent publication on the role of members ('We Can't Go on Meeting Like This', 1990) tackles some of these dilemmas of changing role emphasis without satisfactorily resolving them. The double-meaning in the title is a reflection of the Commission's view that in most authorities, the number of committees (and subcommittees), their frequency, their length of meetings and the level of detail they address is quite incompatible with the changing role of local authorities. Although the withdrawal of many of the detailed service-delivery responsi-bilities typically undertaken by committees because of CCT and other legislation would in itself lead to this conclusion, the Commission have long argued that a withdrawal from manage-ment detail on the part of councillors is necessary anyway for the more effective operation of local authorities. The publication makes the case for an enhanced member emphasis on strategy-formulation, policy-planning and performance monitoring and review, in a way which is broadly compatible with the Clarke and Stewart analysis. The report emphasises also the increased importance of the *board-member* role, both in relation to the advent of CCT (concerning which it is generally accepted that the members' role in relation to the operations of internal DLOs and DSOs will necessarily have to move in this direction) and in relation to their authority-wide representative role.

Some have found the role terminology of the Commission – board member/representative/political – confusing and unhelpful (see Jones and Stewart, 1990). This reaction mirrors the role confusion amongst councillors which the post-1987 tranche of

Government legislation (and publications such as 'We Can't Go on Meeting Like This') has generated. The familiar organisational role emphasis, particularly in relation to the effective working of the organisation, is clearly threatened. But it is not yet clear what will, or should, take its place. As Clarke and Stewart argue, the implied shift from an organisational to a representative role emphasis is long overdue anyway and has a number of exciting potentialities. But those potentialities have to be clarified and developed in ways which have meaning for councillors in terms of their own role experiences and preferences. A new emphasis on strategic direction, policy planning and performance review is logical in the context of a move towards 'enabling'. But such processes in so far as authorities have become involved in them in the past, have typically interested and involved only a limited proportion of elected members (this argument is perhaps particularly apposite to a concern with strategy and performance). The main way in which councillors were able to express their representative role was in the detailed (and sometimes locality-specific) agenda items of the committees on which they happened to serve (and through their role as an informal channel of constituents' problems to the officer machinery). A move away from an emphasis on committees, together with the more limited scope in relation to the CCT services to act as an effective redresser of individual complaints, leaves an unmistakable vacuum in the role pattern of the large numbers of councillors whose predominant role orientation has been towards constituency representation.

The Audit Commission publication does little to suggest how the required change in role emphasis can be presented to councillors in such a way that their imagination is captured, and their commitment developed. It is possible to present the concepts of strategic directions and performance review in such a way that councillors do perceive the links between these activities and their political or representative roles. But it usually requires an informal 'weekend away' and skilled facilitation to achieve this outcome. Similarly, Clarke and Stewart (1989b, p.11) have suggested a number of ways in which the representative role of councillors could be enhanced, to compensate for the reduction in emphasis on the organisational role. But their introduction requires in most authorities a major change in emphasis from an inward-looking service-providing perspective to an outward-looking networking perspective related to community needs and preference. Few authorities have yet adopted this change of perspective, although many are moving in this direction.

Conclusion .

The early 1990s are proving a time of instability and change with respect to councillor roles and local authority political management structures. Much of the new legislation implies (or requires) a hands-off approach from councillors in relation to the detailed management of services, and a broad change in emphasis from the organisational role to the representational role. But the manifestations of this change are not necessarily seen as desirable by councillors who are accustomed to the familiar assumptions and operation of the traditional committee system.

New forms of political management are emerging, with a greater emphasis on informal mechanisms for strategy formulation and policy planning. But this process has in turn been hindered by the provisions of the Local Government and Housing Act 1989 which have hindered rather than supported the capacity of majority groups to operate in this kind of way. The Act strengthened local democracy in relation to minority party rights and rights of redress. It did not do so in terms of strengthening the capacity of the majority party (in majority-controlled authorities) to govern effectively. The necessary 'informal cabinet' mechanisms were moved further back into a grey area of informal discussion arenas involving leading members and officers, which are widely known to exist, but which are not represented in the formal structure.

The list of alternatives set out in the recent consultation paper on internal management structures would all (apart from the *status-quo* option) imply the repeal of certain clauses in the 1989 Act. Some would require much more in the way of legislation. None of the alternatives identified – strengthening the committee system (by introducing 'chairman's action' powers or certain types of one-party committee); a separation of powers between a small (cabinet-style) executive and a larger legislative body; a directly elected executive; an elected mayor; and a (non-political) council manager – are likely to become required modes of political management for local authorities, introduced through mandatory legislation. It is more likely that experimentation may be permitted involving small numbers of authorities who wish to introduce one or other of the alternative models. The responses to the consultation paper do not demonstrate much enthusiasm for any of the alternatives; certainly not for elected mayors, and less than might have been expected for the introduction of some form of cabinet government. In many ways the increased politicisation of local government since the late 1970s strengthens the case for local cabinet government. It would be a logical formalisation of a situation which already exists informally (although it would not work in hung authorities). In reality it is difficult to make sensible judgements about the appropriateness of ideas such as an elected mayor until there is clarification about the future role and purpose of local government. This issue is explored further in Chapter 10.

8 Managing People

In this chapter we consider the management of people in local government and the way that it has changed between the 1960s and the 1990s. Local authorities provide highly labour-intensive services, with more than half of their expenditure going on staff costs. Though there has been increasing investment in capital in the 1980s, particularly in information technology (IT), it is unlikely that local government services will ever be other than labour-intensive; labour is more than simply a means of producing the service, but is a basic part of the service. It is difficult to imagine teaching without teachers or social care without carers. The local authority labour force is extremely diverse, comprising professional staff such as social workers and teachers, administrative and clerical staff, skilled manual and non-manual staff, and a large number of semi-skilled and unskilled manual staff such as cleaners. A high proportion of the workforce is part-time, with women filling the majority of part-time posts. The local authority is also a large employer, often the largest in it locality; even the smallest authority has a relatively large workforce. The local authority workforce is highly fragmented, being spread through a number of workplaces such as residential homes, schools, libraries and other service-delivery sites. Though a high proportion of the workforce is concentrated in the town or county hall, large local authorities will have staff working in perhaps thousands of sites. The consequence is that a large proportion of the workforce is either isolated or works in small groups, and communication between staff and between management and staff is difficult.

The management of local authority staff is also differentiated by being the management of professionals. Despite the growth of a more managerialist orientation, the local authority is still organised along professional lines. The nature of the training of different professions varies considerably, and the commitment of staff is at least as much to their profession as to the authority which employs them. The management of manual staff has received relatively little attention, and the divide between manual and non-manual staff is wide. Only in the second half of the 1980s did there begin to be some change in the way that manual staff were managed and some questioning of the radical differences in the way that white- and blue-collar staff were treated.

It is often impossible directly to control the activities of staff in detail, because of the fragmented nature of the work. The exercise of discretion is a feature of the work of a high proportion of staff and not just of the senior manager. Nor can the activities of the police officer, the teacher, the social worker or the environmental health officer easily be controlled by technology. As Lipsky has argued 'street-level bureaucrats' will, of necessity, exercise considerable discretion in their work, and will, to a degree, be able to determine the policies of the organisation. As we will show, control over the local authority front-line worker has been increasing – for example, through the use of formal work-allocation systems and through communication processes such as the use of radio systems. But there will always be a need for a significant degree of autonomy because of the nature of the work.

We consider, first, the growth of formal systems of personnel management and the shift from establishment control to more sophisticated managerialist approaches. Next we consider the development of industrial relations. Traditionally the public service has been seen as a sector of low industrial militancy, but in the 1970s local government came to be the site of significant industrial action, influencing many of the changes of that decade, but especially the views of the government towards public-sector unions in the 1980s. The third major section of this chapter is concerned with the key issue of equality in local authority employment. The final section of the chapter takes up the issue of the flexible organisation in the case of local government, and argues that there has been movement towards a particular pattern of flexibility, which is dependent on increasing the discretion of the organisation at the expense of its least powerful and most disadvantaged members.

Personnel management

Despite the labour-intensive nature of the activities of the local authority, the concept of personnel management came late to local government. The large workforce obviously required management, but that was largely left to the individual departments until the reorganisation of 1974, with the centre providing no more than an establishment control function, keeping a record of staff numbers, and providing a small amount of overall coordination and control. The professional, isolationist culture of departments made a centralised approach to the management and control of staff unacceptable to powerful departmental officers. The approach to the management of staff varied greatly from department to department, with different pay-scales and conditions of employment. Local authorities saw themselves as good employers, providing relatively high rates of pay and generous conditions on such matters as holidays and superannuation. Local government provided safe, if somewhat unadventurous, jobs.

The traditional local authority approach to the management of staff began to change in the 1970s for two reasons, organisational change and growing militancy. The Bains Report laid a great deal of emphasis on the local authority, as a large employer, having a properly developed personnel system, which was seen as involving the creation of a central personnel department and a relatively highly graded personnel officer. In many cases the personnel officer was appointed relatively early to the shadow authorities that operated immediately before the reorganisation took effect, and were able to wield influence in the appointment of other staff. The second important factor was the development of industrial militancy, which, however slowly, had begun to grow in local government from the mid-1960s. By the 1970s the level of militancy had risen considerably in individual authorities, and the extent of local bargaining had grown. The development of personnel management reflected the dual pressures that arose from the development of commonly accepted ideas and the pressures particularly of industrial relations.

Following the reorganisation of local government the majority of local authorities created an explicit personnel function. This was a significant change. The situation before reorganisation is characterised by Fowler as follows:

By 1970 there may well have been more professional personnel management expertise employed in LACSAB (Local Authority Conditions of Service Advisory Board) and the LGTB (Local

Government Training Board) than in the rest of local government put together (Fowler, 1975).

The position had changed by the late 1970s, when a survey by the Society of Chief Personnel Officers in Local Government found that only 14 per cent of local authorities, predominantly small shire districts, did not have a personnel officer. Many of the larger authorities established extremely large central personnel departments, which mainly reported to the Chief Executive. Most authorities also had central personnel committees responsible for all staff except for teachers, fire and police. The approach adopted to personnel management was highly centralised both at officer- and member-level and became more so as resources became more constrained. The influence of personnel officers came more from their access to central powerholders in the authority than their own position, and increased as centralisation grew.

Despite the argument of Bains for the development of a modern personnel function, focusing on the positive development of staff, and seeing itself as human resource management, the approach that quickly became established, in the latter half of the 1970s, one of control, largely as a result of financial constraints. In many cases all staff vacancies had to be cleared through the personnel department and the personnel committee. Processes for the appointment and recruitment of staff were also highly centralised. Training, though it had been emphasised by Bains received very little attention, commonly being left up to individual departments. There was little, if any, significant planning on staff matters. A major concern was the development of uniformity in the staff policies of the authority. The position was institutionalised through the establishment of formalised procedures on matters such as recruitment and selection which were standardised across the authority. The result of these various centralising pressures was a system that was slow and seen by officers in service departments as unresponsive and control-oriented.

The nature of personnel management has changed under the conflicting pressure. On the one hand there has been continuous pressure on staff numbers because of the increasing financial constraints. These pressures have tended to heighten the tendencies for a control-oriented approach to the management of staff, though with somewhat less standardisation and formalisation. On the other hand the pressures for change in approaches to management, and particularly the devolution of control, have tended to lessen both the appropriateness and possibility of formalised central control. The need for new skills and changed patterns of work has led to some emphasis on the importance of developing staff, and improving the ability of individuals. Attempts to change organisational culture, in particular, have led to an emphasis on staff training and development. The contradictory pressures for positive and negative approaches to the development of staff are apparent in conflicting tendencies within the development of the personnel function, both in terms of its policy and the organisation.

Personnel policy

In total there has been some growth in the level of employment within local government, but this overall growth conceals the cuts in staffing that have resulted from changes in the pattern of employment. For example, there have been shifts in the pattern of employment in education as a result of demographic changes and changes in the nature of the curriculum. The result of the introduction of competitive tendering in building and highway construction and maintenance in 1981 was an increase in the proportion of non-manual staff employed. Local authorities, in the early 1980s felt the need to develop policies that gave them greater flexibility in the control of their staffing level.

By the mid-1980s the majority of large authorities had developed policies for redeployment, premature retirement and temporary contracts. The number of staff affected by such policies was large. For example, in education 2 per cent of the total teaching force were redeployed between 1979 and 1981, and 2.5 per cent of teachers were on fixed-term contracts. Few authorities were willing to contemplate compulsory redundancy of full-time permanent employees and many, particularly those that were Labour controlled, had 'no-redundancy' policies. But within this overall constraint local authorities were attempting to develop greater flexibility in the management of staff numbers and costs.

Most of these policies are still in force but have become increasingly hard to maintain, because the authority now has less control over the workforce, as in the case of schools, because circumstances have changed, or because of legal restrictions. For example, local authorities cannot force schools to accept redeployed teachers, and losing contracts under competitive tendering may make redundancies inevitable. In the 1980s and early 1990s even left-wing Labour authorities which were strongly influenced by trade unions found it necessary to reduce staffing. The tightening of the financial regime, and the gradual closing of the loopholes that were utilised by authorities pursuing policies of creative accounting, forced cutbacks in staffing, even in authorities such as Lambeth, Haringey and Liverpool. The introduction of competitive tendering for a number of manual services forced authorities to cut back on staffing if they were to win contracts and led to redundancies where contracts were lost. The protected nature of local authority employment has gradually been eroded, particularly for manual staff.

Paradoxically, at the same time as many staff were finding their employment threatened by financial constraint and government moves to reduce the security of local authority employment, there were also severe staff shortages. There were absolute shortages of certain professional staff such as environmental health officers, lawyers, social workers, surveyors, valuers, and teachers of specific subjects such as mathematics, and also computer staff. There were also shortages of skilled craftworkers, such as plumbers and electricians. These shortages were exacerbated in the south-east of England where the labour market was generally buoyant. In London in particular it was difficult to recruit staff, a problem which was worst in some of the Labour boroughs which were regarded as extremist. The Audit Commission in a report on the management of London authorities argued that:

> local government salaries and conditions make it difficult for inner-London authorities to compete with the private sector or less-stressful authorities in the provinces – where housing and travel to work costs are generally much lower (Audit Commission, 1987).

There were also problems of retaining staff and gross turnover rates of non-manual staff rose from 12 per cent in 1977–8 to 15.1 per cent in 1986–7. The result was to encourage authorities to search for ways of enhancing their ability to recruit and retain staff.

Staff were placed higher on pay-scales than would otherwise have been the case. Performance pay was introduced in a number of cases, at least as much in order to increase levels of pay as to reward measured performance. Pay for senior managerial staff increased markedly in many authorities. Employment packages were introduced that were intended to tie the individual more effectively to the organisation by providing non-transferable rewards such as cars and private health insurance. The conflicting pressures of staff shortages and the need to reduce staff numbers has contributed to the development of multiple labour markets, in which different groups of staff face different employment regimes within the local authority.

Changes in the management of staff within the local authority have resulted not only from external pressures, but also from internally generated changes. Three changes have been particularly important:

- the arguments for the development of a more responsive approach to the consumer;
- the development of decentralised approaches to the delivery of service;
- development of devolved systems of management.

The growing consumer-orientation means that front-line staff have to be more able to deal with the needs of citizens, and more responsive to users. A number of authorities, particularly district councils such as the Wrekin, have made an improved responsiveness to users a key part of their service strategy. At its best this has involved extensive training and revision of the respective responsibilities of back-line and front-line staff. Attempts were made to ensure that front-line staff had the competence to deal with people's problems rather than having to refer them to professional staff in the back office. More common was an attempt to develop a superficial customer-friendliness, with little improvement in competence or performance. It was relatively rare that manual staff were involved in training or other programmes to increase customer satisfaction, despite the fact that they tend to have high levels of public contact. For example, housing-repair workers rarely had any involvement in customer-care programmes. While the degree of change has been limited the movement for improved quality of public service has focused attention on the way that work is organised, and the way that 'street-level bureaucrats' can be given more ability to influence services.

Decentralisation also involved challenges to traditional assumptions about local authority employment. First there was the need to consider the operation of task demarcations both horizontally and vertically. The question of horizontal demarcation lines arose because decentralised offices were expected to work across sections of departments or across departments. Professional divisions – for example between housing and social services – fitted ill with the need for integrated services at departmental offices. Vertical demarcation lines had to be considered because staff in the local office needed to be able to deal with problems without having to refer back to central office staff. In practice the result was frequently conflict. Decentralisation also tended to disrupt traditional career patterns, which were based on the concepts of hierarchy and centralised control. The result has been that in many cases there has been strong trade-union resistance to the decentralisation of service delivery.

The present movement towards the devolution of managerial control raises similar issues, though even more acutely. Managers who are responsible for their own budgets tend to want to have control over their own personnel management, since the major determinant of expenditure is staff costs. They are likely to feel that centrally negotiated pay and conditions do not recognise their particular needs. This view is strongly held in the majority of direct labour organisations (DLOs) which must win tenders in competition with the private sector. The impact of devolved control on the management of staff is most apparent in the case of schools which now have their own budgets, and are able to make their own decision about levels of pay. Since finance is allocated to schools on the basis of average teacher costs, individual schools in which costs are higher, have faced acute dilemmas in matching staff to finance. The result of devolution of financial control is divergence of the way that staff are treated in different parts of the authority. This development raises questions about the nature of the local authority as a corporate employer, which are considered below in examining multiple labour market and the question of organisational flexibility.

Each of these developments in local government management has been mirrored in personnel management. It is less possible to maintain uniform hierarchical approaches in an organisation that is led by concepts of decentralisation and responsiveness. There are also implications for career paths, in that there is no longer a clear match between organisational hierarchies and managerial advance. For example, the division between client and contractor or purchaser and provider roles creates divisions within the organisation that challenge traditional career development paths. The impacts are particularly strong at the middle-management level, where staff see their authority being eroded and their opportunities for advance reduced.

The development of personnel management in local government tends to mirror the general pattern of organisational change to a greater extent than in the manufacturing sector, because of the labour-intensive nature of the public service. In the case of more technologically based organisations it is possible to replace the less-tractable human resource with the machine. In the public service, because the staff are to a considerable degree part of the service, every other organisational change tends to be reflected in the issues of staff management. The development of approaches to staff management is the development of the organisation. Organisational conflicts are also played out as differences in the way that staff are managed, and the development of organisational change inevitably involves questions of industrial relations.

Industrial relations

In 1968 the Donovan Commission Report argued that much of the difficulty of industrial relations in Britain followed from the fact that local institutions for the regulation of bargaining were underdeveloped and that, in consequence, conflict at the local level was common. What was needed, it argued, was a recognition of the realities of industrial relations and a restructuring of institutions to cope with those realities. The Report made almost no reference to the public sector, where, despite the same lack of local institutional framework for bargaining, there was very little industrial conflict. Ironically, almost immediately after the publication of the Donovan Report the level of industrial unrest in local government began to increase markedly. The 1970s and 1980s were characterised by a significant rise of militancy throughout the public service, from the National Health Service to education. This rise in militancy has contributed significantly to the strategy that has been adopted by the government towards the reorganisation of the public service and the approaches to change that have been adopted by individual authorities.

The lack of an institutional framework for local bargaining, on which the Donovan Commission had based its diagnosis of the ills of British industrial relations in the private sector, became apparent in local government as industrial militancy grew in the 1970s. Just as personnel management was little developed at the local authority level, so there was little development of a local industrial relations system. The level of dissatisfaction in the local government work-force had, in fact, been growing since the early 1960s, largely because of the actions of central government in its attempts to control inflation and balance-of-payments problems. Incomes policies introduced both by the Labour and Conservative governments of the time had been focused particularly on the public sector. The studies of the National Board for Prices and Incomes highlighted the fact that, though local authorities might see themselves as good employers, levels of pay were low. The rising inflation of the late 1960s had a relatively strong effect on public-service workers who were held more closely to pay norms. Increasing dissatisfaction and militancy was apparent in the growth of trade-union membership in local government from the mid-1960s, in affiliation of local-authority unions to the Trades Union Congress, and in an increase in the number and size of strikes.

In the 1970s the level of industrial action in local government increased. In 1973–4 there was strike action in the fire service and the ambulance service, then still controlled by the local authorities, which showed that even workers in the emergency services were prepared to take action to forward their interests. Moral commitment could no longer be relied upon to restrain the workforce from taking action. In 1974 NALGO took action through strikes and overtime bans in pursuit of a higher London weighting, showing that traditionally non-militant white-collar workers were becoming more militant. In the second half of the 1970s there was significant action at the national level involving local government staff, notably the fire officers and the social workers. There were also frequent local strikes. Militancy was growing even amongst the police who threatened strike action even though it would have been illegal.

The growth of militancy in local government led to the development of local industrial-relations systems, a development heightened by the pressure for a more developed personnel system. In the 1960s there had been few shop stewards in local government, and they were concentrated in small pockets of relatively isolated manual workers, such as refuse collectors. Key local-authority unions such as the National Union of Public Employees (NUPE) and the National and Local Government Association (NALGO) operated without shop-steward systems, which only existed in general unions, such as the Transport and General Workers Union. The representation of employees, which was usually concerned with individual rather than collective matters, largely took place through union officers. In the event of local action it was difficult to know with whom to negotiate. The problems were enhanced by the fragmentation of local-authority union membership, with a large number of unions organising staff and no clear spheres of influence.

The development of a lay structure in the unions at local level was rapid in the 1970s, partly as a response to local pressure and partly because of encouragement by national leaders such as Jack Jones. The number of General and Municipal Workers Union shop stewards trebled and NUPE made strong attempts to expand the strength and depth of its shop steward system. The development of a local system came later amongst the white collar workers and the National Association of Local Government Officers, developing only slowly from the mid-1970s. There were problems of clashes between full-time officials and multi-unionism remains a problem, but bargaining committees with lay representation were established. By the late 1970s the majority of urban and many non-urban authorities had developed local systems for dealing with industrial relations matters.

The systems that developed were relatively bureaucratic and hierarchical, reflecting the dominant culture of local government itself. Formal systems of bargaining operated on a relatively centralised basis. Most authorities had central joint consultative committees for manual and for non-manual staff, on which elected members, union officials and lay representatives met. There were separate systems for teachers and for fire officers. Larger departments had their own consultative committees. There was little integration of industrial relations systems across the manual non-manual divide, either at management or union level. Bargaining was slow and often tortuous. The difference between bargaining and consultation was not especially clear, with Conservative authorities emphasising consultation and Labour authorities bargaining. The degree of proceduralisation grew as grievance, disputes and other procedures were enhanced. Industrial relations became a specialised function, conducted by personnel officers and union officials or shop stewards who often had significant time off to pursue union duties. Those involved in industrial relations had their own organisational interests, expressed in the institutional framework that had been established for bargaining.

The action of the 'winter of discontent' in 1978–9 and the pay rises that followed the recommendations of the Clegg Comparability Commission made both the newly elected government and many Conservative authorities determined to control the local government workforce, but the immediate effect was limited. The attack on the unions since 1979 has been rather slower to impact on the public sector than the private. While unions recruiting in the private sector faced a rapid and significant decline in the level of membership, local-authority union membership kept up. There were some differences between non-manual staff and manual staff. In the first half of the 1980s the number of manual workers reduced while the number of non-manual staff increased. Particular groups of workers, such as school meals staff, faced erosion of their pay and conditions. But generally the industrial-relations legislation has had only limited effects, and the bargaining systems were little affected. Manual trade unions were very effective in working together during this period. Militancy in the public service generally, and in local government in particular continued throughout the 1980s, with significant action being taken particularly by white-collar workers and by teachers. The developments of the second half of the 1980s and the early 1990s eroded the position of the local-authority unions quite significantly.

The action taken by the government after the election of 1987 was aimed directly at reducing the power of the producer, and the hold of the trade unions over the nature of local authority work. The introduction of competitive tendering has had a major impact on the employment of manual workers in such services as cleaning, refuse collection and grounds maintenance. Staffing levels have been reduced by between 20 and 30 per cent, patterns of work have been changed to improve productivity, and pay and conditions of service have often worsened. The proportion of manual staff who are members of trade unions has decreased. The effect of competitive tendering on non-manual staff has been limited though it will become greater as competition is extended to services such as computing and housing management. The prospect is one of increasing competition from the private sector with consequent continuing pressure on the local government workforce. The principles of competition are also being operated in other services, such as social services. Though pay and conditions are worse for comparable work in the private sector, competitive tendering has forced local authorities to move to less-favourable employment conditions.

Change can be illustrated by the case of the teachers. The delegation of control of finance and staffing to the schools and colleges, with the latter in any case being taken out of local government, means that there is now little point in the operation of bargaining at the level of the authority as a whole. The power of schools to opt out of local-authority control and become grant-maintained, enhances the tendency. Though most teachers are still technically the employees of the authority decisions about appointment and dismissal and to a lesser extent pay are made at the school level by the headteacher and the governing body. Trade-union membership amongst teachers has been declining. The power of the teachers to control their work is reduced by the introduction of the national curriculum, which lays down in some detail what is to be taught in schools at each level. The traditional autonomy of the teaching profession is also eroded by the development of performance appraisal. Finally, the government abolished the national bargaining system for teachers in 1987, and the Secretary for State for Education now sets teachers' pay, after considering the advice of an appointed panel. The development of the school as the key site of industrial relations will weaken the teachers further, because of the fragmentation of the established institutions of educational bargaining.

More generally the gradually tightening central control over local government finance has made it difficult for local authorities to be able to avoid worsening employment policies. Redundancy has become relatively commonplace. Reorganisation of working methods often leads to an increased pace of work, and reduced staffing levels. The workforce is now much less able to prevent change which it feels is against its interests. Management has seen the changes as allowing the reassertion of the right to manage which was seen as having been lost in the 1970s as industrial militancy grew. Politicians, particularly in the Conservative Party, see the developments as allowing them to gain control over the nature of service, and to be able to make service policy independently of producer control. The result of these changes has been that the institutional framework of industrial relations that had been established in the 1970s and early 1980s has come under increasing pressure, both locally and nationally. The change is the result partly of changing external circumstances, and partly the result of changes within the organisation as politicians and senior managers have taken the opportunity to reassert control.

Central and local bargaining

Bargaining in local government remains relatively more centralised than in the private sector, despite the pressures for local bargaining. Bargaining is conducted along Whitley principles, with about forty negotiating bodies, made up of equal numbers of employers' and employees' representatives. The employers' representatives are drawn predominantly from local councillors who sit on the national representative bodies and the Provincial Councils. Centralised bargaining has come under pressure in recent years for two reasons:

1. authorities, particularly in the south-east of England, which have faced recruitment difficulties have felt that their needs were not adequately represented by the national negotiating bodies. London authorities in particular have been dissatisfied with national bargaining.
2. the shire counties and the metropolitan authorities have felt that their interests were not adequately considered because of the overdominance of representatives of the smaller shire districts.

The result has been that some authorities, such as Kent County Council, have partly broken away from national bargaining and made their own settlements. More generally authorities have found it difficult to maintain national pay and conditions in services that are subject to competitive tender and where there is a strong private sector.

Within the local authority there has been decentralisation of bargaining, partly because of the strategic attempt by many authorities to devolve managerial control, and partly because legislation such as the Education Reform Act 1988 and the requirements for competitive tendering make centralised bargaining impossible to maintain. The need for more rapid decision-making, because of financial cutbacks and the need to compete also puts pressure on relatively slow-moving centralised bargaining systems. Managers with devolved budgetary control are pressing for the right to manage their own staff without the involvement of central industrial relations staff and outside the formal bargaining systems. A number of authorities have actually disbanded some of the structure of centralised bargaining. There is a movement away from formal systems for the management of industrial relations towards more *ad hoc* approaches reflecting the organisational interests of management.

The developments of the period since the election of the Conservative government of 1987 have begun to weaken the formalised and centralised system of industrial relations that had developed in the 1970s and 1980s. Trade unionism has begun to decline, and the unions have been unable to resist major changes. There are variation between authorities in the pattern of development. In some Labour authorities, in metropolitan districts more than in London, the trade unions have played a leading role in the development of strategies for dealing with competitive tendering. But in general the unions have found themselves poorly organised to resist the changes which are now being faced. The formal systems of bargaining are both too slow and too centralised to be able to respond to rapidly changing local circumstances. The development of competitive tendering raises the prospect of the local authority without staff. The development of decentralisation and devolved management serves to divide staff, by creating a multiplicity of interests, so that its difficult to mobilise. The breakdown of traditional bureaucratic approaches to the organisation of local authorities is also the end of the institutional system of industrial relations that developed in the 1970s and 1980s.

The pursuit of equality

In the public sector the requirements for greater accountability and the commitment, however notional, to the pursuit of justice, make equality in employment a crucial matter. In local government it is also of great practical importance, because of the high proportion of women employed in the lower levels of the organisation, and the fact that the vast majority of managers are men. The importance of equality has been recognised by local government as a whole and has been a key value for a small number of authorities, particularly in London and the major cities. Equality in employment in local government is most commonly considered with regard to the position of women, ethnic minority groups and people with disabilities. In a small number of cases the concern for equality of opportunity extends to a consideration of the position of gay men, lesbians, and specific religious groupings. The discussion of equal opportunities has been characterised by high levels of rhetorical excess, and the results have been very limited. It is not our intention to consider the whole issue of equal opportunities here, but to examine the interplay between the way that local authorities have managed equal opportunities issues and the overall organisational management of the local authority. Generally the pursuit of equal opportunities has remained at the level of rhetoric. As Young argues:

> Discussion of equal opportunity in employment is bedevilled by ambiguities and confusions which typically characterise areas of public policy where a powerful rhetorical commitment to change exists. In such areas, a shared language may mask multiple and conflicting meanings . . . While ambiguities may facilitate agreement at the symbolic level, they preclude clear specification of the ends of policy and so inhibit the proper identification of feasible means for its achievement. Ambiguity can assume major importance where – as in this case – it serves to obscure sharply divergent implications for the practicalities of policy (Young, 1987, p.94).

It seems that a similar process has happened in the introduction of equal opportunities policies as occurred with the change in management structures in the 1970s; policies and practices were adopted in a largely symbolic and ceremonial form as a means of ensuring external legitimacy, while organisational realities changed little.

The approach to developing equal opportunities in local authority employment has had two main strands. First, there was the introduction of relatively centralised procedures to control recruitment and selection in order to try to ensure that there was equality of opportunity. These procedures had some limited success, but were frequently resented by managers who felt that they involved delay and expense in the appointments procedure. Second, there was the introduction of central units and committees to forward equal opportunities in employment and in policy more generally. These units were most common in the London boroughs and the metropolitan districts. They were frequently the source of tension and conflict with departments, which saw them as interfering with, and threatening, their independence.

The impact of equal opportunities policies and units has been limited. The spread of the adoption of initiatives has been slow; in 1983 a D. of E study of a sample of authorities found that slightly less than half had an equal opportunities policy. There has been some change in the pattern of employment – for example with the appointment of a small number of Chief Executives who are women or members of ethnic minorities, but it is still the case that women and ethnic minorities are concentrated at the lower level of local authorities and in manual jobs. Even in professions where the majority of employees are women, such as social work and primary-school teaching, the majority of managerial positions are filled by men. There have been some small changes in the opportunities that are available to people with disabilities, but, again, their opportunities for advance are relatively constrained. The culture of the local authority is still predominantly one of white, male, able-bodied control. In part, of course, this is a result of the nature of the labour market and of career structures. In many cases women and people from ethnic minorities do not have the initial qualifications that would allow them to compete equally for posts in the most prestigious career lines. But even where they are represented it is difficult to ensure equality. Women, members of ethnic minorities and people with disabilities face both overt and covert barriers. The process of professionalisation itself, one which has been fundamental to the development of occupational groups in local government, is inherently disadvantaging to women and members of ethnic minority groups, because of the difficulty of obtaining initial qualifications and the requirement to be organisationally mobile. Similarly the hierarchical structure of departments disadvantages women, who because of career breaks, cannot so steadily climb the organisational ladder.

A study for the Local Government Training Board has distinguished four types of barrier that serve to prevent equality in a study of the position of women in local government:

1. People may be disbarred from employment by a range of job requirements – for example unpredictable or inflexible working hours, or the way that job descriptions are phrased.
2. People may be deterred by the absence of the necessary facilities such as child-care provision or adaptations to help people with disabilities.
3. The workplace environment may deter by the nature of relationships with fellow-workers or by unrealistic expectations.
4. The management style of the organisation may be a barrier because of stereotyping and cultural expectations.

Each of these barriers is likely to be faced by members of ethnic minority groups and people with disabilities as well as women. The essential determinant of discrimination is not the conscious intention of organisational actors, though this may be significant, but the way that disadvantage is built into the institutional framework of the organisation.

The development of the more devolved form of management that is beginning to characterise local authorities has implications for equal opportunities. Managers who have resented the central policies on recruitment, training and selection that have been developed to try to improve equality have argued that decentralised cost-centre management makes such approaches inappropriate. Managers faced with financial constraint, particularly those faced with competitive tendering, have argued that they cannot afford expensive policies that are aimed at equal opportunity. The introduction of an ideology of commercialism has made it easier to argue against the commitment to equality. Labour authorities, particularly in London, have been unwilling to abandon or weaken their policies for equality in the face of commercial arguments, and have developed skills analysis, retraining programmes and redeployment in an attempt to alleviate the problems of commercialism and financial constraint. The ability to maintain equal opportunity policies has also been limited by legislation making many aspects of contract compliance policies illegal.

Young and Connelly, in their study of equal opportunity policies in local government, argue that it was not in the interests of those with the primary responsibility for developing staff, the personnel officers, actively to pursue equal opportunities. Their position forces them to balance conflicting pressures.

> The general impression that arose from our contacts with and observation of personnel directors is of a profession whose ethos and training inclines them to a management role which perceives two distinct needs; the manpower and functional needs of the authority as an organisation and the personal development needs of their individual staff. Their professional skill lies in their ability to balance or reconcile these needs within a tradition of consultation with unions and staff associations. Such competing pressures and loyalties doubtless provide personnel directors with a testing and often unpredictable working environment. To expect them to take the lead-role in developing the more positive type of equal opportunity practice may be unrealistic; their professional ethos and their managerial role are understandably at odds with the concept of a responsive local authority operating in a multiracial environment (Young and Connelly, 1981, p.54).

The relative failure of the holistic and centralised approach to the development of equal opportunities in local government in the 1980s is consistent with experience in other employment sectors. Jewson *et al.* (1990) in their study of ethnic minority employment practice have argued for an approach to equality that builds on the processes of 'deformalisation, decentralisation and the devolution of managerial responsibility'. The difficulty with this strategy is that discrimination is likely to result more generally from poor employment practices such as the casualisation of employment.

Flexibility, trust and surveillance

There have been frequent arguments that the nature of organisations is changing as we enter the more differentiated and less monolithic world of post-modernism. The modern era has been the age of 'Fordism' in which organisations were characterised by large size, mass production, technology, the deskilling of the workforce, and the control of staff primarily through Taylorist methods. In the post-modern ear, it is argued, organisations will be much less monolithic, and the aim will be for flexibility and responsiveness to a much more diverse and rapidly changing market. In the post-modern organisation there will be less bureaucratic control of staff, and hierarchy will give away to much more flexible systems of staff organisations and management.

Studies of the development of the flexible organisation have identified three ways in which flexibility can be obtained within the workforce; flexibility in the use of skills, flexibility of staff numbers and flexibility of staff costs. The first implies the breaking-down of traditional skill demarcations and the use of deskilling through the introduction of new technology. Pressures on manual workers as a result of competitive tendering have led to some erosion of the barriers between crafts, for example, in grounds maintenance and in the building trades. At the white-collar level there is only very limited evidence of deskilling as a result of the introduction of new technology (Crompton and Jones, 1984). There is little evidence to support other, more tendentious, arguments that there has been deskilling amongst professional staff. What has been happening to a greater degree is that the degree of professionals' control over their own work has decreased. There are two reasons for this:

1. methods have been developed for monitoring professionals' work more closely, for example through work measurement schemes, performance targets and appraisal systems.
2. There have been movements to make professionals more accountable, for example through increasing the influence of parents on the governing bodies of schools or through increasing tenants' rights in housing.

Neither of these developments reduces professional skill, but they do reduce autonomy. There has been a decline in the trust that is placed in staff and particularly professional staff, rather than a reduction in their professional skills.

There is much stronger evidence that there has been a development of greater flexibility in the numbers of staff employed. This has been accomplished through the use of short-term contracts and the use of more casual labour. Most authorities have introduced schemes of redeployment and premature retirement in order to be able to reduce numbers or move staff from one area of work to another. Redundancy has become relatively commonplace as a result of competitive tendering, changing patterns of work and financial difficulties. The total number of staff employed in local government has changed very little over the course of the 1980s, but the changes in particular areas of work have been considerable – for example, the number of staff employed in cleaning buildings has declined markedly as a result of tenders for work being lost to the private sector and because authorities have reduced numbers in order to reduce costs. Authorities have also been changing the basis on which they employ staff by privatisation and buy-outs for services such as computing and architecture. The shortage of staff in some authorities has also led to greater use of external consultants. Flexibility of staff is partly attained by changing the basis on which people are attached to the organisation. The contractual relations between staff and the organisation for which they work are becoming much more varied.

Flexibility in staff costs has been important particularly in those areas that are subject to competitive tendering. Traditional work-measured bonus systems have been criticised as being too complex and out of date. Many systems had been introduced in the 1970s and had never been revised since, despite changes in work methods and materials. They were costly to administer and were felt to bear little actual relationship to productivity. Competitive tendering has led many authorities to revise their bonus systems in order to make them simpler and more closely related to output. A common development has been to introduce attendance bonus systems. Other changes have involved changes in sick-pay procedures and the introduction of more part-time workers.

There has also been some attempt to introduce more flexibility in the way that staff are paid through the introduction of performance-related pay particularly for senior staff. Changes are being made with the introduction of cashless pay, and paying on a fortnightly or monthly, rather than weekly basis. The local authority is seeking to increase its discretion by reducing that of the workforce.

Local authorities have made some limited move towards greater flexibility, largely at the expense of manual and lower-paid staff. There is the emergence of a multi-tiered labour market within the local authority. At the core are the central staff concerned with the maintenance of the organisation as a corporate entity – for example, the Chief Executive, the finance officer, and policy staff. Next there are the client-side staff concerned with the management of contracts, which may have been let either to internal or to external contractors. Third, there are internal contractors, whose attachment to the organisation is dependent on the winning of tenders. Finally there are external contractors. Within these various groups there will be further gradations: for example, there will be distinctions between permanent and temporary staff both for internal and external contractors. In some cases, in authorities such as Berkshire, these changes have gone quite a long way. In others the change has been much more limited. In all cases there has been a move away from traditional patterns of bureaucratic uniformity in the employment relationship.

There has also been change in the way that staff are controlled in the organisation. The traditional approach to the management of staff in the local authority was a combination of hierarchical authority and professional and street-level autonomy. The developments of the late 1980s and early 1990s point towards the development of a system that is based less on processes of direct control and more on arm's length surveillance mechanisms. These methods are a combination of work measurement and performance management systems, by which the core senior members of the organisation set targets against which performance is monitored. Managers and staff in cost centres have freedom, but only in so far as they meet the targets that have been set. Toleration of failure is much less than was the case in the traditional, paternalistic, bureaucratic system, in which, in practice, limited sanctions were operated. The reasons for this change are partly ideological development, and partly contingent circumstances. The idea of the flexible organisation that is made up of relatively independent cost centres is an idea in good currency. But, equally, changed financial conditions have removed the slack that allowed the traditional hierarchical bureaucratic system to operate.

Cutting across these changes is the segmentation of the organisation in terms of race, gender and disability, with those groups that are most disadvantaged by the development of a multi-tiered labour market being further disadvantaged by their personal characteristics. Many of the advances that were being made in the 1980s in the pursuit of greater equality have been brought up short by the external constraints that financial and legislative changes have brought about. There are then two dimensions along which the local government labour force is segmented, namely, the mode of attachment to the organisation and the equalities dimension. These two dimensions are likely to reinforce each other, unless there is positive action to ensure that institutional processes that maintain disadvantage are overcome.

Conclusion

In a labour-intensive organisation such as a local authority it is inevitable that changes in the nature of the organisation will find a direct expression in the way that staff are managed. The management of staff in local government reflects the conflicting pressures and strategies that are being pursued. On the one hand there are pressures to build a more responsive organisation in which staff are conscious of the needs of the service-user and are able to act on their own initiative to meet them. This sort of organisation implies that staff are strongly committed and self-motivated. On the other hand there are the pressures towards less security, closer monitoring of work and cuts in pay and conditions of service. In part these conflicting pressures can be overcome by separating out core staff who need to be positively motivated, and who are members of the primary labour market of the organisation. On the other hand there are those who are more peripheral and whose attachment to the organisation is much less secure. It is difficult to maintain such distinctions when it is often relatively weakly integrated staff who are crucial to the development of effective service.

The development of flexible patterns of organisation in the manufacturing sector is dependent on an appropriate combination of labour and technology In the case of the highly labour-intensive local government sector there is only a very limited possibility of using technology. Where in the manufacturing sector much of the flexibility that is wanted can be created through the development of appropriate technology, creating freedom for the worker, in the local authority it is the worker who must be flexible creating freedom for the organisation. Local authorities, in the management of staff, have moved from methods that are based on authority and command, to control through systems and contracts. The traditional bureaucratic approaches of extensive hierarchies are giving way to managers with devolved budgets who have responsibility for their own staff. The emphasis is less upon direct control than on informal control through targets and sanctions.

These changes are placing considerable pressures on managerial staff within local authorities. As a recent report on well-managed authorities put it:

> In some authorities a concern with staff had become out of balance with other elements of managerial change. In one authority we were told that the pace of change had created demotivation amongst staff, and that there had been a lack of attention to managing the process of change, investing in human resources and workforce care. In all cases, there were to be found amongst middle managers perceptions of tighter expectations, increasing pressure, longer hours and the need to develop a range of new skills relatively quickly. One sensed that further increases in pressure could result in a more widespread process of fairly rapid demotivation (Leach, Walsh *et al.*, 1993).

Local authorities now face a major period of change which will lead, if anything, to increasing pressure.

9 The Inter-Organisational Dimension

It was argued in Chapter 2 (pp.37–43) and Chapter 3 (pp.63–6) that in the current circumstances facing local authorities, the inter-organisational dimension is becoming increasingly important, both for local authorities themselves in achieving their objectives, and for those seeking to understand the emerging patterns of organisation and management in local government.

A local authority has always been part of a network of other organisations – both private and public – with whom it has necessarily had a set of relationships. Many of its functions involved control over, or provision of, services to other organisations. Equally, other organisations have always provided services to, or had control over, local authorities. Local authorities have had goals which conflicted with, or complemented, other organisations. Long before the enabling role was written about Friend and his colleagues studied the Town Expansion Scheme at Droitwich as 'the intercorporate dimension' and recognised the need for reticulist skills in handling the network of relationships (Friend *et al.*, 1974).

Although the work of local authorities involved relationships with other organisations, their own organisation and management focused on the direct provision of services based on the assumption of self-sufficiency. Traditionally it has been assumed that joint action, even between different local authorities, was not easily achieved. The ideal of the all-purpose authority coupled with the belief that the minimum size of local authorities should be at least 250 000 (Redcliffe-Maud, 1969) reflected that belief.

In Chapter 3 we discussed the concepts developed by inter-organisation theory for understanding such relationships. It discussed inter-organisational networks distinguishing the degree and nature of the coupling:

The more tightly coupled a set of organisations, the more those organisations can be seen as forming an explicit network which involves organisations cooperating in order to build on complementary strengths. Networks will tend to be based upon concepts of reciprocity, rather than competition, and to require a degree of trust between parties to the network. It is more difficult to operate through networks than through hierarchies because the sanctions that are available within an organisation are not available and because knowledge and information is widely spread (p.66).

Rhodes has used the concept of networks to explore the complexities of what he describes as subcentral government. He makes clear that local authorities are 'embedded in complex patterns of interdependence' (Rhodes, 1988, p.207). He stresses the need to recognise the

complexity, indeterminacy and interdependence as defining characteristics of the system. The plurality of organisations and the indeterminacy of the system's structure cannot be assumed away as political inconveniences. Strategic flexibility is an essential prerequisite of effective intervention.

It is useful in this connection to focus on the role of 'interests' in inter-organisational behaviour. In Chapter 3, the work of Benson (1975) was briefly discussed. Benson argues that public-sector organisations operating in a network are oriented to the protection (or ideally, enhancement) of scarce and valued resources, predominant amongst which are 'money' and 'authority'. Thus local authorities will strive to protect or enhance *both* the flow of financial resources available to them, *and* their right to operate exclusively within established domains of authority (e.g. the legal right to provide certain kinds of services). Inter-organisational relationships which threaten the stability of the flow of financial resources or threaten established domains are likely to become a source of conflict rather than cooperation. Conversely, relationships which are likely to lead to enhanced financial resources, or are premised upon 'domain consensus' (i.e. mutual agreement concerning domains of responsibilities) are more likely to proceed on a more consensual basis. A redistribution of resources and domain responsibilities may also be an important influence on the quality of relationships in the network established following the redistribution. For example, after the 1974 reorganisation, the values and interests of key actors at both county and district level were influential in generating (or failing to generate) trust and a predisposition towards cooperation between authorities. In authorities which felt that they had lost power and status in 1974 (e.g. former county boroughs) trust of, and cooperative predisposition towards, the other tier were scarce commodities.

Thus, as we argued in Chapter 3, managing in an inter-organisational network differs from management within an organisation. Whereas within a local authority, there is a common organisation, which in principle, if not always in practice, should make possible joint action by different parts of the organisation, that cannot be assumed for joint action by different organisations in a network. Certain conditions favour joint action, while certain conditions make it more difficult (see pp.218–20).

The growing significance of inter-organisational relations

While inter-organisational relations have always been important to a local authority they have gained a new significance due to changes in society and to changes in the structure of government. The changes in society discussed in Chapter 2 have led local authorities to a greater recognition of the complexity of the networks in which they operate. The issues that faced local authorities in a changing society necessarily involved them in developing new relationships. For example, the emphasis given to economic development meant that local authorities had to work with and through the private sector.

It was not merely the new concern for the local economy, emerging concerns for environmental issues also led to a recognition that while local authorities had a key role, many other agencies and organisations were involved. Whilst Sutton Council:

> has taken many direct steps to make that contribution, it has also worked through many other people and bodies in order that its overall goal for the quality of the environment can be achieved. That may be one reflection of the Council enabling others to

contribute to an overall objective; another is the way which the Council has [influenced] and intends to influence others, individual and organisation. In using a variety of means of influence from regulatory powers, shifts in the application of Council resources and the development of incentives through to straightforward education, campaigning, and advocacy, the Council recognises that the overall objective can only be achieved by the efforts of a wide range of individuals and organisations (Ennals and O'Brien, 1990, p.65).

If new problems and issues have led to a greater emphasis on inter-organisational relations, so have changes in the structure of government at the local level. The creation of new agencies such as Training and Enterprise Councils generally or Urban Development Corporations in particular areas has increased the complexity of the network of agencies. As Stoker has written:

The Thatcher governments have also encouraged the growth of non-elected agencies through their attempts at restructuring and reforming the practice and performance of elected local authorities to create companies to manage their participation in bus and airport operations . . . With their election for a third term the Conservatives are in the process of making it possible for public-sector tenants and schools 'to opt out' of the local authority system. This will lead to the creation of a further range of non-directly elected local agencies to take over the management of these services from local authorities (Stoker, 1991, p.62).

The list of separate institutions includes some apparently under the control of local authorities. The abolition of metropolitan counties led to the creation of Joint Boards for the police service, for the fire service and for public transport (Leach *et al.*, 1992). Even where schools remained in the local authority, the provisions of the Education Reform Act gave them a semi-autonomous status so that the roles of the local authority became in the words of the Audit Commission:

leader of the education service;
partner to schools and colleges;
planner of facilities;

provider of information to those who use the service:
regulator of quality in schools and colleges;
banker to educational institutions (Audit Commission, 1989).

As opting out for grant-maintained status extends, the role of the local education authority will be further reduced. Its responsibilities for planning provision will be at first shared with the Funding Agency for Schools and will be taken over by them if and when 75 per cent of schools opt out (Department for Education, 1992).

The recognition that local authorities were part of a network of agencies and organisations with which they had to work if they were to resolve the problems and issues faced by local communities supported the development of the enabling role in the wider senses of that term discussed in Chapter 2. The fragmentation of the government of local communities created a need for integrative mechanisms which local authorities cannot meet by direct action, but only by action through a network of organisation.

The recognition of the importance of inter-organisational relations has been increased by financial pressures. These have led to local authorities recognising that they had to work with other organisations that could bring additional resources in dealing with problems faced in local communities as housing authorities worked with housing associations and with development firms to meet housing need.

Legislation has placed its own requirements upon local authorities. Compulsory competitive tendering requires local authorities to put out certain specified services to tender and to award the contract on the basis of commercial decisions. This can mean that work previously carried out by the local authority is now carried out by a private contractor, although in practice by far the majority of contracts have been awarded to direct service organisations (DSOs) within the local authority. Such DSOs are in their own way becoming almost separate organisations, governing their relations with the local authority by a contract in the same way as a private contractor.

In similar ways the legislation on community care has led to the government encouraging local authorities to develop a mixed economy of care. Local authorities will deliver services directly but should also make increasing use of the voluntary sector or of the private sector.

Under the pressures of legislation and of financial constraints, faced with new challenges in what is an increasingly complex legislative framework, the model of local authorities structured for the provision of services through their own organisation is increasingly inappropriate as a guide to the working of local authorities.

For all these reasons the role of inter-organisational networks and relationships in the operations of local authorities has increased enormously in significance over the past decade. A local authority operates in many different ways in inter-organisational relations. Services can be delivered on behalf of the local authority through private contractors, cooperatives, companies formed through management buy-outs, voluntary bodies or through a joint agency formed with other local authorities or public bodies. A local authority can form companies or enter into partnerships with other organisations. A local authority regulates, inspects and licenses other organisations. It will use its statutory powers to:

- assist initiatives by other organisations;
- act as advocate or lobbyist, influencing other organisations;
- advise and guide, providing information and insights into opportunity.
- can be a forum for raising issues about other organisations
- be a stimulus to other organisations to come together.

Brooke (1989) has set out a categorisation of the different forms that 'networking' can take:

> *control*: contracting out
> *partial control*: the 'arms-length' agency
> *partnership*: joint operations
> *part ownership*: joint boards and committees
> *purchasing*: the use of the market
> *support*: the voluntary sector
> *regulatory*: enforcement by compulsion
> *influence capacity*: persuasion and networking.

All these forms of relationship have come to be of increasing importance in the work of a local authority. In this chapter we highlight three of these forms of relationship which have been of particular significance recently: part-ownership (joint boards and committees); the capacity to influence (especially in relation to economic development and the environment); and control (contracting out).

Part ownership (joint boards and committees)

The impact of reorganisation

The reorganisation of 1974 rejected the recommendations of the Redcliffe Maud Report for the creation of unitary authorities (outside the three metropolitan areas it proposed). It created a two-tier system of local government with different divisions of functions in the metropolitan and non-metropolitan areas. But the 1974 local government reorganisation was itself only part of a wider reorganisation. At the same time new water authorities and new health authorities were created, taking over some of the functions of local government. The changes were most marked in the former county boroughs, whose functions were divided between four different authorities, but affected the whole of local government. It meant that local authorities had to recognise not merely that they operated in a network of organisations, but that those organisations were a part of the system by which local communitites were governed.

The response was a new interest in relations between local authorities and other governmental organisations. This was reflected in the emphasis given by the Bains report to the community approach. It focused on the relations between county and districts:

> In the course of our enquiries we have seen and heard a great deal about the conflict and general lack of cooperation which is said to exist between authorities in some areas at the present time, and there has been, in the evidence submitted to us, a recognition that authorities must in the future establish much closer working relationships than in the past . . . We have throughout this report urged local authorities to adopt a corporate approach to the management of their affairs. We believe that there is in many ways an equal need for what has been termed a 'community' approach to the problems and the needs of areas . . . the need as we see it is for each authority to be aware of, and take into account, the interaction between plans,

policies and functions for which it is responsible and those of other authorities (Bains, 1972, p.92).

The 1974 reorganisation highlighted the reality that local authorities had always operated as part of a wider network of organisations. It made that reality much more visible and created pressure for new approaches. The response adopted was the creation of joint committees and initiatives in joint planning. The Bains Committee recommended the creation of joint committees as a means of community planning. The legislation that set up the new health authorities which divided community health services from the services run by local authorities set up a formal framework for joint planning and required the setting up of joint consultative committees between health authorities and local authorities (Webb and Wistow, 1986).

These attempts to deal with the issues posed by the new divisions in the structure of agencies at local level proved an inadequate response, probably because of their emphasis on formal mechanisms of coordination or joint planning, rather than on the relationships on which they depended. However, the experience of joint working which followed from the 1974 Act – particularly that between counties and districts – has become a particular focus of interest in relation to the abolition of the Greater London Council and the six Metropolitan County Councils (MCCs) in 1986, and the setting-up of the Local Government Commission in 1992 to review the structure of local government – England outside the metropolitan areas and Greater London.

Joint action between authorities can take a number of different forms. It is important in the first instance to distinguish between *professional/technical* and *political* forms of joint action. Table 9.1 sets out a typology of the different possibilities.

There is no implication that joint arrangements at the *professional/technical* level necessarily require joint arrangements at the *political* level. They may or may not. It depends on the level of *political salience* of the activity concerned. In general it is true to say that inter-authority cooperation over problems with a *wider territorial dimension* (e.g. the planning/provision of public transport) does normally require political machinery, whilst inter-authority cooperation over *specialist skills/facilities* does not, although there have been several exceptions to both these generalisations.

TABLE 9.1   Typology of joint action

Professional/technical level		Political level
A Joint 'contracting out' to a private sector or voluntary sector organisation		D Informal political co-operation
B Agency arrangements		E Joint Committee
C 'Specialist units'		F Joint Board
C1 Jointly financed		
C2 Self-financing		
C3 Seconded from participating authorities on temporary/ irregular basis		

The distinction between joint committees and joint boards is an important one, and merits further explanation. A Joint Board is a

> corporate body, created by order of a Minister, and in many cases requiring the approval of Parliament. It has perpetual succession, a common seal, and it can hold land. It has independent financial powers, including the power to borrow, and obtain, the money it needs from constituent authorities by means of precepts. The term of office of members of a Joint Board depends on the provision of the Order by which it was established (Cross, 1982, p.78).

On the other hand, Joint Committees:

> have no corporate status independent of their constituent authorities, and cannot hold property, borrow or precept. They may be set up under the general power in S.102 of the 1972 Local Government Act, whereby authorities are empowered to discharge their functions through joint committees. Expenses are defrayed amongst constituent authorities as agreed. Joint committees are the creatures of the authorities creating them. Both their constitution and the powers are controlled by and may be terminated by the constituent authorities (Cross, 1982, p.79).

Thus the key distinction is that whilst joint committees are the creatures of authorities participating on a *voluntary* basis (and can be withdrawn from or disbanded within agreed 'notice' provisions), joint boards are in effect *permanent* 'single-purpose' executive bodies, with considerable powers of decision-making and expenditure in their own right.

Circumstances governing the effectiveness of joint action
On the basis of work by Flynn and Leach (1985), Leach *et al.* (1987) and Leach (1992) it is possible to develop a framework setting out the circumstances in which joint action (of any kind) tends to be relatively effective (i.e. to achieve what it is set up to achieve) and those in which it is relatively ineffective (i.e. fails, to a greater or lesser extent, to do so). The framework, which has important implications for the current debate about the need for, and likely effectiveness of, joint action in 'unitary' systems, is set out in Table 9.2.

Two caveats should be made in relation to this framework. First, it is probabilistic, not deterministic, in nature. It is (for each component) based on an 'all other things being equal' assumption. A factor generating a tendency towards ineffectiveness (e.g. high political salience) may be outweighed by a factor generating a tendency towards effectiveness (e.g. joint financial benefit).

Second, the framework was developed at a time when the financial context in which local authorities operated, although perceived at the time as 'difficult' (and requiring close attention to the costs of joint action) was, in retrospect, considerably less critical than the present circumstances of 'universal charge-capping'. This means that cost issues involved in joint action (how the costs of support of a joint unit are to be distributed amongst the authorities involved) are likely to be an even more significant part of local authorities' calculations than they were in the early 1980s, and are more likely also to be drawn into the political arena than they were then.

It should be noted that the higher the level of political salience of an issue requiring joint action, then the more likely it is that the joint action will be problematical *unless* the issue is made the responsibility of a separate executive body (e.g. a joint board) in which case, however politically contentious the decisions involved, there will exist an explicit mechanism for resolving them. The

TABLE 9.2 The conditions of joint action

Variables affecting joint action	Circumstances implying higher potential for effectiveness	Circumstances implying lower potential for effectiveness
(1) Circumstances in which joint action is proposed	Voluntary choice by participants	Joint action 'enforced' or strongly recommended
	Status context of limited significance	Recent history of status change at political and/or professional level
(2) Characteristics of the political network	Subject of joint action has low political salience	Subject has high political salience
	Political network consensual, with no major differences of interest	Political network conflictual, with major differences of interest
	Small number of agencies	Large number of agencies
(3) Financial context	Subject of joint action generates income	Subject involves costs to participating authorities
	Clear basis for cost-apportionment	Disputed basis for cost-apportionment
(4) The nature of the task	Information collection and analysis	Policy-making or the preparation of plans
	Operation of an ongoing concern	Topic involving resource allocation

greater the extent to which high political salience is combined with a situation in which the authorities involved are controlled by parties with different political ideologies and interests, the more problems there are likely to be, and the less likely it becomes that anything less than a joint board will be able to resolve them.

The 'post-abolition' experience in the metropolitan areas
The arguments about the conditions of effective joint action are well-illustrated by the evidence of the operation of the joint arrangements in the metropolitan areas following the abolition of the GLC and the six metropolitan county councils in 1986 (see Leach *et al.* (1992)). The circumstances in which joint action was proposed were generally favourable in that all the districts felt that their status had been enhanced on the disappearance of the county, and (with some exceptions) districts felt an equivalence of status in the interactions (which was not true of the county/district interaction previously). Although joint action over strategic guidance was 'required' by the DoE, the potential benefits – control of the agenda and minimisation of the 'imposition' of DoE guidance was apparent to all districts. The remaining potential topics of joint action – e.g. the establishment of joint research and intelligence units (S.48 of the 1985 Local Government Act) were genuinely voluntary, and the districts judged whether or not to cooperate on the basis of financial or technical considerations. However, the nature of the task – the identification of (policy) guidelines and the preparation of plans is not one for which voluntary joint action is typically effective and this was illustrated by the relatively bland and anodyne nature of the guidance agreed. Consideration of the 'nature of' the task' also explains why research and information units have been so firmly directed toward the collection and analysis of information and precluded from drawing out its policy implications. It is also pertinent in this connection that whilst joint *studies* on the scope for future shopping development have been agreed, joint action on the *location of new developments* has been much more difficult to achieve, as the experience in Greater Manchester shows. The high political salience of this kind of shopping decision was relevant also. As soon as the choice of sites was highlighted the district planning officers were no longer able to control the agenda, and

'political' considerations began to dominate. Finally, in almost all the MCC areas, the nature of the political network has been conducive to effective joint action with Labour control dominant within the districts, but with the few Conservative-controlled or hung authorities generally able to forge good working relationships with the other districts in the area (Merseyside 1986–8 providing a notable exception).

The previous experience of joint boards and committees suggests that *Joint Boards* have under many circumstances proved relatively effective in the discharge of their functions; they have not, however, proved successful in involving the constituent local authorities in the processes of decision-making; nor have they proved effective at overcoming problems of joint planning and coordination with other bodies, when these have arisen. On the other hand, *Joint Committees* have proved much more successful at involving their constituent authorities. This, however, has frequently been at the expense of the efficient and effective discharge of the function for which they were set up. It is almost as if a choice has to be made between the effective involvement of the local authorities and the effective discharge of the function (see Stewart, 1985).

The growth of 'influence capacity'

In economic development, local authorities have increasingly worked with and through private sector firms. They have assembled land and have provided factory units, and can provide grants or loans, or promote the area in exhibitions or events, often with chambers of commerce or other representatives.

But it is not merely in economic development that new forms of inter-organisational working have developed, beyond the traditions of direct provision. In Glasgow the Housing Department success-fully negotiated on behalf of its tenants for tariff and other concessions from the Electricity Board through a heating-with-rent scheme. A strategy for Thamesdown argued that:

An agreed and accepted vision of the kind of overall community we are seeking to achieve is vitally necessary both to motivate the Council's organisation and to enlist the support of many interests (Thamesdown, 1984, p.58).

It recorded:

> a firm determination to maintain and, where necessary, intensify a strong advocacy role on behalf of Thamesdown and its residents, businesses and workers (ibid, pp.5–6).

Gwynedd County Council has played a lead role in promoting the use of the Welsh language in other public organisations and in the community generally. Reading Borough Council in its strategy statement has argued:

> Partnerships with other agencies, benefiting Reading residents by alternative means will be even more important (we have not, for example, the capital resources required to construct the Council housing which would meet the demand for public-sector rented housing). So we must create effective relationships with housing associations to ensure the maximum amount of rented housing development in Reading (Reading, 1988).

Wiltshire County Council, like many counties, has developed a rural strategy;

> containing a vision of the future for Wiltshire's rural areas, in the face of growing threats to the viability of communities and to the natural and manmade environment (Wiltshire, 1988).

It recognised that it had to work with the district councils and other bodies who must therefore join in the preparation of the strategy. Amongst the agencies it sees as involved are the:

> Community Council for Wiltshire; Rural Development Commission; Council for the Protection of Rural England; Government Departments . . . Countryside Commission; Health Authorities; Tourist Board; Manpower Services Commission; Wiltshire Trust for Nature Conservation; Sports Council; National Farmers Union; Transport and General Worker's Union (Agricultural Section); Dioceses of Bristol and Salisbury; Housing Commission; Forestry Commission etc. (ibid).

Tendring District Council 'has created an enabling division to act as a resource for local voluntary and amenity groups in fulfilling community needs' (Ennals and O'Brien, 1990, p.37).

Kirklees Metropolitan Council cooperated with the Friends of the Earth in the preparation of a State of the Environment Report published in 1988. It was designed to be:

a fully integrated study of the Kirklees environment in order to provide a comprehensive overview of environmental conditions and trends, with particular reference to

(a) helping people to understand the factors which affect the quality of the environment in which they live;

(b) assisting the public, private and voluntary sector to develop a further understanding of, and concern for, the environment alongside an appreciation of the impact of their policies on the Environment.

(Kirklees, 1988)

While its recommendations are to the local authority, those recommendations do not necessarily involve direct action by the local authority. They involve, for example, the council lobbying Yorkshire Water on the application of measures to prevent pollution.

Control (contracting out)

Contracting-out has traditionally been little used as a mode of service delivery in British local government, but is now becoming increasingly important. In some cases, notably community care, local authorities are required to contract with the private and voluntary sectors; in others local authorities themselves are adopting a strategy of 'externalisation'. Contracting-out is being applied not only to manual services, such as refuse collection, but, increasingly, to professional services such as legal, personnel or property services. A number of local authorities have chosen to contract-out housing management to existing or specially established housing associations. Some have also contracted-out some residential care. A variety of approaches are being adopted, including contracting with external private companies, buy-outs, buy-ins, and facilities management systems. There are, as yet, no cases of total contracting-out of service delivery, but a number of authorities, such as Berkshire and Rutland, have gone a long way in that direction.

The decision on contracting out is, essentially, the 'make or buy' decision – whether it is more efficient and effective to purchase on the market, or to produce what is needed within the organisation. As Williamson has argued, the ease with which purchasing on the market can be used will depend upon uncertainty and opportunism. The greater is certainty about future needs, and the more clearly those needs can be described, the easier it is to write contracts and specifications, and for contractors to know what is required. Opportunism refers to the motivation and opportunity for contractors to pursue their own interests at the expense of the contracting organisation. The more difficult it is to measure performance, and to be clear about the relationship between the contractors' actions and result, the more possible is opportunism. The greater is uncertainty and opportunism, the more difficult is contracting-out.

Local authorities have used both competitive bidding and negotiated contracts. Where the market is relatively well-established, and it is relatively easy to evaluate contractors and to specify services, competitive bidding is more likely to be used. A number of authorities have adopted the competitive-bidding approach in voluntary contracting of building, cleaning, and refuse collection. In other cases, notably professional services, a negotiated contract may be seen as more appropriate. The difficulty of writing a specification can be overcome by detailed cooperative work with the contractor. Management buy-outs and buy-ins generally involve negotiated contracts, with the contractor guaranteed a proportion of work for a specified period.

The motives behind contracting may vary. In the smaller local authority it may be used because of the difficulties of recruiting staff and the dis-economies of small scale. The most common reason is the belief that services will be provided more cheaply by external contractors. Other motives include the wish to avoid the difficulties of staff management, to gain access to capital funding not available to the local authority, and to allow services access to a wider market. Different motives tend to lead to different approaches to contracting.

The contracting-out process involves the local authority in specifying what service is to be provided, letting the contract, and managing and monitoring contractor performance. Specification and contract-letting are complex processes, especially the first time they are done, and contract management can be expensive. Osborne and Gaebler (1992), quote figures of up to 20 per cent as the costs of adequate client-side management services. The costs of management of contracts let under the Local Government Act 1988 has generally been between 5 and 10 per cent of the annual contract value. These figures suggest that contracting-out is not likely to be a cheap option.

Contracting-out is easiest when outputs and outcomes can clearly be specified, but this is rarely totally possible, and many contracts specify, for example, methods and frequencies, rather than performance. In practice the majority of contracts are specified both in terms of performance and method. Most contract management systems relate payment in some way to performance, deducting money from payments if there is failure to perform adequately. Performance may be specified either in terms of specific outputs, or in terms of user satisfaction. Those local authorities that have contracted out have generally been satisfied with the performance that has resulted. Indeed, it is commonly argued that contracting-out improves performance, because it requires greater clarity on standards and quality than has traditionally been the case.

The approach to the management of contracts may be based on either trust or 'punishment'. The latter approach depends upon checking on performance, and exercising sanctions when there is a failure to meet adequate quality levels. This approach is most commonly used for relatively simple services, such as building, cleaning, or refuse collection. Most contract managers emphasise the importance of trust, even in relatively simple contracts. They argue that effective performance depends upon cooperative relations between the local authority, as client, and the contractor. The argument is in line with more general findings on the operation of contracts. Authorities tend to see their role as being not so much to control contractors, but to work with them to ensure proper provision. Contract management then involves:

- regular client–contractor meetings to discuss performance and spending;

- service improvement meetings and service review;
- dealing with variations to the specification;
- payments;
- dealing with complaints and failure.

Simple services tend to emphasise inspection and monitoring, but more complex services such as social care, require a much more developed contract-management process.

Contract-management has developed in a fairly ad hoc fashion, focusing predominantly on direct monitoring and control. Skills of client-side management will take some time to develop. The ability to manage services has, traditionally, been based upon close contact with service provision, but that contact will be reduced in the enabling, contract-based, authority. The ability to manage services at arm's length will require the development of new processes and abilities. The move to more extensive contracting-out will raise issues about the appropriateness of traditional patterns of departmental organisation. Authorities may, for example, choose to set up central client-monitoring units. Many authorities, following the development of contracts under the Local Government Act 1988, have felt that there is a need for more integration on the client-side, to ensure that the contract management and monitoring role receives adequate attention.

The development of contracting-out leads to the contrasting dangers of excessive contractor power, and loss of interest. Power may arise from monopoly, especially where the contractor gains information that puts them at an advantage in future rounds of contracting. So far, this danger does not appear to be very great, and there seems to be a growing market in most services. The danger of loss of interest is that the contractor will tend to give lower priority to the local authority, if more lucrative markets emerge. There is some indication that this happened in some cases with computer contracts. The greatest difficulty is likely to arise if contractors go into liquidation as happened in the case of a major leisure contractor in 1991, and local authorities have to deal with a sudden gap in service provision. It is easier to cope with such problems if the contractor does not have a monopoly, and other providers can extend their provision. Alternatively local authorities may choose to keep a proportion of service in-house to act a brake on contractor opportunism, and to be able to step in should external contractors fail.

The move to much more extensive contracting-out raises issues about the nature of public-service motivation and how it links to private provision. Service motivation may conflict with commercial interest. Work on the provision of health services in various countries has shown the difficulties of creating systems of provision that deal adequately with the relation between payment and the quantity and quality of service provided. Contracting-out also leads to issues of accountability, because the clear reporting lines that characterise internal provision are broken. Issues of probity will need to be dealt with in contract-management systems.

The development of contracting-out as a mode of service delivery forces local authorities to be clear about what is core and what is peripheral. Authorities are, increasingly, developing a strategic core organisation that has responsibility for strategy and contracting. What is developing is an organisation that becomes a nexus of internal and external contracts. The boundary between organisation and market is becoming increasingly permeable.

Implications for internal management structures

Brooke has argued that the new emphasis on *external* relationships will lead to change in the organisational structure of local authorities:

> Committee structures will be changed not only to reflect the client/contractor split, but also to correspond to the larger preoccupation with overall welfare . . . the traditional structure and role of local authority departments will also not necessarily be appropriate to the needs of the enabling authority. A local authority free from executive responsibility can restructure its departmental organisation more easily to correspond to its overall strategy. The professional base can disappear; indeed a professionally oriented department may present that one-dimensional view which the local authority is anxious to reject in favour of a total approach. The Chief Executive is key to the change (Brooke, 1989, p.100).

As Brooke also makes clear, such a role would require new skills and changed attitudes. It will require skills in networking and understanding of other organisations and a readiness to operate in different modes of working. The management of influence has to be developed alongside the management of action and that implies an acceptance of the limitations of direct control by the authority.

Ennals and O'Brien studied the extent to which new ways of working outside the traditional departmental structure had been established to reflect the outward-looking enabling role. They found some examples which reflected an explicit response to this change in role emphasis. For example, Berkshire County Council is splitting staff into three categories: service strategists, service commissioners and service providers:

> Service strategists, normally the authority's most senior officers, work closely with members to analyse and assess needs in the community and identify potential sources for meeting that need (Ennals and O'Brien, 1990, p.36).

Generally, however, their conclusion was that, apart from the impact of compulsory competitive tendering there was:

> little evidence that structures at officer- or member-level have altered radically as a result of a move towards an enabling role . . . A number of authorities, however, recognised that change would be required in order for them to operate effectively as enabler on issues that did not fall neatly within traditional departmental or professional boundaries. A number also recognised that the role played by elected members would need to change to reflect what was expected of them in a new environment. Many authorities reported that they were considering how best to meet those requirements, but so far traditional structures have remained largely intact (Ennals and O'Brien, 1990, p.39).

The Ennals and O'Brien survey was carried out in 1989. From other work carried out since (Walsh, 1991; Leach *et al.*, 1992) we would except that there has been some acceleration in the erosion of traditional structures. These surveys confirm the crucial role of the Chief Executive in establishing an implementing the wider role discussed above. At member-level, the logical focus for the development of this perspective is the Policy and Resources Committee. In our judgement the Policy and Resources Committee will increasingly be recognised as having a community remit and a responsibility for network management. A community remit recognises that the council advised by the Policy and Resources Committee has a concern for problems and issues facing local communities that extends beyond the services provided. Responsibility for network management means that the Policy and Resources Committee has a responsibility for structuring and managing the relationship between the authority and outside agencies and organisations as well as structuring the units and the relationships within the authority. The Chief Executive clearly has a key role in advising the Policy and Resources Committee on these tasks, because his or her own responsibilities are not tied to particular units or services.

The new emphasis on the local authority as a central focus in a network of organisations implies a strengthening of strategic planning and management processes. These have been discussed at length earlier in the book, particularly in Chapters 4 and 6. But it is worth singling out here the particular relevance of 'strategic review' processes to the management of external relationships.

Strategic review

Strategic review is, in effect, a stocktaking in which the authority appraises its environment, public expectations and aspirations, political priorities and organisation capacity. As a process, it requires a broad perspective to be taken. In turn this requires an *organisational pause* – a distancing from the ordinary concerns of the day-to-day or operational management. Strategic review is a broad scanning process to enable key issues to be identified. Review must therefore be wide-ranging, looking beyond the activities of the local authority to the problems, needs and opportunities faced in the environment (Clarke and Stewart, 1991, p.31).

Such a process will necessarily encompass the changes in the environment and public aspiration beyond the needs at which its current services are directed. Appraisal of organisational capacity will cover not merely the local authority, but the network of organisations within which the authority operates. For example,

Coventry's State of the City Report aims to create a shared understanding, not merely in the council but in the city, of issues faced and citizens' views.

Managing in a network of organisations requires new understanding, skills and attitudes.

> An increasing part of the local government management task lies in working across organisational boundaries. This means that management objectives will often be achieved only if the manager is capable for working 'sideways' – that is influencing and persuading rather than instructing and directing. Managers must, therefore, acquire the skills and confidence necessary to cross
>
> - internal boundaries (i.e. within the authority and between departments);
> - external boundaries (i.e. with other organisations and agencies on the public, private and voluntary sectors).
>
> Local Government Training Board, 1988, p.18

The new emphasis on external orientation in local government requires organisational understanding beyond the local authority, which can come, in part, from officers with experience in and with other organisations – making the case for new career patterns. Amongst the skills required for the enabling role are negotiation and bargaining, networking, contract management. New forms of financial analysis will be required, bridging organisations and showing the total resources being used in dealing with shared issues and concerns. The enabling authority will need staff with a tolerance of uncertainty, a capacity for learning and listening across organisational boundaries and a readiness to work in new ways.

Conclusion

There are two issues which merit emphasis in this concluding section:

1. the importance in retaining a balance between the inter-organisational and intra-organisational dimensions in revising the internal structures and processes of local authorities;
2. limits to organisational networking.

Balancing inter- and intra-organisational dimensions

In this chapter, we have deliberately emphasised the way in which local authorities have been using external networks to achieve organisational goals. Yet provision of services *directly* is likely to continue and would be seen by many as one means of enabling local communities to meet their problems. The organisation and management of the local authority therefore has to combine a capacity for direct provision with the capacity for different modes of operation and the ability to choose between them.

Managing in and through a network of organisations involves indirect management rather than direct management and that requires new ways of working. The key point that has to be faced is that local authorities lack direct control. Except when using their regulatory powers or enforcing a contract, they lack the ability to instruct other organisations. The authority that lies within the organisation does not carry outside the organisation. There the management of influence may be more important than the management of action, and yet the organisational assumptions of local authorities have been formed by the management of the direct provision of services.

The local authority has important resources that it can use – finance, staff, land and property – but also information, powers and the public status to command attention and the political skills to use their position. These resources can be used in managing in and through a network of organisations, but that places its own requirements on the organisation. The language reflects the different requirements of the management of influence from the management of action. 'Networks' become more important than 'hierarchies'. 'Suggestions' are at the heart of management in a network rather than 'defined responsibilities'.

Limits to organisational networking

We have in this chapter provided a wealth of examples which illustrate the success with which local authorities have operated on a 'networking' basis. Successful partnerships have been established with the private sector and the voluntary sector, which local authorities have played a lead role in setting up. Contractual relationships have been established with private firms to provide a range of services. Joint action between local authorities has often been effective both between the tiers (county/district) or amongst authorities of the same status (inter-district). However, developing from these undoubted successes there is a danger of a glib conclusion that policies which require cooperation between agencies will invariably be successful. As illustrated in Table 9.2, the ease with which successful joint action can be achieved – or whether it can be achieved at all – depends crucially on the circumstances surrounding it. Opportunities for joint action – or indeed any other form of inter-agency working – which threaten a local authority's self-image, status, financial position or established domains of responsibility are much less likely to be well received than opportunities which sustain or strengthen any or all of these different attributes. The difficulties of inter-agency working should not be underestimated, and a realistic assessment of the gains and losses (in terms of finance, status and power) involved for other agencies in any proposal for inter-agency working is an essential attribute for an authority committed to a networking approach.

10   Changing Directions

In this concluding chapter, we first examine the extent to which the changes which we have described in local government management structures and processes can be seen as a movement towards a new type of management approach in local government. We argue that what is happening is that different local authorities are selecting contrasting priorities from amongst a set of wider core values, which, if then pursued consistently, will lead ultimately to varying patterns of organisational structure, strategy, systems and staff orientation. We identify three alternative types of strategic role (within the general ambit of 'enabling') – the *residual enabler*, the *market-oriented enabler*, and the *community-oriented enabler* – and show how these roles can be linked to an emphasis on management approaches emphasising the values, structures and systems of *business*, *customer* and *citizens* respectively. Finally, we return to the concept of 'organisational balance', and argue that rather than making a series of choices between polar oppositions (formal/ informal, centralised/decentralised, etc.), the key task is a search for a balance between each of a pair of different characteristics, *and* a balance in the development of, and emphasis on, strategy, structure, systems and processes, and staff-orientation respectively.

The pervasiveness of change and the concept of enabling

A theme which has become central in the previous chapters is the dominance of change and instability in the environment in which local authorities now operate. It is clear that the institution of British local government is in a state of flux, and has, since the mid-1980s, been operating in what organisational theorists term a 'turbulent environment'. The amount and scope of legislative change which has impinged upon local government, especially since 1987, has been unprecedented. As we conclude this book (October 1993) the Local Government Commission, which has been given the job of proposing structural changes in the local government system outside Greater London and the six metropolitan areas, has made its first recommendations. Local authorities are facing up to a further set of services to which compulsory competitive tendering (CCT) will shortly be introduced, including, for the first time, several professional and central support services such as architectural design and computing. Ways of streamlining internal management systems are being considered in the wake of the 1991 DoE consultation paper on that topic. Schools are continuing to 'opt out', though less rapidly than before and further education and careers guidance are to transfer out of local government. Councils have recently made the transition from one form of local government finance – the community charge – to another – the council tax – and began to implement the requirements of the 1991 Community Care Act. The composition of police authorities is to change. Many authorities are facing their most severe financial crisis in living memory.

These changes have raised important issues for the ways in which local authorities organise themselves, and the choices of management structures and processes which are appropriate to the new, but constantly changing, circumstances in which they operate. Change and instability appear endemic. This raises the question of to what extent there is a *pattern* in the changes which are taking place. Are we witnessing a period of transition between one form of a local authority and another, guided by a 'vision' of where local government is going, so that by the mid-1990s a new 'stable state' will have been reached? Or is the pattern of change less consistent and less guided by a common vision that this? Are we witnessing instead the destabilising effect of a series of *ad hoc* measures which do not 'add up' to a coherent whole, and which will leave local government as unclear about its role and purpose in the mid-1990s as it seems to be today?

The answer, in our view, lies somewhere between these two extremes. The government would no doubt argue that it does have a 'coherent vision' for local government, in which the key element is the concept of the 'enabling authority'. But as we have already seen, the 'enabling authority' is a loose and unspecific concept (we have described it elsewhere (Leach, 1992) as a 'concept of infinite elasticity') which does not, unless it is much more explicitly defined by the government, and unless its implications are much more systematically thought through and applied, provide either a new vision for local government, or a new approach for management.

In 1987–9, when Margaret Thatcher was Prime Minister, Nicholas Ridley was Secretary of State for the Environment, and the Adam Smith Institute was power in the land, it did seem that a coherent vision of local government was beginning to emerge. It was epitomised by the Adam Smith Institute's 'Wiser Counsels' and Nicholas Ridley's pamphlet, *The Local Right*. It was a vision which implied a 'residual' role for local government. Local authorities were seen as 'enablers' in the extremely limited sense of agencies which made arrangements for the provision of the limited number of services which the market could not provide, acting as a kind of 'safety net'.

Fortunately for local government, this particular vision has lost its force, even if it has not totally disappeared, in the wake of the disappearance from the centre-stage of British politics of all its main enthusiasts and advocates! However, the essence of the current Government's concept of 'enabling' is still very much focused on the separating provision and production of services; enabling is concerned in this sense with finding new ways of delivering services through agencies other than the local authority itself.

As we have seen, the concept of enabling developed by Michael Clarke and John Stewart (1989a) involves a very different interpretation of the concept (see p.39 above). Clarke and Stewart define enabling in terms of:

> *strengthening the capacity for self-governance within a local community*, using whatever resources and channels (internal or external) seem most appropriate. (emphasis added)

The starting point here is the identification of community needs. The enabling authority uses a wide range of powers, including the powers of civic leadership, networking, influence and campaigning, to meet those needs.

Thus, given the wide variety of potential interpretations of enabling – finding new ways of delivering services, stimulating local economic activity, providing a regulatory framework for private sector production and distribution, meeting community needs, and civic leadership – we do not regard the mere use of the word as in itself a convincing basis for a new vision of local government's role and purpose.

A choice of future directions?

There is something of a hiatus in the debate about the future direction of local government, which the general election result of April 1992 did little to change. It is possible, however, to give some structure to the discussion by identifying a number of key themes and dimensions of the debate. By pinpointing these dimensions and exploring the effects of possible combinations thereof, important areas of choice are clarified. Three such dimensions are identified here:

1. the economic dimension;
2. the governmental dimension;
3. a dimension concerned with the form of local democracy (see Leach and Stewart, 1992).

The economic dimension

In the Conservative Government's legislative programme since 1987 there has been an increasing emphasis on the role of the market in local government, both as an alternative source of provision of the services which had for a long time been regarded as more appropriately provided by the public sector, and as a set of conditions which should be replicated as far as possible for the provision of services – the concept of quasi-markets. It is possible to argue that a key dimension of the current debate is the choice between market emphasis in the production and distribution of local goods and services and emphasis on public-sector agencies in the production and distribution of local goods and services.

The governmental dimension

This dimension distinguishes between a *weak* role for local government (in the sense of a narrow range of functional responsibilities, a reactive mode of operation, a low level of autonomy/

discretion within those functions, and a high degree of external control), and a *strong* role (implying a wider range of functions, a positive mode of operation, high levels of autonomy/discretion and limited levels of external control). It reflects the familiar dilemma of central–local relationships which has long been a central feature of debate about the role of local government, although under-pinned, since the early 1980s, by a move towards the 'weak' local government position.

The form of democracy dimension

This dimension distinguished between two different bases on which local authorities reach decisions. At one extreme there is an emphasis on *representative democracy*, a system in which community preferences are expressed through the local electoral system. Once elected, the successful party – or cooperating parties in a hung council – regards itself as having a mandate to implement the policies set out in its election manifesto. At the other extreme, there is an emphasis on *participatory democracy*, in which the participation of local communities, and democratic forums is seen as an essential ingredient in local decision-making, within a framework of policies legitimised through electoral success.

One of the ways of presenting these dimensions is through a three-dimensional matrix (see Figure 10.1). To identify extreme points of what is, in effect, a continuum of possible ideological positions is helpful for pinpointing the basic choices implicit in discussions about the future of local government. In practice, most political parties, most of the time, are likely to argue that they favour a more 'balanced' approach, a position around the middle point of each continuum identified. In real life, arguments about the need for a balance between the role of markets and the role of the public sector in the provision of local goods and services, a balance between central direction and local autonomy, and a balance between representative and participatory democracy are likely to be presented. However, our aim in this final chapter is to draw out the implications of some of the extreme positions, to help to highlight the underlying choices involved in the future of local government, and to analyse the significance of these choices for approaches to internal organisation and management.

FIGURE 10.1 Dimensions of choice

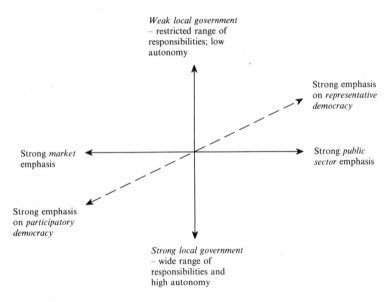

To simplify the argument and strengthen its relevance it is most helpful to concentrate on a selection of 'ideal types' of local government systems which have actually been advocated by those seeking to clarify the role of local government over the past few years. Four models – the *traditional bureaucratic authority*, the *residual enabling authority*, the *market-oriented enabling authority* and the *community-oriented enabling authority* can be identified on this basis. Their positions on the matrix are depicted in Figure 10.2.

The 'traditional bureaucratic authority' combines a relatively strong public-sector emphasis with a relatively strong local governance role and an emphasis on representative democracy. Although this model was the predominant form of system in the 1970s and early 1980s, and is one which still finds favour today amongst many local authorities, it is very difficult to sustain in the light of government legislation, exhortations to move towards an enabling role, and the loss of real power. It is best seen as the starting-point for change, from which a movement in another direction is now required. The three directions most commonly canvassed are the *residual enabling authority* (which combines

FIGURE 10.2   Dimensions of choice and ideal types

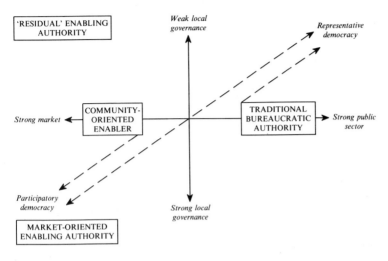

Note: Because of the difficulties of depicting a three-dimensional matrix in two
         dimensions, it should be pointed out for the purposes of clarification that
         both the community-oriented enabling authority and the traditional
         bureaucratic authority are intended to be depicted at the midpoints of the
         strong/weak market and strong/weak local government continua.

strong market emphasis, weak local governance role and a neutral
stance on form of democracy), the *market-oriented enabler* (strong
market emphasis, strong local governance role, representative
democracy emphasis), and the *community-oriented enabler* (strong
participatory democracy emphasis, and at least a mid-point
position in relation to local governance and market/public sector
emphasis). We provide below pen pictures of the four types of local
authority implied by these terms.

The 'traditional bureaucratic' authority

The 'traditional bureaucratic' organisation can be seen as the
archetypal local authority of the period 1945–80, striving for high
self-sufficiency (the combination of strong public-sector emphasis/
strong local-governance role) but never really being granted the

financial and policy autonomy to achieve it. In this type of authority there was a strong emphasis on service delivery and on the local council as direct provider of a set of discrete services, rather than as a vehicle for community governance. Statutory duties were seen as the *raison d'être* of the council; professional disciplines formed the basis of departmental and committee organisation. Public needs were interpreted by professional officers who tended to view service recipients as clients in a passive sense. This type of authority did not spend much time identifying community needs which did not fit with the current pattern of service provision. There was a strong emphasis on the benefits of public-sector provision and an expectation, though not necessarily a high degree of utilisation, of a high level of local discretion in the service provision. Representative democracy, expressed organisationally through service committees, was seen as the major vehicle for local democracy and local accountability. Participatory democracy was not favoured.

It was this form of local authority, which formed the basis of many of the public attacks on local government by successive Thatcher governments in the 1980s. Indeed, it can be argued that the impetus for the recent legislative changes was as much a reaction to bureaucracy, as a positive application of market philosophies to the world of local government.

The residual enabling authority

The term 'residual' refers to the emphasis placed in this 'ideal type' upon the local authority as a 'provider of last resort', responsible only for a limited set of services, which cannot be provided directly through the private market or through some other, more appropriate, mechanism, for example, quango, development corporation, or a local office of central government. Even in the case of those 'residual' services for which a local authority would retain responsibility, it would not be expected that their responsibility would be exercised directly. Rather, the authority would be expected to specify the level of service required, 'contract-out' the service to a private contractor, or exceptionally to a local authority in-house contracting agency, and then to monitor the contractor's performance. There would also be some regulation of private-sector activity, but even this role would be minimised, because from this ideological standpoint, the market can be trusted as the most efficient and effective mechanism for providing goods and services, with only few exceptions and with only a limited need for regulation.

The key accountability relationship would be between the individual council tax-payer and the local authority, the exchange being viewed as involving as close an approximation as possible to a 'supermarket transaction' between customer and market organisation. Notions of community, in the sense of a wider 'social network' or territorial identity, are not seen as significant. As Margaret Thatcher said, 'there is no such thing as society'. The idea that a local authority should play any wider role, in defining and meeting local community needs, is seen as inappropriate. The local authority merely enables the provision of a limited range of public goods and services, which the external market cannot provide. The idea of the 'residual authority' is implicit in several of the publications of the Adam Smith Institute (see Adam Smith Institute, 1989) and the Institute of Economic Affairs (see Mather, 1989).

The market-oriented enabling authority

This ideal type emphasises, in common with the 'residual' authority, the primacy of the market in the affairs of the local authority, but from a very different starting-point. The philosophy of the 'market-oriented enabler' places the local authority in a much stronger and more active role in relation to the economic future of its area than does that of the residual authority. The local authority is seen as the key planning and coordinating agency for local economic development, providing a series of mechanisms and incentives through which the local economy can flourish. The planning role of the authority is given much more emphasis, embodying a view that a longer-term planned approach to land-use, infrastructure and transportation links is necessary for the effective operation of the local economy. The relation between the local authority and local economic concerns is seen as a two-way process. Social responsibility on the part of local employers is emphasised and 'planning agreements' between developer and local authority expected and actively negotiated. The concepts of 'leverage' and 'pump-priming' are emphasised in the local author-ity's approach to the encouragement and support of private enterprise.

Although the market would normally be relied upon in relation to the 'consumption' services which were the responsibility of the 'market-oriented enabler', primarily through the 'contract' me-chanism, the approach of this type of authority to the contracts involved would be different from that of the 'residual' authority. Attempts would be made to negotiate contracts which maximised the benefits to the local authority, rather than the adoption of the more passive 'least cost' contract-letting mechanism for a limited number of specified services emphasised by the residual authority. There would be more recognition of the need to regulate the activities of the private sector, premised on a lesser degree of implicit trust in the ability of the market to deliver, or at least to do so without undesirable externalities. The importance of the local authority as a focal point in a network of external, primarily private sector, linkages would be emphasised.

The 'market-oriented enabler' view of local government was implicit in several of the statements of Michael Heseltine in his earlier term of office as Secretary of State for the Environment (1979–82), although agencies other than local authorities for development corporations, were sometimes identified as alterna-tive focal agencies. Although this 'ideal type' is, by definition, more closely aligned with the approach of the Conservative Party than with the Labour Party, it is ideologically 'wet' or 'One-Nation' Conservatism rather than the dry/Thatcherite variant.

The community-oriented enabler

This 'ideal type', towards which it appears increasing numbers of authorities are now striving (see Ennals and O'Brien, 1990), is derived from the writings of Clarke and Stewart (1988, 1989 and 1989b) who argue that even in the apparently restrictive context of local authority operations caused by the post-1987 legislative programme, there remains an 'alternative' interpretation of the 'enabling authority' role. This 'ideal type' is premised on the view that a local authority exists, or should exist, to meet the varied needs of its population, using whatever channel of provision –

local-authority direct provision, private sector, voluntary sector, or influence – seem most appropriate.

There are emphases on this 'ideal type' – on collective, as well as individual, needs – and especially on the idea of communities. There is an emphasis on the role of the local-authority resident as citizen which goes beyond the implications of consumer/ customer roles. This ideal type implies a heightened emphasis on participatory democracy, although within a framework set by a more effective representative democracy (i.e. involving a greater emphasis on accountability than is possible through periodic elections) and community accountability. It implies an outward-looking, 'networking' role through which influence can be exerted. It is the alternative within which decentralised forms of local government most logically fit.

In principle, the emphases on participatory democracy and on effective representative democracy which form the essence of the community-oriented enabling role could operate in conjunction with either a weak or strong local governance role and a strong public provision or a strong market emphasis. It is, perhaps, less compatible with a weak-governance/strong-market emphasis than the alternatives. We have assumed a mid-point position in relation to each of the two other dimensions.

The main implication of this analysis is that there currently exists a significant degree of choice in the way in which local authorities can and do interpret the meaning and implications of the enabling role. A few have enthusiastically moved in the direction of the residual authority. Many more have operated in a way which is consistent with the position of market-oriented enabler. But the majority of authorities have come to see themselves as community-oriented enablers, at least in the sense of embracing responsibility for identifying and dealing, directly or indirectly, with a wide variety of community needs. The emphasis on the value of participatory democracy itself has typically been less marked. Although there appears to be something of a gap between vision and reality in some of the authorities which have taken up this position, and increasing financial constraint is reducing the scope for response to 'a wide variety of community needs', the 'community-oriented enabler' can still be regarded as a 'legitimate' position for a local authority to take up. Figure 10.3 illustrates the processes of choice involved.

FIGURE 10.3 Local government – direction of change

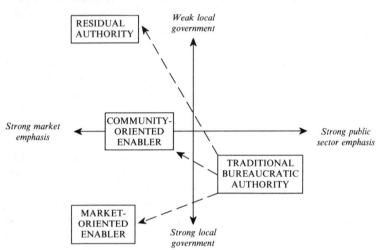

Patterns of dominant values

Further evidence of the way in which local authorities are interpreting this scope for choice has emerged from a recent research project carried out by two of the authors into the ways in which local authorities with a reputation for good management have adjusted their management approaches in response to the changing environments in which they operate (Leach, Walsh *et al.*, 1992). Different patterns could be identified in the structure, strategies, systems and culture of the authorities visited, depending on the dominant 'core values' which had been identified in that authority.

Three primary patterns could be identified: one organised around a set of core values which emphasised commercialism and a *business*-orientation; a second organised around values which were concerned with *responsiveness to customers*; and a third which was organised around the key value of *citizenship*.

There is, of course, a good deal of overlap between the three categories. A strong commitment to a business orientation necessarily implies that the needs and preferences of customers will be taken seriously. A strong commitment to customers implies a concern with business values, such as efficiency, and is often linked with a concern with citizenship. The important point is not the degree of overlap but the *starting-point*. Some of the authorities visited emphasised a primary commitment to a business-orientation, others to a citizen-orientation, and another group (the largest) to a customer-orientation.

There is a conceptual relationship between the three 'ideal types' of authority, reflecting different interpretations of enabling, and the three primary orientations identified in the research. The orientation towards business/commercialism has close philosophical links with the residual enabling authority. The community-oriented enabling role has strong philosophical links with an orientation towards citizenship. The authority with a primary orientation towards customer-responsiveness can not be so straightforwardly equated with a single ideal type, but would be closest to the market-oriented enabler. The stances taken toward the market and governmental roles did not necessarily reflect a positive enthusiasm for these value positions. More typically they reflected a grudging acceptance of reality! Figure 10.4 sets out the relationship between primary role orientation and dominant values.

FIGURE 10.4   Role-orientations and dominant values

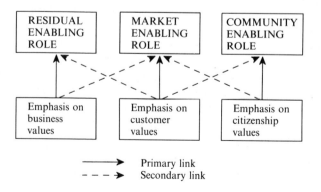

In the next section of this chapter we first explore the implications of the three primary role-orientations for the management and organisation of local authorities. We examine, in turn, the key principles of internal organisation, political management structures and roles, approaches to strategic and service planning, management systems and external relationships involved. The patterns of management discovered in those authorities emphasising, as dominant values, business methods, customers and citizens respectively, are then set out and interpreted.

The residual enabling authority

In the residual enabling authority the key principle of what would be a limited internal organisation would be contract-specification and management, with strong organisational separation of client and contractor roles if the latter were retained within the authority. Except in large authorities, the distinction between the strategic centre and service department would become unnecessary. There would be a minimal strategic/coordinative role for the centre, which could be combined with the contract specification and management role. The whole, small, organisation would in effect be 'the centre'.

In such an authority, operating a limited range of services almost wholly through contracts, a small management board of councillors, meeting at most two or three times a year to agree specifications, let contracts, receive monitoring reports and set the level of council tax is all that would be necessary. Because the strategic role and scope for policy choice in the residual authority would be extremely limited, councillors' roles in these activities would be correspondingly reduced. Similarly the representative role of councillors would not be required to any significant extent because of the limited responsibility of the authority. There would be little point in a system of elected mayors in this option because the political salience of the authority's activities could hardly be viewed as necessitating such a high-profile role. An appointed 'city manager', of the kind which operates in the Republic of Ireland, as the key reference point in the authority would be more in keeping with this ideal type.

Strategic, authority-wide, long-term planning, would be unnecessary in the residual enabling authority, where the most that would be required, beyond the purchase of a set of services, would be a minimal level of inter-service coordination. In relation to service planning, as the primary role of the residual authority is to 'fill gaps in the market', the main element would be the identification of such 'gaps'. Such an attempt could in theory be made on a medium-term basis. However, it has to be recognised that the residual enabling authority, by its very nature would be largely reactive to the market in its operations, and hence the scope for planning of any kind would be very limited, reflecting the familiar tension between 'market' and 'planning' approaches.

The systems which would be emphasised in the residual enabling authority would be those which had a primarily commercial or business focus such as business planning and marketing. Although systems of delegation of managerial control and devolved budgeting are also in principle appropriate in such an authority, the scope for this introduction would be limited because of the small number of *internal* employees within the organisation (the scope for service-level agreements would also be limited, for similar reasons). The small numbers of direct employees involved would, however, make the development of a set of common organisational values potentially relatively straightforward.

The main external relationships would be relationships with contractors. These apart, given the limited scope of activities and the minimal governmental role, there would be very little need to develop a wider set of linkages with other organisations.

The market-oriented enabling authority

Contract specification and management would also be one of the key organisational bases of the 'market enabler', but this type of authority would also need a stronger, separate strategic centre and active networking and advocacy roles. There would normally be a programme-area-based departmental structure, reflecting its greater range of service responsibilities. For an equivalent population size, its number of directly employed staff would be significantly higher than the residual authority (although lower than for the 'community enabler', or existing local authorities).

An executive management board would also be appropriate to the 'market-oriented enabling' authority, but would be a much more powerful political entity. It would play an active role in the development and operation of the economic development strategy emphasised in this 'ideal type'. In this context, the 'elected mayor' role would have its attractions. There would be a good deal of scope for a strong 'figurehead', with a high public profile and considerable entrepreneurial bargaining and networking skills. Equally, an executive board could play a strong role in such an authority. The political management structure, whatever form it took, would need to meet far more frequently than its counterpart in the residual authority. Although there would still be a strong emphasis on the politicians as 'board member' in this type of authority, equally important would be the roles of strategist, enabler and advocate. In neither the residual nor the market-oriented enabler, however, would there be much scope for the operation of the constituency role of members and its associated activities.

In the 'market-enabling' authority the key strategic emphasis would be on economic development. A planning document which provided 'strategic parameters' for the market would constitute an essential component of such an authority's work. Compared with the residual enabling role, the 'market enabler' role would imply a greater commitment to planning and development, partnerships, emphasising market regulation and selective market intervention. Longer-term service planning in the conventional sense would still be limited by the strong market emphasis of this 'ideal type', but, because of its more active enabling role, the commitment would be greater than in the 'residual' role. Similarly, the basis for service provision would be the 'mixed economy', rather than the market.

The management systems which would be emphasised in this model would include marketing, strategic management, inter-organisational management, and business planning. There would be more need and scope for devolved systems of managerial and financial control, reflecting the scope of this type of authority's activities, and its correspondingly larger number of employees. There would also be likely to be a greater emphasis on systems concerned with customer responsiveness – for example, quality assurance systems, customer contracts, given the significantly higher level of direct involvement of the market-enabling authority in service provision.

In the market enabler, the external relations role would be much stronger than in the residual enabler, with the local authority increasingly seen as 'ring-holder' within a network of primarily private-sector interests.

The community-oriented enabling authority

In the 'community-enabler', the appropriate principles of internal organisation would be matrix management; decentralisation; area-based, rather than profession-based, departments, and inter-professional cooperation. There would be a small, but influential, 'strategic centre'. As in the market enabling authority, strong political executives would be implied, but a different sort of political executive, allowing more space for wider political participation. In this case an 'elected mayor' would not be appropriate. A different type of two-tier political management system would be implied for the 'community enabler' authority; a central executive with responsibility for overall strategy and policy formulation responsibilities, and a set of area committees with considerable devolved powers to achieve those policies, which would emphasise the 'representative' role of the majority of council members, but a representative role that gained strength from the active involvement of the community, rather than based on the fact of election alone. In these circumstances, a relatively large number of councillors would be appropriate, compared with the relatively small numbers necessary to operate the residual and 'market enabling' models.

The local representation, or constituency, role involving local decision-making, casework, and local advocacy, would be much more important in the 'community enabler' authority – where it would be given institutional recognition through the 'area' or 'neighbourhood' committee – than in the other two alternatives. There would also exist relatively strong strategic and policy-making roles for elected members to provide a framework for local choice. In general, party politics *per se* would play a much stronger role in community-enabling and, to a lesser degree, market-enabling authorities than in the 'residual' enabling authority.

A 'community strategy', starting out from an attempt to identify community needs comprehensively, whilst recognising that the authority was not directly empowered to deal with all the needs identified, would be an essential element in the operations of the 'community-enabler' authority. There would also be a variety of forms of service provision varying with differences in local need and preference and with local communities playing an active role in service provision wherever possible. There would be less emphasis on the authority of the professional, and on the boundaries of professional disciplines, than in the traditional bureaucratic model. Service planning would be decentralised and based on local needs, interpreted within broad, centrally defined guidelines.

On management systems, the emphasis in the community enabling authority would be on mechanisms which reflected the wide scope of the authority's role – for example, strategic management – in setting frameworks; and on citizenship – for example citizen's charters, but charters that interpreted citizenship as being more than customer equity in service delivery and decentralisation. This does not imply that customer-oriented systems or business methods would be neglected, but rather that the emphasis would be different. In this type of authority one would also expect a relatively strong emphasis on systems for developing and motivating staff.

In the 'community enabler' authority there would be a wide network of external relations built around the central-enabling role of the local authority itself. There would be links not just to local people, but also to local agencies, for example, the private sector, other public sector and voluntary sector agencies of all kinds.

What we have attempted to demonstrate in this section, is that the future direction of change in relation to the organisation and management of local authorities cannot be seen as a linear development. The emphasis on different types of structure, process and system will differ depending upon what stance an authority is taking to its primary role and purpose (see Figure 10.3). The differences involved have been analysed and illustrated in the preceding pages. Central government may, in future, specify a preferred direction, based on a more explicit conception of role and purpose, or it may introduce legislation which make any of the existing choices of direction more or less difficult. However, few clear signals of this kind have emerged from central government over the past few years. Indeed, it can be argued that different central initiatives have implied different directions of change. The extension of CCT, the further measures to encourage opting-out in education and the pressures to set up 'arm's-length' housing management agencies are all compatible with a move towards the residual authority. However, the emergence of elected mayors and 'cabinet government' on the DoE agenda is clearly not compatible with this kind of direction. The strengthening of the political executive role at the local level is much more consistent with a more active interpretation of enabling, particularly with the market-oriented enabler role. In contrast, the new emphasis on the importance of community in the Policy Guidance to the Local Government Commission, and the proposals to strengthen town and parish councils, indicates a growing interest in participatory democracy and, possibly, a community-oriented enabling role for local authorities.

Patterns of management under different core values

There is a further way in which the variety in management approaches currently being adopted by local authorities can be illustrated. In the work by Leach and Walsh (1992) on well-managed authorities, it was possible to relate different patterns of core values to different patterns in the introduction of management systems and processes. Three primary value groups have been identified – business/commercial values, customer values and citizenship values. Local authorities were asked to rank a list of sixteen organisational values in priority order. Table 10.1 sets out the rank order of the values concerned. Two questionnaires were used in the research; one on the relative priority given to different organisational values; the other on the extent to which different types of organisational system had been introduced.

There are a number of interesting features of this ranking. It reveals how far local government has moved from the values of the late 1970s and early 1980s, when it was highly likely that consensus and professionalism would have appeared in a higher position, and responsiveness to the public and creativity in a lower position. It is, perhaps, surprising how low a ranking the value of commercialism achieves. This finding is, in fact, in line with the evidence from interviews, that in authorities which had embraced a commercial approach most enthusiastically in the past, there had recently been something of a retreat from an emphasis on 'commercialism' in itself. Indeed, in one authority we were told 'we have been moving away from a predominantly commercial and competitive approach

TABLE 10.1   Rank order of organisational values

1.	⸙ Effectiveness
2.	Responsiveness to the public
3.	Accountability
4.	Fairness
5. =	ℓ Efficiency
	Political sensitivity
7.	Communication with the public
8. =ℓ	Economy
	Creativity
	Realism
11. =	Caring for staff
	Communication with staff
13.	ℓ Equality
14.	Professionalism
15.	Commercialism
16.	Consensus

to a more corporate and managerial one'. The relative position of the four Es is also significant: Effectiveness at the top, Efficiency and Economy close behind, which reflects the recent worsening of local authorities' financial circumstances and room for manoeuvre, and Equality languishing, relatively speaking, in thirteenth position.

The analysis was extended by grouping the values concerned in categories comprised of values which are similar, or which reinforce one another. The results are shown in Table 10.2 (some values can be interpreted in different ways and are included in more than one category).

These findings suggest that the group of core values given the highest ranking are those associated with a customer-orientation. In this category *all* the relevant values enjoy a relatively high ranking. In relation to groups of core values associated with a citizen-orientation and a business-orientation, average rankings are lower. But more telling perhaps are the differences which emerge between the 'lead values' within each broader category. In our judgement the best single indicator of customer-orientation is 'responsiveness to the public'; of citizen-orientation 'equality'; and of business orientation 'commercialism'. These three values ranked 2, 13 and 15 respectively, demonstrating again the strength of the customer ethic which currently pervades authorities. A

TABLE 10.2 Categorisation of core values

Core Values (Customers)		Core values (citizens)		Core values (business)	
Responsiveness to the public	2	Equality	13	Commercialism	15
Accountability	3	Accountability	3	Economy	8 =
Efficiency	5 =	Fairness	4	Efficiency	5 =
Effectiveness	1	Communication with the public	7 =		
Communication with the public	7 =				

254 Changing Organisation and Management of Local Government

concern with staff (as measured by 'caring for staff' and 'communication with staff' respectively) invariably comes further down the list for those authorities stressing the 'customer' values. In many authorities it would appear that the interests of customers are now clearly ranked above those of staff.

The extent to which the groups of values within the broad categories of 'consumerism', 'citizenship' and 'business-orientation' hang together is borne out by a study of the responses of individual authorities. Those authorities which place a relatively high emphasis on *commercialism* also tend to emphasise the values of 'economy' and 'efficiency'. Those which place a relatively high value on *equality* also tend to emphasise fairness, accountability and communication with the public. And those which place most emphasis on *responsiveness to the public* invariably also rank efficiency, effectiveness and accountability highly, although not communication with the public, which does not follow the pattern of the other variables in the group.

These findings are consistent with the more qualitative impressions gained from interviews. The three alternative patterns of cultural emphasis – customer, citizen and business orientation – did fit broadly with the authorities' own perceptions of core values. Although no authority ignored the values' association with the other two orientations, in many cases the primary emphasis was clear.

Other conclusions from the questionnaire and interview data are worth highlighting. In some authorities it was our strong impression that a concern with staff had become out of balance with other elements of managerial change. Middle managers were not always clear in which overall direction the authority was going, or how the mass of new initiatives which had been generated by the centre interrelated. Sometimes this bemusement reflected a lack of clarity at the centre about such issues, but in other cases the problem was one of communication.

In all authorities visited there was to be found, amongst middle managers, perceptions of higher expectations, increasing pressure, longer hours, and a need to develop a range of new skills relatively quickly. Although in almost all cases, motivation remained high, one sensed that further increases in pressures/demands could result in a process of fairly rapid demotivation, in those authorities where middle managers felt that they were not adequately supported or valued.

In several authorities it was recognised that the level of formal commitment to a 'customer orientation' within the authority was not yet matched by an ability to put it into practice. In one authority it was noted that 'there is a lot of talk about customers, but very little work on customer care, consultation or user involvement'.

The relative ease with which business systems could be introduced compared with those which emphasised customers, citizens or staff was recognised in many authorities, together with an awareness of a resulting imbalance in the array of systems currently developed. Indeed, in a few authorities, a concern to rethink the appropriateness of some of these business systems had emerged. Service-level agreement systems, for example, were the subject of some criticism. They were often seen as over-bureaucratic. Delegation of managerial control was sometimes not working well because of the lack of adequate management and financial information.

In some authorities, one of the most fundamental processes of all – the budget process – had not yet been remodelled to bring it into line with other elements of the changed approach to management. In those authorities which had developed strategic planning systems, there is a self-evident need to link this system with the budget process, if the strategy is not to become an empty symbol. But whatever dominant value perspective is adopted – business, customer or citizen – it is highly unlikely that a traditional incremental budget process would be appropriate. Most authorities we visited had recognised this and had either developed a policy/priority-led budget process or were working towards this end. Some, however, had hardly begun to tackle this issue.

The important general point to be emphasised is again the point about *selectivity*. There currently exists a wide array of management systems which have been advocated widely, many of them relatively recent developments as far as local government is concerned. Their relevance, or at least relative priority, to individual local authorities depends, in most cases, on the choice of authority role, residual enabler, market enabler, community enabler and so on – and the set of core values – business, customer, citizen – with which the choice of role is associated. A certain amount of consistency of pattern in the relative emphasis placed on different systems is apparent from the evidence. Well-managed local authorities ensure that their choice of systems reflects their conception of identity.

The characteristics of the well-managed authority

Despite the emphasis on the importance of local authorities making choices between primary roles, core values and arrays of management systems, it was noticeable in the survey described that there were a number of qualities which all or most of the well-managed authorities seemed to possess, whatever choice of direction they had made. A 'composite picture' of the qualities of a well-managed authority, well-managed in the sense of demonstrating a capacity to respond appropriately to the pressures facing it, whilst retaining a strong proactive sense of its own direction/vision can be developed. The qualities are listed in summary form below:

- A clear sense of direction expressed in the form of a 'strategic vision' or similar statement, which is specific to the particular circumstances of the authority concerned.
- Common ownership of a hierarchy of values in which a particular philosophy of local government can be identified.
- An emphasis on 'customer care' within the core values, without this concept necessarily forming the central element thereof.
- A development of customer-care (and other customer-oriented) systems and procedures to implement the formal commitment to this value.
- A commitment to informing, developing and motivating staff, to create a climate of identity and motivation which can deal effectively with the pressures of change.
- A system of performance review which is central to the operation of the authority and accepted by those operating it as a benefit rather than an imposition.
- A capacity to identify and readiness to acknowledge failures as well as successes.
- A budget process which reflects strategic priorities and is capable of challenging existing patterns of expenditure.
- A wariness about embarking on structural change as a panacea for problems which may be better dealt with by other means.
- A clear sense of leadership from the centre.

- A concern to develop management solutions which reflect the particular circumstances, that is, the uniqueness of the authority concerned.
- A balance in developmental emphasis between the key elements of shared (core) values, strategy, staff, structure and systems.

The last of these features of the 'well-managed authority' takes us back to the key dimensions of analysis of the book, first introduced in Figure 1.1 (p.8). A well-managed authority, whatever strategic choice it makes as a starting-point, must maintain a balance between the five key features of organisation design identified – strategy, structures, processes and systems, culture and staff management. It is a mistake to overemphasise any one dimension, and to expect that changes in that dimension alone will transform the effectiveness of the authority. Similarly it is counterproductive to ignore or under-emphasise any dimension, whilst focusing organisational energy on the other four. It is not unusual, for example, to find issues of culture and staff management relatively neglected, in circumstances where major changes of structure and process are being implemented. Or it may be that insufficient attention is paid to how a major change in strategic direction can be incorporated into the culture of the authority (i.e. came to be owned collectively by the organisation's staff, including elected members).

The concept of 'organisational balance'

The concept of 'organisational balance' discussed above is important in other ways also. As we have seen throughout the book, local authorities face organisational dilemmas posed by the different demands made on them. To deal with these dilemmas, the *relativity* of *organisational characteristics has to be appreciated.* No organisational characteristic is absolute. Each characteristic, such as centralisation or competition, has to be balanced against its opposite. While organisational balance is not easily identified, organisational *imbalance* can be. The task then becomes that of redressing the balance.

It is important to emphasise that the concept of 'organisational balance' does not imply that all authorities should seek an optional 'equilibrium position' which balances the underlying principles of each variant of enabling (residual, market and community). On the contrary, as we have emphasised throughout this final chapter, it is important that each individual authority should develop a clear view about its dominant orientation and use that as a starting-point. To give equal weight to the principles of commercialism, customer-orientation and community would involve an unhelpful evasion of choice and is not recommended. Rather, the argument about 'organisational balance' acknowledged that even if a dominant principle is identified and used as a starting-point for organisational design, it will be important to recognise that compensatory mechanisms will be necessary if a local authority is to operate effectively. For example, an authority which wishes to decentralise decision-making – either to business units or local community forums – will need to pay careful attention to the range of decisions that should be retained at the centre. Such compensating mechanisms do not dilute the commitment to the original strategic choice; they merely recognise that in organisational terms, the real choice is not between absolutes (centralisation, decentralisation) but between positions on a continuum. It follows that the appropriate 'point of balance' will be different for different authorities, depending on the strategic choice they have made.

As we have seen, local authorities have to be capable of *change*, both in their policies and in their ways of working. They also require continuity. They are still responsible for delivering those services reliably – whether directly or indirectly – and on a continuing basis. The key organisational dilemma is thus the dilemma of change and continuity. A local authority has to be capable of both. The problem is to build both into the working of the organisation. The two competing pressures – change and continuity – have to be balanced.

Within this central dilemma, many other issues of balance can be identified. Local authorities have to be both governmental agencies, *and* providers of services. They have to make collective choices and yet meet individual needs. They have to enhance representative democracy and yet sustain participation. Different approaches will require different emphases and balance.

So often, organisational characteristics are seen as absolutes. Advocates of decentralisation, or of competition, or of corporate working have been seen as advocating that mode of working as though it were an end in itself. One cannot meaningfully discuss the introduction of decentralisation in an organisation, without considering the need for centralisation. Nor can one sensibly examine the case for competition in the internal workings of services, without understanding the case for cooperation. Failure to do so leads to organisational problems. Local authorities considering decentralisation have sometimes acted as though it were possible to decentralise the whole of the working of the organisation. If the role of the centre is not carefully considered before decentralisation is embarked upon, it will certainly be discovered in experience! (Consider, for example, the implications for decentralisation of an equal opportunities policy to which there is a strong political commitment.)

Local authorities – and indeed all organisations – can move on a switchback process, whereby a management reorganisation is undertaken to emphasise one particular organisational characteristic, leading in due course to the need for a further reorganisation to correct the problems of the earlier over-emphasis. Organisational characteristics should be seen not as absolutes but as points on a dimension. Seen this way the response to the over-centralised authority is not to create the totally decentralised authority, but to move toward, or give greater weight to decentralisation. Similar choices of balance can be identified between a departmental and a corporate emphasis; between formality and informality of structure and process; between an emphasis on specialist staff and an emphasis on generalist staff; between standardisation of practice and variation in practice and between uniformity of policy and diversity within policy. The exploration of these issues in terms of balance transforms the way of thinking about them. It does not lessen the case for organisational change but deepens the approach to that change. The tendency is to swing between poles; maintenance of balance in the sense we have defined it, is needed to counter this tendency.

Conclusion

The contrast between traditional approaches to local government management, and emerging new patterns of management, can be highlighted by a characterisation developed in one of the authorities visited in the LGMB's 'Well-Managed Authority' research (Leach *et al.*, 1992).

TABLE 10.3 Old and new approaches to management compared

Old approach to management	New approach to management
* traditional, static	* change-oriented
* insular	* open, communicating
* centre-focused	* customer-focused
* incremental short-term	* business-oriented, planned
* rule-driven	* flexible
* passive employment policies	* active employment policies
* no recognised corporate culture	* corporated culture geared to management style and purpose
* finance/treasury-driven	* more policy-driven

The characterisation of traditional and emerging approaches will vary. But all the authorities studied were clear about the differences, as they saw it, between the past and the present and future. Clear perspectives on the past have helped to orient authorities in the process of change.

Our final conclusion refers back to the three types of strategic role – residual enabler, market enabler and community enabler – which have formed the basis of our analysis of the choices currently facing local authorities in the 1990s. Although all of these choices represent a plausible interpretation of strategic role (in that they are compatible with the broad 'enabling' parameters set by central government) it is important to recognise the implications of these choices. Whilst 'market enabling' and 'community enabling' acknowledge a continuing 'governmental' role for local authorities (indeed, the community enabling role would have the effect of strengthening this emphasis) the same cannot be said of the residual enabling role, which plays down the governmental role of local authorities, and focuses almost exclusively upon the service provision (or rather the service specification/purchasing) role. A more widespread adopting of (or central government insistence upon) this role would imply a fundamental change in the role of local authorities, minimising the *governmental* role (with its relatively wide connotations of local choice) and restricting local choice to choice between different bundles of local services.

The significance of these differences is further illustrated by the choice of core values which different local authorities choose to emphasise. We were struck by the different climate in those authorities we visited which had emphasised a governmental interpretation of the local authority's role, as opposed to those which emphasised a business approach. In the former an active examination of concepts such as 'empowerment', 'community leadership', and community governance was providing a strong counter-balance to the fragmentary effects of central government legislation. It also provided an important basis for motivation of authority staff. Local authorities were still recognisable as agencies of *local governance*, even though the way in which the role was carried out had changed markedly over the past few years.

In authorities dominated by a business culture or ethic, we sensed that the new interpretation of the authority's overarching purpose was less of a strong motivational force. Authorities which have espoused this philosophy have a particular problem in counteracting the fragmentation of the authority into a set of relatively separate businesses. Indeed, such authorities typically recognise this problem and talk of slimmed-down strategic centres. Yet 'strategic' in these circumstances has a much more limited meaning than the sense in which we used the term earlier – it becomes similar to the role of a multinational company in relation to the constituent units which comprise it. For the authority which continues to emphasise, or reinterpret, a governmental role, strategy is interpreted in a way which responds to community needs in a much wider sense. There is an important sense in which business systems ought, in the local government world, to be clearly subservient to a wider community governance role. If they are not, but become instead a dominant value in their right, there are crucial concerns about where that particular road will ultimately lead.

Bibliography

Adam Smith Institute (1988) *Wiser Counsels* (London: Adam Smith Institute).

Ahmed, M. W. and Scapens, R. W. (1991) 'Cost Allocation Theory and Practice: The Continuing Debate' in Ashton, D., Hopper, T. and Scapens, R. W., *Issues in Management Accounting* (Hemel Hempstead: Prentice-Hall).

Aldrich, H. E. (1979) *Organisations and Environment* (Englewood Cliffs, New Jersey: Prentice Hall).

Alexander, Alan (1982) *Local Government in Britain Since Reorganisation* (London: Allen & Unwin).

Alford, R. (1975) *Health Care Politics* (Chicago: University of Chicago Press).

Audit Commission (1984a) *Code of Practice* (London: HMSO).

Audit Commission (1984b) *Economy, Efficiency and Effectiveness*, Vol. 1 (London: HMSO).

Audit Commission (1987) *The Management of London's Authorities: Preventing the Breakdown of Services* (Bristol: HMSO).

Audit Commission (1988) *The Competitive Council* (London: HMSO).

Audit Commission (1989a) *Losing an Empire, Finding a Role: The LEA of the Future* (London: HMSO).

Audit Commission (1989b) *More Equal than Others: The Chief Executive in Local Government* (London: HMSO).

Audit Commission (1990a) *Building Maintenance DSOs in London* (London: HMSO).

Audit Commission (1990b) *We Can't Go on Meeting Like This* (London: HMSO).

Bains Report (1972) *The New Local Authorities, Study Group on Local Authority Management Structure* (London: HMSO).

Barley, S. R. and Kunda, G. (1992) 'Design and Devotion: Surges of Rational and Normative Ideologies of Control in Managerial Discourse', *Administrative Science Quarterly*, 37 (3) September, pp.363–99.

Barnard, C. I. (1938) *The Functions of the Executive* (Cambridge, Mass.: Harvard University Press).

Bass, B. M. (1985) *Leadership and Performance* (New York: Free Press).

Benson, J. K. (1975) 'The Inter-organisational Network as a Political Economy', *Administrative Science Quarterly*, vol. 20, no. 2 (July).

Bolton, J. E. (1974) 'Corporate Management after Bains', *Local Government Chronicle*, 7 June 1974, pp.548–50.

Brooke, Rodney (1989) *Managing the Enabling Authority* (London: Longman).

Burns, T. and Stalker, G. M. (1961) *The Management of Innovation* (London: Tavistock Publications).

Butler-Schloss, E. (1988) *Report of the Inquiry into Child Abuse in Cleveland 1987* (London: HMSO) Cmnd. 412.

Caulfield, I., Schultz, J. (1989) *Planning for Change: Strategic Planning in Local Government* (Harlow: Longman).

Challis, L., Fuller, S., Plowden, W. Webb, F., Whittingham, H. and Wistow, C. (1988) *Joint Approaches to Social Policy: Rationality and Practice* (Cambridge: Cambridge University Press).

Chandler, A. D. (1962) *Strategy and Structure* (Cambridge, Mass.: MIT).

Chandler A. D. (1977) *The Visible Hand: The Managerial Revolution in American Business* (Cambridge, Mass.: Harvard University Press).

Child, J. (1987) 'Information Technology, Organisation and Response to Strategic Challenges', *California Management Review*, 30, 1, pp.33–50.

Citizen's Charter (1991) *The White Paper on the Citizen's Charter* (London: HMSO).

Clarke, Michael (1991) 'Foreword' in *Strategic Management in Focus* (Luton: Local Government Management Board).

Clarke, M. and Stewart, J. D. (1988) *The Enabling Council* (Luton: Local Government Training Board).

Clarke, M. and Stewart, J. D. (1989a) *Challenging Old Assumptions* (Luton: Local Government Training Board).

Clarke, M. and Stewart, J. D. (1989b) *The Councillor and the Enabling Council: Changing Roles* (Luton: Local Government Training Board).

Clarke, Michael and Stewart, John (1990) *General Management in Local Government: Getting the Balance Right* (London: Longmans).

Clarke, Michael and Stewart, John (1991) *Strategies for Success* (Luton: Local Government Management Board).

Clegg, S. (1990) *Modern Organisations: Organisation Studies in the Post-modern World* (London: Sage).

Coopers and Lybrand Associates (1981) *Service Provision and Pricing in Local Government: Studies in Local Environment Services* (London: HMSO).

Crompton, R. and Jones, G. (1984) *White Collar Proletariat, De-skilling and Clerical Work* (London: Macmillan).

Cross, C. A. (1982) *Principles of Local Government Law* (London: Sweet and Maxwell).

Crozier, M. (1964) *The Bureaucratic Phenomenon* (Chicago: University of Chicago Press).

Daft, R. (1974) 'A Dual-Core Model of Organisational Innovation', *Academy of Management Journal*, 21, pp.193–210.

Davis, Howard (compiler) (1986) *The Future Role and Organisation of Local Government* (Birmingham: Institute of Local Government Studies).

Department for Education (1992) *Choice and Diversity* (London: HMSO).

Department of the Environment (1973) *The Sunderland Study: Tackling Urban Problems: A Working Guide* (London: HMSO).

Department of the Environment (1974) Consultation Paper sent to urban authorities in England with a population of 200 000 (London: HMSO).

Department of the Environment (1983) *Local Authorities and Racial Disadvantage: Report of a Joint Government/Local Authority Association Working Group* (London: Department of the Environment).

Department of the Environment (1988) *The Conduct of Local Authority Business: The Government Response to the Report of the Widdicombe Committee of Inquiry* (London: HMSO).

Department of the Environment (1991a) *The Structure of Local Government in England* (London: HMSO).

Department of the Environment (1991b) *The Internal Management of Local Authorities* (London: HMSO).

DiMaggio, P. and Powell, W.W. (1983) 'The Iron Cage Revisited: Institutional Isomorphism and Collective Rationality in Organisational Fields', *American Sociological Review*, 48, pp.147–60.

Donovan Commission (1968) Royal Commission on Trade Unions and Employers Associations, *Report* (London: HMSO).

Douglas, M. (1987) *How Institutions Think* (London: Routledge & Kegan Paul).

Duke of Edinburgh, (1985) *Inquiry into British Housing* (London: National Federation of Housing Associations).

Dunleavy, P. (1991) *Democracy, Bureaucracy and Public Choice: Economic Explanations in Political Science* (Hemel Hempstead: Harvester Wheatsheaf).

Elster, J. (1978) *Logic and Society* (London: John Wiley).

Elster J (1983) *Sour Grapes: Studies in the Subversion of Rationality* (Cambridge: Cambridge University Press).

Ennals, Ken and O'Brien, John (1990) *The Enabling Role of Local Authorities* (London: Public Finance Foundation).

Etzioni, A. (1961) *Comparative Analysis of Complex Organisations: On Power Involvement and Their Correlates* (New York: Free Press).

Evan, W. (1976) 'An Organization-Set Model of Inter-organizational Relations' in Evon, W. (ed.) *Inter-Organizational Relations* (Harmondsworth Penguin).

Fisher, Ed. (1983) *The Entrepreneur in Local Government* (Washington, DC: International City Management Association).

Flynn, N. and Leach, S. (1985) *Joint Boards and Joint Committees: An Evaluation* (INLOGOV, University of Birmingham).

Fowler, A. (1975) *Personnel Management in Local Government* (London: Institute of Personnel Management).

Fox, A. (1974) *Beyond Contract: Work, Power and Trust Relations* (London: Faber).

Frater, Michael (1991) 'Kent County Council', in Clutterbuck, David, *Going Private: Privatisations Round the World* (London: Mercury Publications).

Friend, J.K., Power, J.M. and Yewlett, Chris (1974) *Public Planning: The Intercorporate Dimension* (London: Tavistock).

Gaster, L. (1993) *Organisational Change and Political Will* (Bristol: School for Advanced Urban Studies).

Goldsmith, Michael and Newton, Ken (1986) 'Local Government Abroad' in the Widdicombe Report Research, vol. IV, *Aspects of Local Democracy* (London: HMSO).

Goold, M. and Campbell, A. (1987) *Strategies and Spoils: The Role of the Centre in Managing Diversified Corporations* (Oxford: Blackwell).

Gouldner, A. (1954) *Patterns of Industrial Bureaucracy* (New York: Collier Macmillan).

Gouldner, A. (1957) 'Cosmopolitans and Locals: Towards an Analysis of Latent Social Roles', *Administrative Science Quarterly*, vol. 2.

Granovetter, M. (1985) 'Economic Action and Social Structures: The Problem of Embeddedness', *American Journal of Sociology*, 91, pp.481–510.

Greenwood, R. (1983) 'Changing Patterns of Budgeting in English Local Government', *Public Administration*, vol. 61, pp.149–68

Greenwood, R., Hinings, C. R., Ranson, S., Walsh, K. (1976) *In Pursuit of Corporate Rationality* (University of Birmingham: INLOGOV).

Greenwood, Royston, Norton, Alan and Stewart, John (1969a) *Recent Reforms in the Management Arrangements of County Boroughs in England and Wales* (London: Institute of Local Government Studies).

Greenwood, Royston, Norton, Alan and Stewart, John (1969b) *Recent Reforms in the Management Structure of Local Authorities – the London Boroughs* (London: Institute of Local Government Studies).

Greenwood, Royston, Norton, Alan and Stewart, John (1969c) *Recent Reforms in the Management Structure of Local Authorities – the County Councils* (London: Institute of Local Government Studies).

Greenwood, Royston and Stewart, John (1974) *Corporate Planning in Local Government* (London: Charles Knight).

Greenwood, R. Hinings, R. and Brown, J. (1990) 'P2 Form Strategic Management: Corporate Practices in Professional Partnerships', *Academy of Management Journal*, vol. 33, no. 4, pp. 725–55.

Gulick, L. and Urwick, L. (eds) (1937) *Papers on the Science of Administration* (London: Institute of Public Administration).

Gyford, J. (1985) 'Political Change' in M. Loughlin, D. Gelfand and K. Young (eds) *Half a Century of Municipal Decline* (London: Allen & Unwin).

Gyford, J., Leach, S. N. and Game, C. (1989) *The Changing Politics of Local Government* (London: Unwin Hyman).

Hadley, Roger, and McGrath, Morag (1984) *When Social Services Go Local* (London: Allen & Unwin).

Hadow Report (1934) *Report of the Committee on Qualifications, Recruitment, Training and Promotion of Local Government Officers*, (London: HMSO).

Handy, Charles (1985) *Understanding Organisations* (Harmondsworth: Penguin).

Henry, Edmund (1984) 'Decentralisation in Islington' in Robin Hambleton and Paul Hoggett, *The Politics of Decentralisation* (Bristol: School for Advanced Urban Studies).

Heseltine, Michael (1991) Speech to the Annual Conference of the Association of District Councils.

Hickson, D. J., Lee, C. A., Schneck, R. E. and Penning, J. M. (1971) 'A Strategic Contingencies Theory of Intraorganisational Power', *Administrative Science Quarterly*, pp.216-19.

Hickson, D., Butler, R., Gray, D., Mallory, G. R. and Wilson, D. (1986) *Top Decisions: Strategic Decision-Making in Organisations* (Oxford: Blackwell).

Hill, C. W. L. (1988) 'Corporate Control Type, Strategy, Size and Financial Performance', *Journal of Management Studies*, vol. 25, pp.403–16.

Hinings, C. R. and Greenwood, R. (1988) *The Dynamics of Strategic Change* (Oxford: Blackwell).

Hinings, C. R. Greenwood, R. and Ranson, S. (1975) 'Contingency Theory and the Organisation of Local Authorities: Part II Contingencies and Structures', *Public Administration*, vol. 53, pp.169–90.

Hinings, C. R., Greenwood, R., Ranson, S. and Walsh, K. (1980) *Management Systems in Local Government* (INLOGOV, University of Birmingham).

HM Government (1987) *Housing: The Government's Proposals* (London: HMSO).

Hoggett, Paul and Hambleton, Robin (eds) (1987) *Decentralisation and Democracy* (Bristol: School for Advanced Urban Studies).

Hood, C. (1976) *The Limits of Administration* (London: John Wiley).

Hughes, Peter (1987) 'Decentralisation in Tower Hamlets', *Local Government Policy Making*, September.

International City Management Association (1990) *Service Delivery in the 90s: Alternative Approaches for Local Government* (London: ICMA).

Jewson, N., Mason, D., Waters, S. and Harvey, J. (1990) *Ethnic Minorities and Employment Practice: A Study of Six Organisations* (London: Employment Department).

Johnson, G. (1987) *Strategic Change and the Management Process* (Oxford: Blackwell).

Jones, G. and Stewart, J. D. (1989) 'Dividing the Member's Role into Three is Misleading', *Local Government Chronicle*, 14 December 1990, p.17

Kinsey Lord (1989) *Cambridgeshire County Council into the 1990s* (London: Kinsey Lord).

Kirklees Metropolitan District Council (1989) *Kirklees: State of the Environment Report* (Kirkless: Metropolitan District Council).

Labour Party (1989) *Meet the Challenge: Make the Change* (London: Labour Party).

Labour Party (1991a) *Devolution and Democracy* (London: Labour Party).

Labour Party (1991b) *Citizen's Charter* (London: Labour Party).

Laffin, M. (1986) *Professionalism and Policy: The Role of the Professions in Central Local Government Relationships* (Aldershot: Gower).

Laffin, M. and Young, K. (1985) 'The Changing Roles and Responsibilities of Local Authority Chief Officers', *Public Administration*, vol. 63, pp.41–59.

Leach, S. (1989) 'Strengthening Local Democracy? The Government's Response to Widdicombe' in J. Stewart and G. Stoker (eds) *The Future of Local Government* (London: Macmillan).

Leach, S. (1992) 'Strategic Land-Use Planning: The Implications of Post-Abolition Experience in the Metropolitan Counties for the Current Reorganisation Debate', *Strategic Government*, Winter 1982.

Leach, S., Davis, H., Game, C. and Skelcher, C. (1992) *After Abolition* (INLOGOV, University of Birmingham).

Leach, S. and Stewart, J. (1992) *The Politics of Hung Authorities* (London: Macmillan).

Leach, S. and Stewart, M. (1992) *Local Government: Its Role and Function* (York: Joseph Rowntree Foundation).

Leach, S., Vielba, C. and Flynn, N. (1987) *Two-Tier Relationships in British Local Government* (INLOGOV, University of Birmingham).

Leach, S., Walsh, K., Game, C., Rogers, S., Skelcher, C. and Spencer, K. (1993) *Challenge and Change: Characteristics of Good Management in Local Government* (London: Local Government Management Board).

Lipsky, M. (1980) *Street-Level Bureaucracy* (New York: Russell Sage).

Local Government Commission (1993) *The Future Local Government of Derbyshire* (London: HMSO).

Local Government Management Board (1991) *Achieving Better Management* (Luton: Local Government Management Board).

Local Government Management Board (1992) *Getting On With It* (Luton: Local Government Management Board).

Local Government Training Board (1987) *Getting Closer to the Public* (Luton: Local Government Training Board).

Maclean, A. and Marshall, J. (1983) *Intervening in Culture*, Working Paper, University of Bath.

Mallaby Report (1967) *Report of the Committee on Staffing in Local Government*, (London: HMSO).

March, J. G., Olsen. J. P. (1986) 'Garbage-Can Models of Decision-Making in Organisations', in J. G. March and R. Weissenger-Baylon (eds) *Ambiguity and Command: Organisational Perspectives on Military Decision Making* (Cambridge, Mass.: Ballinger).

March, J. G. and Olsen, J. P. (1989) *Rediscovering Institutions: The Organisational Basis of Politics* (New York: Free Press).

Mather, Graham (1989) 'Thatcherism and Local Government: An Evaluation' in John Stewart and Gerry Stoker (eds) *The Future of Local Government* (Basingstoke: Macmillan).

Maud Report (Committee on Management in Local Government) (1967) *Report*, volumes 1–5 (London: HMSO).

Mayer, Maud and Zucker, L. (1989) *Permanently Failing Organisations* (London: Sage).

Morgan, G. (1986) *Images of Organisation* (London: Sage).

National Community Development Project (1977) *Gilding the Ghetto: The State and Poverty Experiments.*

National Consumer Council (1986) *Measuring Up: Consumer Assessment of Local Authority Services – A Guideline Study* (London: NCC).

Niskanen, W. A. (1971) *Bureaucracy and Representative Government* (Chicago: Aldine-Atherton).

Osborne, D. and Gaebler, T. (1992) *Re-inventing Government: How the Entrepreneurial Spirit is Transforming the Public Sector* (Reading, Mass.: Addison-Wesley).

Paterson Advisory Group (1973) *The New Scottish Local Authorities: Organisation and Management Structures*, (London: HMSO).

Peters, T. and Waterman, R. (1982) *In Search of Excellence* (New York: Harper & Row).

Pettigrew, A., Ferlie, E. and McKee, L. (1992) *Shaping Strategic Change* (London: Sage).

Pollert, A. (1988) 'The "Flexible Firm": Fixation or Fact?', *Work, Organisation and Society*, vol. 2, no 3, pp.281–316.

Power, Anne (1987) *Property Before People* (London: Allen & Unwin).

Puddephatt, Andrew (1987) 'Local State and Local Community: the Hackney Experience', in Paul Hoggett and Robin Hambleton (eds) *Decentralisation and Democracy* (Bristol: School for Advanced Urban Studies).

Quinn, J. B. (1980) *Strategies for Change: Logical Incrementalism* (Home-wood, Illinois: Irwin).

Reading Borough Council (1988) *Why a Strategy?* (Reading: Borough Council).

Redcliffe-Maud Report (1969) *Report of the Royal Commission on Local Government in England 1966–69* (London: HMSO).

Rhodes, R. A. W. (1988) *Beyond Westminster and Whitehall* (London: Unwin Hyman).

Ridley, Nicholas (1988) *The Local Right* (London: Conservative Political Centre).

Schon, Donald (1971) *Beyond the Stable State* (Harmondsworth: Penguin).

Seebohm Report (1968) *Report of the Committee on Local Authority and Allied Services* (London: HMSO).

Shelter (1972) *Another Chance for Cities* (Liverpool: Shelter Neighbourhood Action Project).

Simon, H. A. (1945) *Administrative Behaviour* (New York: Free Press).

Shepherd, Cliff (1987) 'The Middlesbrough Community Councils', *Local Government Policy-Making*, September.

Society of Chief Personnel Officers in Local Government (1980) *The Role of the Personnel Officer in the Management of the Authority* (Institute of Local Government Studies, University of Birmingham).

Stewart, J. D. (1985) 'The Conditions of Joint Action', *London Journal*.

Stewart, John (1986) *The New Management of Local Government* (London: Allen & Unwin).

Stewart, John (1989) 'A Future for Local Authorities as Community Government', in John Stewart and Gerry Stoker (eds) *The Future of Local Government* (London: Macmillan).

Stewart, John and Stoker, Gerry (1988) *From Local Administration to Community Government* (London: Fabian Society).

Stewart, John and Walsh, Kieron (1989) *In Search of Quality* (Luton: Local Government Training Board).

Stoker, Gerry (1991) *The Politics of Local Government* (London: Macmillan).

Stoker, Gerry and Lowndes, Vivien (1991) *Tower Hamlets and Decentralisation: The Experience of Globe Town Neighbourhood* (Luton: Local Government Management Board).

Surrey County Council (1992) *Option for Local Government in Surrey: Prospectus* (Kingston: Surrey County Council).

Thamesdown Borough Council (1984) *A New Vision for Thamesdown* (Swindon: Thamesdown Borough Council).

Treasury (1951) 'O and M Reports on Coventry' as quoted in *Public Administration*, Spring 1954.

Tushman, M. L. and Romanelli, E. (1985) 'Organisational Evolution: A Metamorphosis Model of Convergence and Reorientation', *Research in Organisational Behaviour*, 7, pp.171–222.

Walsh, K. (1991) *Competitive Tendering for Local Authority Services: Initial Experiences* (London: HMSO).

Webb, Adrian and Wistow, Gerald (1986) *Planning Need and Scarcity* (London: Allen & Unwin).

Webster, Barbara (1982) 'Area Management and Responsive Policy Making', in Steve Leach and John Stewart (eds) *Approaches to Policy Making* (London: Allen & Unwin).

Wendt, Robin (1987) 'The Value of Cheshire's Values', *The County Councils Gazette*, November.

Widdicombe, D. (Chairman) (1986a) *The Conduct of Local Authority Business*, Report of the Committee of Inquiry into the Conduct of Local Authority Business (London: HMSO).

Widdicombe, D. (Chairman) (1986b) *Research Volume 1: The Political Organisation of Local Authorities* (London: HMSO).

Williamson, O. E. (1964) *The Economics of Discretionary Behaviour: Managerial Objectives in a Theory of the Firm* (Englewood Cliffs, New Jersey: Prentice-Hall).

Williamson, O. E. (1970) *Corporate Control and Business Behaviour* (Englewood Cliffs, New Jersey: Prentice-Hall).

Williamson, O. E. (1975) *Markets and Hierarchy* (New York: Free Press).

Williamson, O. E. (1985) *The Economic Institutions of Capitalism* (New York: Free Press).

Wiltshire County Council (1988) *Development of a Rural Strategy for Wiltshire: Report to the Policy and Resources Committee* (Trowbridge: Wiltshire County Council).

Young, K. (1986) 'Party Politics in Local Government: An Historical Perspective', in Widdicombe, D. (Chairman) (1986) *The Conduct of Local Authority Business*, research volume IV.

Young, K. (1987) 'The Spaces between Words: Local Authorities and the Concept of Equal Opportunities', in R. Jenkins and J. Solomon (eds) *Racism and Equal Opportunity Policies in the 1980s* (Cambridge: Cambridge University Press).

Young, K. and Connelly, N. (1981) *Policy and Practice in the Multiracial City* (London: Policy Studies Institute).

Young, K. and Davies, E. M. (1990) *Breaking Down the Barriers: Women Managers in Local Government* (Luton: Local Government Training Board).

Index

271